# THE RESTORATION OF THE KETCH-RIGGED TAMAR SAILING BARGE *SHAMROCK* 1974–79

by

ALAN VINER

NATIONAL MARITIME MUSEUM 1983

ISBN 0 905555 68 6



Cover: F. *Shamrock* at anchor at Cotehele Quay, 1982.
B. *Shamrock* derelict at Hooe Lake.

Designed and Illustrated by Lionel Willis
MSIAD

Printed by Eyre & Spottiswoode Ltd
on behalf of the Trustees of the National Maritime Museum

# Contents

## List of Photographs

The National Maritime Museum is grateful to the following who have kindly agreed to the use of their photographs in the production of this book: Dr Basil Greenhill, the late Captain Roe, Mr M H Grosse, Tom Perkins, George Eley, Lionel Willis, John Stengelhofen, Alan Viner.

# Foreword

*The Genesis of the Idea*

It is not the general policy of the National Maritime Museum to own, or become directly involved in, the management of ships afloat. The acquisition of the *Shamrock* was a conscious and deliberate departure from this policy, a departure made for a number of very good reasons.

The work of the National Maritime Museum covers many fields. We are a large general historical museum, with great and diverse collections, with the central theme of Man's Encounter with the Sea. But man's encounter with the sea, until the '70s of the last century, was made virtually exclusively in wooden sailing ships and boats. So the wooden sailing ship, her history, her powers and her limitations, runs as a central theme through a great deal of the Museum's work. The pictures we have in our superb collection of marine paintings are largely of wooden ships; the navigation instruments were used on board wooden ships; the models are predominantly of wooden ships; the archaeology is the archaeology of the wooden ship; the antiquities are the personal effects of the men who sailed in wooden ships, the vast archive comprises largely papers concerning the operation, business management and operation of wooden ships.

But of course the wooden ship as a living entity is on the other side the great technical and social revolutions of the late-19th and 20th centuries. As all of us know, she was an organic being, made up of thousands of separate, relatively small, pieces of wood, fastened together in one way or another — a flexible mass of rotting material and of joints, rigged with natural, biodegradable fibre rope which was constantly stretching and tightening, with wooden spars which required nearly as much attention as the hull and with ironwork which rotted the spars to which it was attached as it corroded. Such a structure needed as much attention to keep it in working order as a herd of cows requires to keep them healthy, or a team of draught horses to keep them working. It required the same degree of expertise and the same total dedication, and never let us forget it.

The thinking behind the Museum's involvement in the *Shamrock* is simple to explain. She is the historian's ship. Because she was chosen carefully for her purpose as of simple hull shape, relatively unlikely to strain, with no long overhanging counter to be a source of tension and rapid decay, and with simple spars and rigging, her maintenance and occasional sailing, it was thought, should not prove an insuperable problem in the long period. At the same time, she would serve the purpose of keeping curatorial staff at least a little in touch with reality, so that they would have something other than the written record to bring home to them the realities of the problems of preparing infinitely more complicated wooden vessels than the *Shamrock* for sea, and handling them and maintaining them there, as merchant vessels, trading all over the world with heavy cargoes, or as ships of war, patrolling a coast perhaps for years on end.

The idea of the historian's ship as a future necessity was first put forward by one of the founding fathers of the National Maritime Museum, Sir Alan Moore, in his book "The Last Days of Mast and Sail" when he wrote, in 1924, "One sailing vessel and one only appears to be necessary for the future, a ship for naval historians and archaeologists. I mean it seriously. No one can follow the naval campaigns and battles of the past or understand the development of the ship unless he realises the limitations of sail and the difficulties with which seamen of former ages had to contend.

"It is true that men who were not sailors have studied these subjects and have written admirably upon them, but they lived in the blaze of the old tradition."

Such was the theory, and I have little doubt but that in the long run the effort will prove to have been fully justified. Future generations will benefit greatly from having the unavoidable responsibility of the conservation of the *Shamrock* as a museum function.

But we have learned a great deal. We have

already learned that the effort of restoring a vessel like the *Shamrock,* especially when the job is properly done to Museum standards, is, to quote Revell Carr, the Director of Mystic Seaport — the museum which has more experience than any other in the world of this kind of work — "a time consuming and costly undertaking . . . that there are no simple expedients that will substitute for doing the proper job. Every compromise threatens the integrity of the vessel being restored and seriously diminishes its historic significance. We have a responsibility to work towards the highest standards in ship preservation and we, like any other group or individual contemplating taking on the responsibility for a ship, must face the reality of that commitment. It calls for rare skills, equipment and materials." And in the *Shamrock*'s case a great deal of research was done before rebuilding was even started, so that we are sure there is nothing on board her that would not have been there in 1926 — she has natural fibre rigging, natural fibre sails, no laminates, no glues, no anachronisms of any kind.

When you do a job like that, the effort is out of all proportion to the necessary effort to achieve more conventional museum functions — special exhibitions, the opening of new galleries, the establishment of new research functions, and so forth. It goes on being out of proportion. We know, now, that to maintain the *Shamrock* and to establish a specialist professional conservation function for that purpose, is going to be a complicated business. The specialist conservation unit we are contemplating setting up to look after the *Shamrock* and our wooden boats looks as if it is going to absorb the full-time energies of three people, about one in ten of all the conservation staff.

The experience of the *Shamrock* has led me to think a great deal about the problems of vessel preservation. The question does arise of how far maritime museums are justified in choosing this particular very expensive form of activity — vessel preservation — rather than other forms of activity which may have a wider educational function, be of greater interest to a greater number of people, be of more importance in preserving examples of human cultural and technical achievement. I think very great care and much thought must be taken in choosing between vessel preservation and other forms of museum activity. Priorities must be very carefully assessed.

Some vessel preservation, or attempted preservation, has not been the result of careful assessment and thought, but of romantic idealism, of an excess of nostalgia, of a desire to escape into a past which never really was. Focus and discipline are needed in the maritime preservation field. To quote Revell Carr again, "Groups should carefully and fully assess the historic significance of the vessels they wish to preserve, and the costs of acquisition, restoration, and an endless preservation obligation. Sources of funding, and sources of the skills and materials needed to carry out the work should be identified so that initial high expectations of success can be met. Without this careful planning the hopes and enthusiasm of volunteers and benefactors will be dashed as the project founders and the vessel is lost. Scarred by such experience, supporters lose confidence and interest, and other worthwhile viable projects may be unable to generate the needed backing."

If the choice, after careful assessment of a museum's priorities, goes to vessel preservation, it is very important indeed to know why that choice has been made. The rational statement of the reasons for preservation of a particular vessel or boat should precede the decision to preserve, and the record of the motives and arguments must itself be preserved for posterity as part of the acquisition. The valuation of significance is an essential part of the whole game. The simple statement that it is vital that a vessel should be preserved can be no more than an emotive smoke screen to hide lack of rational analysis.

The same problems exist on land. They exist for buildings, they exist over the scheduling of archaeological sites, in some cases almost obliterated by deep ploughing, over the preservation of machinery and industrial material in circumstances which make conservation grossly uneconomic. But with vessel preservation the problems are writ larger, because of the cost, and because of the world shortage of expert conservators in this field. A preserved ship, and especially a preserved wooden ship, is a most unnatural object. She was never meant to lie static in still water without natural ventilation, perpetually exposed, without virtually hour-by-hour attention, to the climate pattern imposed on a static object, no longer providing a fierce economic incentive to those responsible for her preservation as a working artefact on which they depended for their very livelihood.

The Tamar barge was a very simple type of wooden merchant sailing vessel. She was small, and her hull form, with flat transom stern, like a gigantic yacht's dinghy, and round bows with no overhang, meant that she was relatively easy to maintain and less liable to decay than more complex vessels. Here working area was restricted to the relatively sheltered waters of the south coasts of Devon and Cornwall between Salcombe and the Lizard. Just how big was the problem of restoring and conserving even so small and so simple a vessel as this is shown very clearly in this book, a record of what was involved in the work. Anybody contemplating the preservation of a wooden ship should ponder carefully the resources, the professional skill and the money needed, not only to restore the vessel but to conserve her for posterity afterwards. Just as no properly planned archaeological excavation should be undertaken unless adequate arrangements have already been made for the storage and conservation of the artefacts recovered, so no vessel should be acquired for preservation unless adequate facilities and resources exist to complete and continue the job. She is probably much better left where she is, to revert to the earth from which she came.

By 1950 only two Tamar sailing barges remained employed in the coasting trade. Each had been fitted with an auxiliary motor, but they were both also still equipped with at least two sails, which they would use on occasion when the wind was favourable in order to economise in fuel. These two barges were the smack-rigged *Mayblossom*, which had been built in Plymouth by David Banks in 1889, and the *Shamrock*, a ketch-rigged barge built at Devonport by Frederick Hawke 10 years later. Besides these two, a Kingsbridge-built smack, the *J.N.R.* sailed in the same trades. She had a markedly sharper and deeper hull than the Tamar vessels and a long transom counter in place of their simple but efficient and economical flat transom sterms.

It was remarkable that these vessels had survived to earn profits in the middle of the 20th century, since they were almost indistinguishable from the vessels that had been engaged in the coasting trade of the south west of England 200 years earlier. Their principal employment was the carrying of granite roadstone from Port Houstock on the eastern side of the Lizard to Tresillian Quay at the head of the Tresillian River, a tributary of the Truro River, where the Cornwall County Council had a distribution point from which the stone was collected by lorries. The vessels earned marginal profits and when she came due for extensive repairs in 1951 the *Mayblossom* was laid up in Turnpike creek on the Penryn River. A local waterman with experience in barges, Mr Jim Morrison, offered £50 for her because he was sure that he could still make money with her in the stone trade, but the owners, a quarry company, turned him down, and the vessel slowly fell to pieces where she lay.

Besides these three vessels in the mid-20th century, a number of other Tamar barges were still working carrying gravel dredged up from the river beds to riverside wharves on the Exe and the Torridge. On the Exe were the Goss-built *Lillie*, the *Dream* and the *Annie*. On the Torridge the *Princess May*, the *Maud Mary*, the *C.F.H.*, the Truro river-built barge *Mary*, and a vessel very similar to the *J.N.R.*, also built at Kingsbridge, the *Marie* of Salcombe, were employed in the local gravel trade. None of these vessels was still equipped with sails.

In the early 1970s, we at the National Maritime Museum decided that the time for the historian's ship had come, and would be gone forever unless action were to be taken soon. To cut a long story short, attention was concentrated on a search for a surviving Tamar barge, because one of these vessels, small, with simple hull form and rigging, but miniatures of the bigger wooden ships in both hull construction and rigging and gear, would be relatively economical to maintain and within the powers of one or two men to keep in first class condition. She could also be sailed occasionally in the restricted waters for which she was designed.

A search conducted by the Museum in the early 1970s revealed that only one of the transom-sterned, flat-bottomed, full-hulled Tamar barges survived, and she was the *Shamrock*. One of the last two or three barges ever to be built, she was also the most sophisticated in design and fittings. It was the Museum's policy to seek to bring about the restoration and maintenance of a local vessel preferably in partnership with a group of local people. The late Frank Booker, then Assistant Editor of the Western Morning News and a considerable authority on the industrial archaeology of the south west, very kindly arranged the publication in his newspaper of a number of items on the preservation of the *Shamrock*. Sufficient local interest was shown to justify the formation of a local committee, of which Frank Booker took the chair. In the event, it was agreed that the idea of restoring the *Shamrock* was technically feasible, providing sufficient funds were forthcoming and providing that a suitable site for the work could be arranged.

The National Trust, which was represented on the Committee, offered to accept the vessel from her owner, Mr John Fildew, and to provide the site for her rebuilding at the quay on its Cotehele Estate if the National Maritime Museum would provide the necessary technical expertise and advice. At the same time the Trust offered the Museum a building on the quay in which to develop a small maritime industrial Museum of the river as an outpost of the Museum. In the event, therefore, the rebirth of the *Shamrock*, now owned 34/64th by the National Trust and 30/64th by the National Maritime Museum, became a joint effort of these two national institutions. Today, by agreement, the Museum is responsible for the maintenance of the vessel and the Trust for the provision of the berth and the maintenence facilities. Jointly, the Quay is slowly being developed as a museum of the boats and life of the river.

The *Shamrock* represents one of the few cases in Europe in which a merchant vessel has been restored to rigorously maintained full Museum standards, as she was at a defined stage in her working life and with no anachronistic materials. The insistence on these high standards led to tensions among those involved in the project from time to time, but in the end they were achieved and the *Shamrock* today is in every respect as she was 55 years ago, but without the auxiliary engine she had by then acquired.

Alan Viner was placed in charge of the Museum's participation in the project. He kept detailed notes of the whole operation throughout the 5 years it took to complete. In the chapters which follow he records the story of the resurrection of the *Shamrock*.

Basil Greenhill

# Chapter 1

*Early history; acquisition and preparation for restoration. February–November 1974.*

*Shamrock* was built by Frederick Hawke of Stonehouse, Plymouth, in 1899 as a sailing barge for a regular specialised trade between Plymouth and the Torpoint Manure Works. She measured 57.6 ft overall by 18.1 ft beam by 5.4 ft depth of hold and was initially registered as of 31.71 tons gross. The *Shamrock*, named after a current challenger for the America's Cup, was the most advanced Tamar sailing barge ever built, the product of a conscious effort to design a vessel which would carry the maximum cargo for her size on the minimum draft and at the lowest operating and maintenance cost.

To increase her lateral resistance when sailing (or to get the grip on the water which her shallow hull could not provide) *Shamrock* was fitted with two steel plate drop keels. Although drop keels were common in small North American merchant sailing vessels (and used in many much larger vessels including the pioneer five masted schooner *Governor Ames*, built at Waldoboro, Maine, in 1878, which rounded Cape Horn) very few British vessels were so equipped for trade in local waters. She was also rigged as a ketch with the heels of her masts secured in tabernacles, and their shrouds set up with steel-bottle-screws instead of the almost universal deadeyes and lanyards to enable her two-man crew to handle her more conveniently when shooting under low bridges.

In 1919 *Shamrock* was sold to a group of stone quarrymen and converted for trading to the coasts of Devon and Cornwall. The steel drop-keels were removed and replaced by a false keel of conventional style, and many other structural alterations were made to enable her to comply with the Board of Trade regulations for coasting vessels of her size and type. A bowsprit and jib were added to her original sailplan of staysail, mainsail and mizzen, and a Blake 30 ihp four-stroke paraffin motor was installed. *Shamrock* worked in the stone trade from the River Lynher, Plymouth and Port Houstock quarries until 1962 when she was sold, equipped with two 65 ihp Diesel engines and converted to a twin screw salvage and prospecting dredger. In 1966 she was sold again and converted for use as a diving tender in Plymouth Harbour. In the early 1970s she was used as a scrap iron store in Hoo Lake, near Plymouth, and it was here that she was discovered by the National Maritime Museum.

*Shamrock* laid up and semi derelict in Hooe Lake 1973.

In 1973 she was sold once more to Mr John Fildew of Plymouth who attempted to restore the vessel privately, and sought the advice of The Maritime Trust, the National Maritime Museum and The National Trust in an effort to save one of the last of the Tamar sailing barges. The age of *Shamrock*'s timbers and the strain of grounding and carrying heavy stone cargoes for over 42 years, plus lack of maintenance during the last 3 years of her working life, made it necessary to have a preliminary survey made of the vessel to establish whether the hull was sufficiently sound to warrant its restoration. This was arranged by Commander Eric McKee OBE, RN, a Consultant to the National Maritime Museum.

After a preliminary survey had been carried out by R. F. Freeman, Marine Surveyor of Plymouth, it was considered that although the *Shamrock* was semi-derelict, enough of her original structure remained to justify an attempt to restore her. But the amount of work that would be required to bring this about could not then be assessed.

Mr Perkins, a shipwright with many years of experience of all types of wooden ship construction, and a member of the Committee to preserve the *Shamrock*, had prepared the vessel for her initial survey prior to her acquisition by The National Trust and the National Maritime Museum, and as a result he was asked by her new owners if he would prepare the vessel for the voyage to Cotehele Quay. This was a formidable task. Most of the seams of the outer planking gaped wide, many of them completely devoid of pitch, or even of oakum, allowing the sea to flow in and out of the hull as the tide rose or fell. The bottom planks showed evidence of attack by gribble, there were areas of wet rot, and numerous fillets, graving pieces, metal tingles and patches which indicated that many repairs had been necessary to keep *Shamrock* afloat during the last years of her working life.

All that could be done at this stage was to stop or patch every leak below the waterline, a tedious task which involved watching the hull drain itself as the tide ebbed away in order to locate the leaks. They were then sealed off either with a soft ready mix of sand and cement which was ideal for stopping, and plastering, and also easy to remove when required or, where such

Alongside Cotehele Quay after removal of the mainmast.

methods were more suitable, with soft-wood plugs and wedges sealed with oakum.

After 2 weeks of patient stopping and patching, Mr Perkins had the satisfaction of seeing *Shamrock* straighten up off her starboard bilge and then float clear on a rising tide. All that remained was to inform the Queen's Harbour Master of her changed condition, so that he could inspect and clear the vessel for the tow up to Cotehele Quay.

Meanwhile, the Museum made all the necessary arrangements for towage, and a 'voyage plan' was worked out to ensure that suitable places to beach the vessel were available should trouble develop on passage. Two 2 in Rotary pumps were put aboard, and on 25 March 1974, manned by Commander McKee and Mr Fildew, *Shamrock* arrived at Cotehele Quay, the pump having to be used only twice during the entire passage.

With the vessel moored in the soft mud berth which had been specially prepared to avoid straining the hull when she grounded on each tide, work could begin on planning the project and preparing the restoration site.

At a meeting between The National Trust and the National Maritime Museum, a policy was formulated whereby the Trust would initially employ Mr Perkins as the shipwright-in-charge of the restoration, and also supply additional labour, tools and materials for the hull. The museum undertook to research the history of the *Shamrock*, to supply plans and photographs, to seek out contemporary fittings, to co-operate actively in the masting and rigging of the vessel, and to monitor and record the progress of the restoration.

A great deal of interest was shown in the *Shamrock* by local people who had known her in her working days and thought she had been sunk or scrapped. Many provided information that was to prove useful at a later date. Holiday makers were equally intrigued by the vessel, the more serious minded offering free advice regarding the way the work of restoration should be carried out, as they watched the preparations going on all around them.

There was only one way in which the work of restoration could be properly carried out, of course, and that was to place the *Shamrock* in a wooden cradle and haul both up a slipway well clear of the highest tides, so that all parts of the hull were easily accessible. To accomplish this task it was first necessary to dig at a right-angle to the water's edge a bed some 25 ft wide for the slipway, which, with a declivity of 1 : 20 would reach 100 ft inshore at the northern end of the quay.

Digging out the bed of the slipway.

Five-inch thick railway sleepers were bedded 4 in deep at 4 ft centres to form the slipway, and their ends were linked together by stapled loops of wire which helped to reinforce blobs of concrete placed there to prevent their movement under stress. Two 4 in × 4 in timber guides were then coach-screwed to each sleeper for the entire length of the slipway, at a distance apart sufficient to allow the cradle containing *Shamrock* to be hauled between them.

The cradle itself needed to be at least 40 ft long, 2 ft deep with a grid 14 ft wide, and because local timber merchants could not supply 12 in × 12 in baulks of elm more than 20 ft long, the cradle was made in two parts. Each half-cradle was constructed of two elm baulks tied together by compression cross-struts housed and tenoned 2 ft from their ends and reinforced by steel tie rods.

To avoid unnecessary handling of the heavy timbers the work of assembling the cradle was carried out on the slipway itself. The two halves were united with 4 ft long iron clamp plates each 12 in wide and $\frac{3}{8}$ in thick, through bolted to the longitudinal baulks. Six 14 ft cross-pieces of 12 in × 12 in oak were then secured to the cradle frame with 4 in × 4 in angle irons and steel bolts to form the grid upon which *Shamrock* was to rest. This arrangement allowed a working space of 2 ft 8 in under the hull bottom.

Assembling the cradle on the slipway track.

Stabilising blocks to keep the hull upright on the grid were next dogged in position, and after greasing all moving parts, the empty cradle was hauled up and down the slipway by two tractors to rub off any high spots of contact, thereby ensuring that hauling up the cradle with *Shamrock* in it would be as smooth as possible.

While awaiting delivery of the timber to make the slipway and cradle, a 50 ft × 20 ft shed which had been in use as a barn at nearby Treehill Farm, was re-erected close by to act as a mould loft, timber store and workshed. Tree trunks were sunk to support the principal rafters, and a framework was constructed which was covered with sheets of corrugated iron. Wide double doors at each end allowed plenty of room for handling large timbers, masts or spars, and a window and work bench was built in along the entire length of the north side. A band-saw and circular saw were to be installed later on to assist in the conversion of heavy timber.

During this period of preparatory work *Shamrock* herself had been regularly pumped out and kept in good order, and as the time drew near for her to be hauled ashore her pitchpine mast was released from its tabernacle and was lowered, stripped of its standing rigging, and taken ashore. A rack was made for its stowage along the inner south side of the shed, and having been inspected for any rot or necessary repairs, the mast was securely lashed, where air could circulate all round it. Thought to be the original, the mast measured 41 ft from keel to truck, $10\frac{1}{2}$ in maximum diameter, and it was fitted with all the ironwork usually associated with the mainmast of a Tamar sailing barge.

Timbers from the barn at Treehill Farm ready for erection as a temporary workshed.

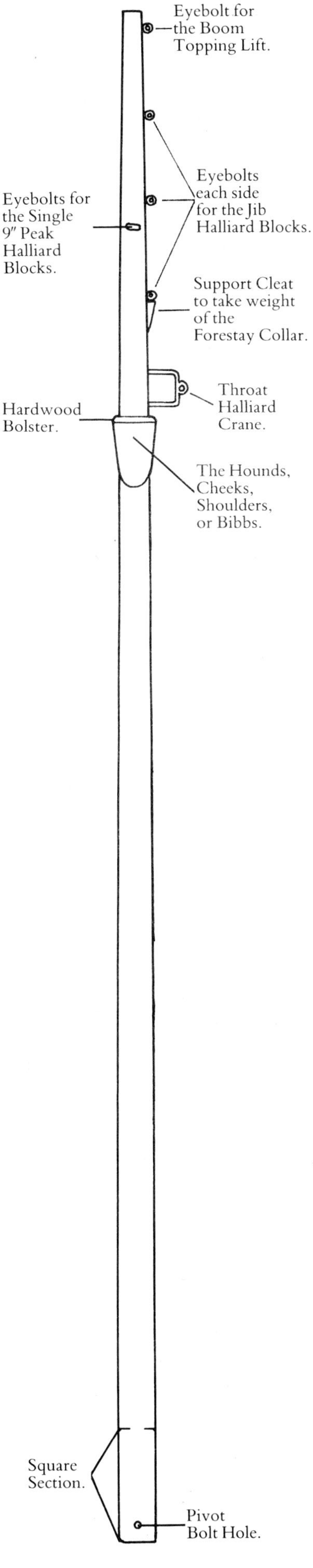


The prediction for the morning tide of Monday 22 July 1974 indicated that *Shamrock* could be hauled ashore on that day, provided that she could be placed in her cradle by the previous evening tide. Consequently, every effort was made to achieve this aim. The actual hauling of ship and cradle was to be performed by a National Trust tractor secured to a strategically placed anchor point. The tractor would use its own powerful winch in combination with a wire purchase of two treble-sheaved blocks rigged to provide a 5 : 1 advantage. A $2\frac{1}{2}$ in steel bar secured to the forward end of the cradle was fitted with two 5 ton chains. These were to be both shackled on to the moving block of the wire purchase which would travel on a sleeper to prevent snagging en route. Dolphins also had to be fixed to No. 2 and 5 cross-pieces of the cradle grid to a tolerance of 12 in of the vessel's beam.

By Sunday 21st all these preparations were completed, and an anchor had also been dropped in mid-stream in line with the slipway so that stern control of the *Shamrock* was available. A necklace of doubled 4 in circumference rope was hung off right round the bull and a wire span from the moving block of the purchase was shackled to it. The cradle itself had been anchored to the slipway to prevent it moving with *Shamrock* as she was hauled upon it.

At 2000 hours *Shamrock* was manoeuvred on to the cradle, her position relative to the dolphins indicating that she was properly centred over the grid.

High water occurred about 30 minutes early, but as the tide neither rose as high, nor lasted as long as predicted, the shipwright-in-charge decided to haul without delay and the hull was literally dragged the last 16 ft into position.

*Shamrock* remained secured in the cradle overnight, and on Monday 22 July after liberal applications of grease to all working parts, removal of the dolphins and the cradle lashings, and a general check to see that nothing could impede the hauling, the moving purchase block with its travelling sleeper was shackled to the cradle chains, and *Shamrock* was slowly hauled up the slipway to her restoration site.

The National Trust Tractor and triple sheaved wire purchase used to haul the cradle and *Shamrock* ashore.

Once the cradle was in position it was anchored with concrete blocks placed between the sleepers at its lower end. All the hauling gear was stripped off and made up and *Shamrock*'s bow and stern overhangs at each end of the cradle were quickly supported by wooden blocks and wedges.

While the preparatory work preceding the slipping of *Shamrock* was going on at Cotehele Quay, the National Maritime Museum on 4 June 1974 had commenced a local research project into the vessel's history. The first step was the inspection of all the official documents relating to *Shamrock* which were lodged with the Registrar of British Ships, Plymouth. Copies were made of these and after studying them, it

Preparation for the final hauling ashore of the vessel to her restoration berth.

*Shamrock* in her restoration berth, 22 July 1974.

became evident that *Shamrock* had undergone several structural changes to her hull, since her completion in 1899, and that she had originally been rigged as a ketch.

The second step was to trace the whereabouts of Mr Hoskings, who had been Master of the *Shamrock* during the twenties, and enquiries quickly showed that he was living at Burraton, Saltash, a few miles down the river from Cotehele Quay. On being informed that *Shamrock* was now owned by The National Trust, and was to be preserved as one of the last of the Tamar sailing barges, he agreed to provide as much information about the vessel as he could remember. Although 92, Mr Hoskings proved to be as alert as ever, and very interested to learn that his old ship had become an object of historical interest.

During the interview that followed, Mr Hoskings was able to answer over one hundred questions relating to the *Shamrock*, which later proved to be of inestimable value in her subsequent restoration. At a second meeting, some 3 weeks later, Mr Hoskings gave the same answers to the same questions without hesitation or reference to notes. By the use of rough sketches based on this information the Museum was able to provide a fairly clear record of how the vessel appeared between 1900 and 1934 when she was rigged as a ketch. However it was Mrs Hoskings, equally interested in the vessel in which she had occasionally sailed with her husband some 50 years before, who triumphantly produced the most conclusive evidence of how *Shamrock* appeared at that time. A small, somewhat battered snapshot, taken by their daughter in 1926, and hidden away amongst family photographs for all these years, showed the ves-

*Shamrock* on her moorings at St. Germans 1926.

sel laying to her moorings off St Germans in the River Lynher. For those with eyes to see, this photograph, when enlarged and studied in detail, provided practically all the information required to rig the *Shamrock* as she appeared at that time.

As a result of this research, by the 6th August the Museum was able to provide The National Trust with six scale drawings of *Shamrock* based on information contained in her official documents, conjectural drawings and sketches made by Mr Perkins, the shipwright-in-charge, together with the photograph loaned by Mr Hoskings. Sketches were also provided of various sail plans based on traditional methods of mastings and rigging a vessel of *Shamrock*'s size and type.

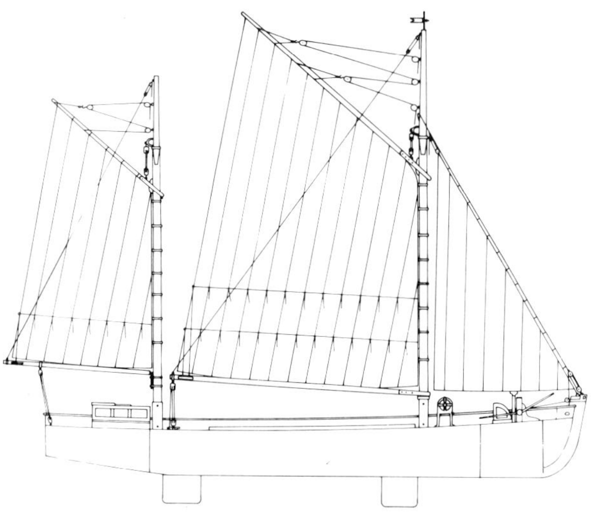

Drawing No. 1 was a conjectural draught of the *Shamrock* as she might have appeared between 1899 and 1920 when she was fitted with drop keels, and rigged as a ketch with a fore staysail, mainsail and mizzen.

The hull drawings were based on a set of lines produced from measurements taken off the hull on 24th July by the late Captain John Roe DSO, OBE, RN of Mary Tavy, who was later commissioned by the National Maritime Museum to build two scale models of the *Shamrock*. The models were for reference purposes and for eventual display in the small museum which was to be established at Cotehele Quay.

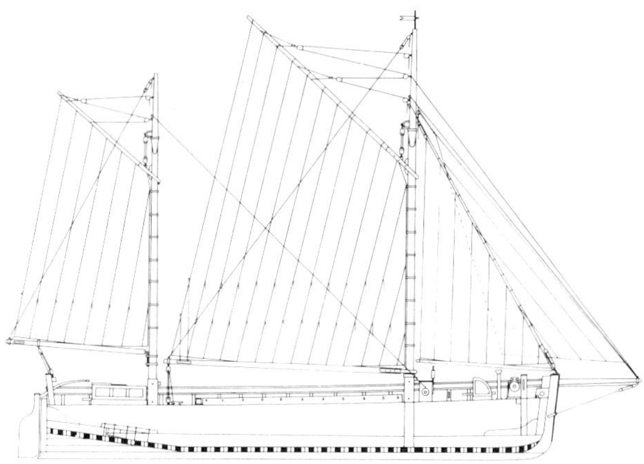

Drawing No. 2 showed how the vessel appeared between 1920 and 1934 after major alterations to the hull, the installation of an auxiliary motor, and the addition to her sailplan of a bowsprit and jib.

A system of close liaison was also established at this time between Mr Eley, the Foreman of The National Trust Cotehele Estate, who was in charge of labour and materials provided by the Trust, Mr Perkins, who was in charge of the actual work of restoring the *Shamrock*, and me from the Department of Ships at the National Maritime Museum. It was the Department's job to provide technical and historical data and materials as required, and to monitor the progress of the restoration for future reference.

Although the preliminary research and preparatory work so far indicated that there was now sufficient data available to justify the restoration, the real state of the *Shamrock*'s hull remained an

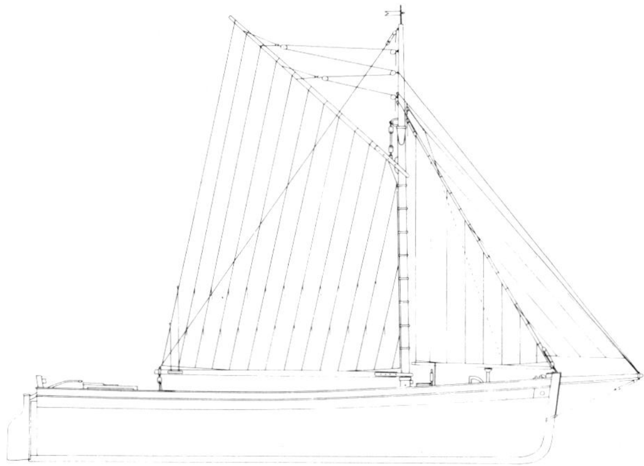

Drawing No. 3 depicted *Shamrock* between 1934 and 1951 as she was mostly remembered in the River Tamar and Plymouth Harbour, without a mizzen mast, and therefore technically smack rigged, with her original mainsail staysail and jib, and the auxiliary motor.

unknown factor. Now that she was safely secured in her restoration berth, however, it was possible for the shipwright-in-charge to work out a method of stripping the vessel systematically to ascertain the state of the frames. Until this operation was completed no one could calculate the extent of the restoration work or the amount of timber and materials that would be required. When building a new vessel such requirements are known well in advance, but in restoring a vessel so as to conserve as much of her original structure as possible, much time is taken up in carefully assessing and removing timbers and fittings without damage, before rebuilding can begin.

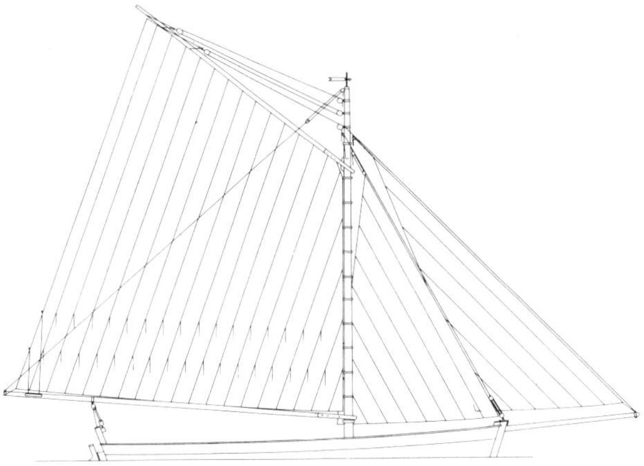

Drawing No. 4 was the sail and rigging plan of *Flora May* built by Hawke of Stonehouse, Plymouth, in 1897; a long boomed smack-rigged Tamar barge typical of this class of vessel.

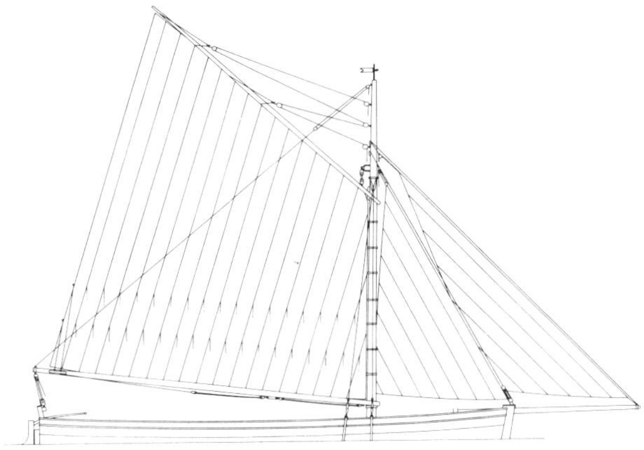

Drawing No. 5 showed the *Shamrock* with a long boom, and high peaked mainsail showing how she would appear if rigged as a typical smack rigged Tamar barge.

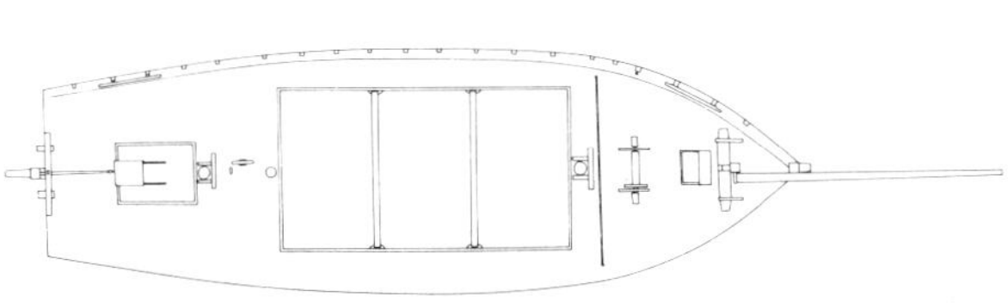

Drawing No. 6 showed the hull and deck layout of the *Shamrock* with the probable positions of the mizzen, mast and other deck fittings.

After a thorough investigation of the hull planking both inside and out, it was decided that the inner or ceiling planking should be lifted. *Shamrock* had 35 frames of close jointed, doubled timbers, and between frame 10 (from forward) to frame 26 it was obvious that the ceiling (that is, the inner lining of planking) was not original. Most of this planking consisted of 4 in × 2 in deal, which was often used for a quick job. It was laid without any attempt at shaping or tapering and secured with 4 in spike nails. At some time in her long career *Shamrock* had been re-fastened with ½ in dia × 10 in coach bolts which passed through outer planking, frame and ceiling plank. A nut and washer counter-sunk into the ceiling plank provided the positive fastening which was required, because the frame was too soft to hold the more usual 6 in spike cut nails. The bolt nuts were rust bound and it was a time consuming job to free or cut them ready for punching out the bolt.

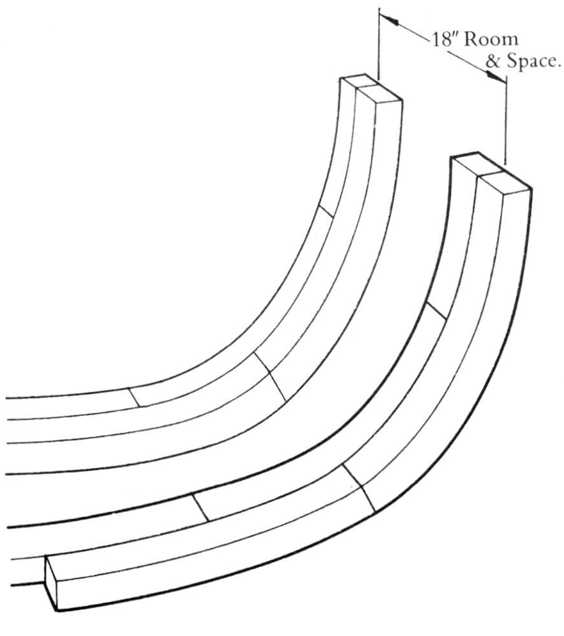


Close joint framing

A start was made on the bottom of the hold on the starboard side, and as the planks were lifted, evidence of fresh water rot was revealed. The spaces between the frames which varied between 5 in and 6 in, were found to be packed solid with a residue of wet black sand. Cleaning out this accumulation of years from the frame spaces was tedious and took a lot of time. Altogether about a ton of the stuff was finally shovelled out from the starboard side. Removal of the hold bottom ceiling planks on the port side followed the same pattern and revealed a similar amount of compacted sand between the frames.

Now for the first time it was possible to see the extent of frame shrinkage and rot, and everywhere it was evident that many of the frames were either too decayed to be retained, or they had been bored for refastening so many times as to render them unfit for further service. In some places the shrinkage of frame faces from the faying surface of the outer planking had caused a gap between them wide enough to admit the fingers of one hand, and the iron fastenings were generally badly corroded throughout. Some of the additional 10 in bolts which had been driven through the butt ends of outside planks were practically eaten away.

The ceiling aft of frame 26 was examined next, and much of this was also of 4 in × 2 in deal.

Removal of the ceiling planks revealed frames in an advanced state of decay.

Some of the original shaped pitch pine ceiling planks remained however, and these were measured, marked, logged and photographed. A plan locating all the original planks was made before their removal and safe stowage ashore.

The starboard engine bearer of oak was next removed, the through bolts of which were heavily corroded. The removal of the port engine bearer proved very difficult — its $\frac{3}{4}$ in diameter iron tie bolts being immovably rusted into oak frames at that point. Loose floors which had carried the weight of the engine and gearbox had been simply wedged to the required height of the propellor shaft line; these and the shaft blocks from the inner to the outer planking were easily removed.

In the fore part of the vessel, the foc'sle or crew accommodation was contained between two bulkheads of tongued and grooved boarding. The forward bulkhead separating the foc'sle from the anchor cable locker did not appear to be original. It extended from the forward face of No. 2 beam to the stem post on the port side, but on the starboard side it was some 17 in further forward, to allow space for a built-in locker. The inner side of this locker formed the division of the bulkhead on the middle line of the vessel. The after bulkhead was positioned at No. 5 beam.

Two built-in bunks, one each side of the foc'sle, shaped to fit the vessel's side and floors and fitted with drop in locker lids were next removed, carefully measured, marked and stowed safely in the workshed.

With the removal of the forward bulkheads and built-in bunks it was possible to strip out the forward section of ceiling. A great deal of the original planking remained and once again each plank was measured, marked and recorded. A plan of the lay of each plank was also made for future reference.

Although it was early August, continuous rain made it necessary to cover the vessel so that work on board could continue. For this purpose a framework of scaffold tubing was constructed around the hull to carry tarpaulin sheets sufficient to cover the deck completely. A strong-

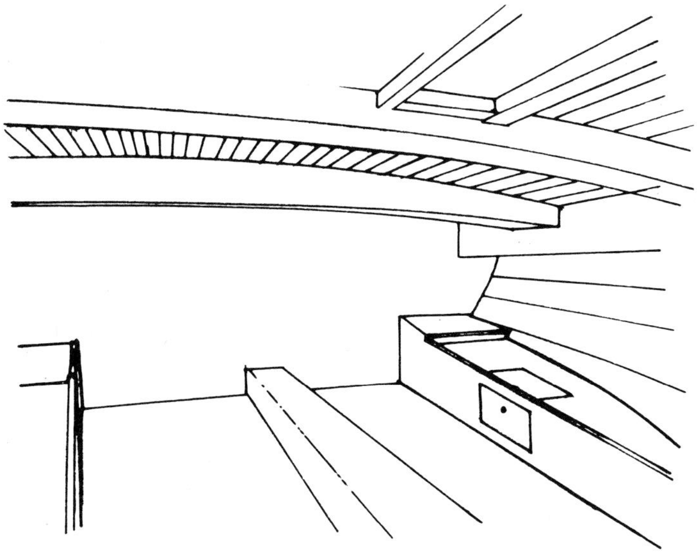

Drawing of the fo'c'sle, taken from a rough sketch before removal of the bunks.

back which ran the entire length of the vessel about 6 ft from deck level provided support along the centre of the cover and allowed sufficient head room to work underneath it. The bottom edges of the cover at the vessel's sides came to within a foot of deck level and were secured by lashing to a temporary lacing rail.

Scaffolding was also placed at 12 ft intervals around the hull to which putlogs were attached which reached to the deck to form a support for the scaffolding boards which formed a working platform. An access and viewing platform was also constructed, some 5 ft 6 in in height with a wide timber ladder leading to a viewing platform 7 ft long and 3 ft 6 in wide. Both the ladder and platform were fitted with strong timber safety rails. As on any site where men at work can be watched at leisure, this amenity proved an irresistable attraction to the Summer visitors to Cotehele Quay. The National Maritime Museum provided photographs, drawings, and a label to illustrate and describe the past history of *Shamrock* and plans for her restoration, and these were displayed on a National Trust Notice board close by the vessel.

Work on the large shed had continued, and by the end of August it had been completely clad with galvanised iron sheets painted with black bitumen.

With the vessel effectively covered against the almost continual rain of this period, it was possible to start work on the removal of the ceiling

The temporary canvas cover completely covered the hull.

The viewing platform allowed the summer visitors to watch the shipwrights at work

from the turn of the bilge to the air courses under the beam shelf. To do this it was necessary to remove 14 wrought iron hanging-knees, seven on each side, which gave support to the side decking in way of the large cargo hatch. The centre hanging-knee on each side was larger and longer than its fellows, and could almost be termed a rider, since it almost reached down the ceiling to the turn of the bilge. Maximum support was therefore provided at the centre of the hatchway by this fitting. Without this, and the additional support of the smaller knees, the hull would soon have lost its shape.

All the iron knees were secured to the sides of the hull with four 12 in × $\frac{3}{4}$ in diameter

Mr Perkins, shipwright in charge, removing the ceiling planks in way of the wrought iron hanging knees.

wrought iron bolts which passed through knee, ceiling, frame timber, and outer plank, the nuts standing proud of the knee. The horizontal or upper limb of the knee was secured to the deck beam or half beams with 6 in × 9 in × $\frac{5}{8}$ in diameter dome or button headed dump bolts. Usually these bolts are pointed and barbed but in *Shamrock* several were simply blunt ended. Many of the beams and half-beams were found to be rotted at their outboard ends, a feature common in all ships of wooden construction.

The port side iron knees were removed first, and all were chipped of rust, wire brushed and given a coat of priming paint before being hung up in the shed ashore. Each one was carefully marked so that it would be correctly positioned when the time came-to replace it.

The subsequent removal of the port side ceiling planks finally revealed the extent of rot and decay in the vessel's frames, and it was evident that not many of the original frame timbers would be serviceable, on this side of the vessel at least.

Next, the iron knees to starboard were removed. They followed the same pattern as those to port, and a 2 in stilson wrench being used to free their nuts, in their corroded state. After carefully marking the starboard ceiling planks were removed, a claw foot bar being used to lever up the bottom edges of the plank. The starboard frames were found to be in an even more advanced state of decay than those to port, and it became obvious at this stage that the task of restoring them would be more in the nature of a rebuilding job.

The next task was to remove all the fastenings that were left sticking up from the frame faces where the ceiling planks had been simply split off. Punching out the secondary fastenings of 10 in × $\frac{1}{2}$ in diameter through bolts also continued, a tedious business which took up a lot of time.

The removal of a steel-plate diving chamber which had been placed on the bottom starboard side of the hold just aft of amidships was the next job. The chamber had been used by divers taking off-shore bed core samples for a Cornish mining company between 1966–73, and was therefore not relevant to the restoration. The quickest and simplest way to remove it was to burn it off with an oxy-acetylene torch, and this was done.

Ashore, a concrete base for the band-saw had been laid in the workshed, workshop, Mould Loft, or just plain shed — according to whoever was describing its function — and by the end of September the band-saw was in position and ready for work.

Meanwhile, the work of research continued and widened. Contact was made with the Senior Surveyor of Ships, Plymouth regarding future classification of *Shamrock*. HMS *Raleigh* assisted the Museum as a training exercise to recover items of ironwork from schooner *Millom Castle* then lying as a hulk in the Lynher River. Wrecks, hulks and shipyards from Falmouth to Maldon in Essex were sought out in the search for traditional fittings, blocks, rope and wire which had either been in use between 1900–30, or which from that period had been hidden away in warehouses, stores, rigging and sail lofts. In a Southampton yard practically every type of block necessary to rig the *Shamrock*, either as a smack or ketch, was located under sheets of steel scrap. Dealing was done on the spot if yards were being cleared of old stock. It was a case of, "there it is, if you want it, you'd better take it today, otherwise it will be gone for ever." The deal was done, cash handed over, and a receipt with covering note was sent to the Museum. Transport was arranged, and away went a 70-year-old anchor, a length of iron shroud wire, still wrapped in oil cloth (meant for a barge and never used), side lights, a set of peak halliard blocks and rigging shackles of various types, for delivery to Cotehele Mill, which The National Trust had put at the Museum's disposal for use as a temporary rigging loft. In this manner genuine traditional gear from working sailing vessels was obtained at a fractional cost, in a manner which was soon to become impossible, since most of the sources for material of this kind have since disappeared. Thus the wisdom of the Museum's decision to proceed with the 'historian's ship' in the early 1970s, and leave it no later, was proved.

By the middle of October 1974 a progress report by the Shipwright-in-charge confirmed that the stripping out of the hull had revealed an advanced state of decay in practically all the frames, and that consideration should now be given to the amount of work involved, and the quantity of new timber which would be required for a virtual rebuilding of the hull.

Work continued on the removal of the rudder post to ascertain the extent of the rot in line of keel. Actually, the visible keel was a false one. It was 'planted' on to *Shamrock*'s original plank or ram keel, when she underwent structural alterations during 1920 to fit her for the coastal trade. The original keel-plank only projected 2 in below the bottom planking and it was pierced by two slots for drop-keels. Its condition was unknown, but highly suspect, as it had been in the vessel for 75 years.

The gaps which were created between the 'planted' keel, the original rounded forefoot, and the run of the vessel aft, had been closed by wedge shaped oak infills — the after ones forming the skeg. The bottom edge of the stem post rested on the keel, which had been cut to half its moulded depth to receive it.

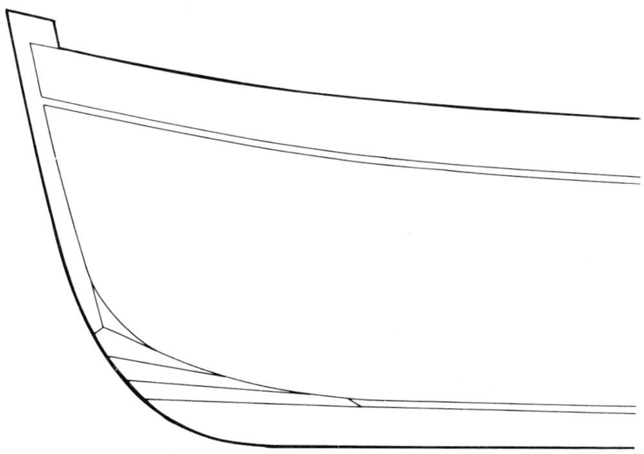

Bow wedges fitted in 1920.

Having removed all the rudder fittings from the stern post, the next major work would be the raising up of the keelson in order to free the frame floors; the dropping of the false keel to examine the original keel, and also to free the skeg assembly. The skeg was through fastened with iron bolts to the keelson, in the same manner as the false keel. The only way to drop both the skeg and the keel was to raise the hull bodily by jacking it up and wedging it about $\frac{1}{2}$ in at a time, then cutting the keel bolts which held the whole assembly together.

Prior to commencing this difficult job, the mainmast tabernacle had to be taken out. The tabernacle consisted of an oak check-board 8 ft 6 in long, 10 in wide and 4½ in thick, on each side of the keelson, the two, through bolted together at their lower ends.

*Shamrock's* original tabernacle.

While preparations for raising the hull were organised, work started on the stripping of the bulwarks prior to the removal of the deck, which was to be the first job after raising the hull, since it would allow more room overhead when lifting the keelson. The hawse pipes, windlass, iron fairleads, bulwark stanchions, planking, main rails and washstrakes were also removed at this stage. Each separate item was measured and marked as required for future reference, and then safely stowed in the shed. The hawsepipes and iron fairleads, which were original, and would be used again, were chipped, wire brushed and coated with a coat of primer.

*Shamrock*'s exposed frames were then carefully checked in order to find out if any through bolts remained in them which might hinder their removal in the near future, and those that were found were punched out.

Three months after the *Shamrock* was hauled out of the water Mr Perkins, the shipwright-in-charge, was able to estimate the quantity of oak that would be required to replace the frames which were clearly unfit for further service, and the material was procured from a local timber merchant.

Ideally, the timbers of the frame should be 9–12 year seasoned English oak with the grain following the curve of frame as closely as possible. These days, it is practically impossible to obtain oak timber of such quality in any great quantity, and it was recognised that many frame floors and foothooks (futtocks) would have to be sawn from slabs of relatively straight grained timber of the required siding (thickness), and wide enough to contain their curvature. Such construction was inevitably of slightly less strength, but acceptable, since although *Shamrock* would require several tons of ballast to trim her, for sailing she would never again be required to carry her full cargo of 50 tons.

To raise the hull it was necessary to acquire two 15 ton hydraulic jacks, and have plenty of timber blocks and packing wedges available. To avoid undue strain on the hull structure it was planned to place the two jacks in selected positions under the false keel and raise the vessel half an inch at a time until her base line was more or less level, then to continue raising her, blocking and wedging all the while, until she reaches a height of 12 in above her previous level.

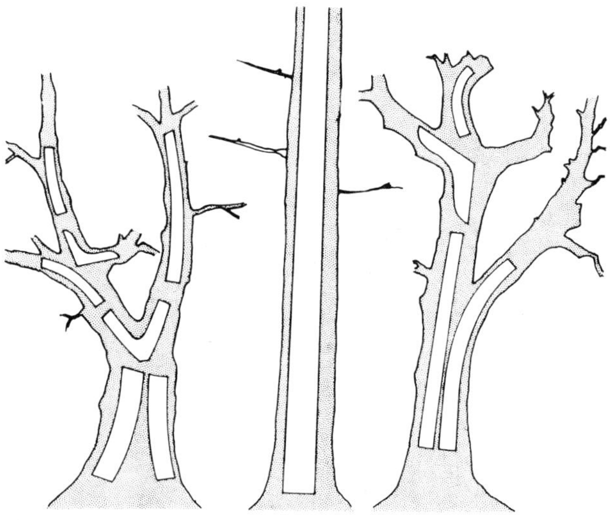

Grown timber. As far as practicable timber for shipbuilding was selected with its grain running true to shape.

Other preparations included the raising of the working platform around *Shamrock*, and also the public viewing platform to accommodate the intended new deck level, together with the addition of another step in the access ladder. Electric lights were also rigged along the backbone of the tarpaulin cover to enable work to be carried on during the approaching winter days. To allow working room for lifting the keelson and removal of frames, the next job after raising the hull, would be the removal of the deck, deck beams and lodging knees. To prevent any distortion of the hull that might result $\frac{3}{4}$ in diameter wires were inserted through holes bored at selected positions between the joint of the original and false keel; their ends were brought up port and starboard and inboard opposite each other; temporary eyes were formed in them with bulldog grips, and bottlescrews shackled to each eye took up the tension required to maintain hull shape. To prevent the wires cutting into the outside planking wooden packing pieces were inserted, to which the wires were stapled.

With everything ready and in place, the task of slowly raising *Shamrock* began in the first week of November.

By the middle of the month *Shamrock* had been jacked up approximately one foot from her former level and was properly cradled with timber blocks and wedges, the blocks being dogged to the cradle to prevent any movement. A necklace of $\frac{3}{4}$ in diameter wire was also placed right round the hull from stern to bow, and well secured to check any tendency for the hull to creep down the slight gradient.

Work now began on the removal of hatch coamings, the hoodway, the waterways, which were in a bad state on both sides of the vessel, and the deck itself. A plan was made of the run of deck planks, and lifting them was begun from the vessel's sides in reverse order to the way that they had been laid. The operation proved to be quite a job, since in addition to the iron fastenings securing the planks to the beams, the pitch which had seeped into the caulked seams had caused the plank edges to adhere to each other. Many planks appeared to be sound enough for future use, and care had to be taken to avoid damaging them during removal.

When all the decking was finally lifted the

Safely blocked up and shored in the cradle prior to stripping the hull.

planks were scraped off, cleaned and marked port and starboard 1, 2, 3 etc. from the centre king plank. A special rack had been constructed in the shed for the deck planks to prevent their twisting or warping, and here they were stowed until required again.

Once the decking had been removed it was possible to see the extent of rot in and around the beam ends, due mostly to fresh water leakage. There are ten beams in *Shamrock* and 20 lodging knees to tie them to the vessel's sides. Some of the grown knees appeared to be serviceable, others, notably, Nos. 9 and 10 starboard appeared soft. On removal extensive rot was found behind them and at the beam ends. The iron through fastenings were completely eaten away.

Work now began on the lifting of the keelson which rested on the upper faces of the frame floors. The only way to get at the bolts which passed through the keelson, original keel, and the false keel, was to split out the floor seatings with a chisel ended steel bar and create enough space to hacksaw through the 1 in diameter bolts. This is simple enough to describe, but it proved to be a tough and awkward job. Once the bolts were sawn through the keelson was jacked up some 2 ft and blocked up with railway sleepers.

The large grown oak stemson was removed entirely and taken ashore for stowage. To allow more working room beams No. 2 and 4 were also removed together with their four lodging knees.

The keelson raised to a height sufficient to allow the removal of the frame floors.

# Chapter 2

*The hull; frame problems. The sail and rigging plans. December 1974–August 1975.*

With the end of the year drawing near, the short winter days with rain and wind proved the value of the tarpaulin cover which allowed work to continue inside the hull. A lamp on a wandering lead was necessary to light up particular areas of work, and by Christmas 1974 everything was ready for the main job of the restoration to begin. This was the almost complete re-framing of the hull, a task which was to test the skill of the shipwright-in-charge and his two man team, since any mistakes here could lead to the loss of hull shape.

New frame timbers in position.

The plan for re-framing the hull was to retain the original frame timbers, where possible, and to make moulds of all those timbers which were unserviceable as they lay still held in place by the outer planking of the hull. Since there are no original drawings or a contemporary half-model of *Shamrock* in existence, every timber replacement had to be copied, even if it had been set up wrongly in the first place.

It was decided to use hard-board for the moulds, since it would be obtained in sheets wide enough to include the curve of any timber. It was strong and flexible enough for handling in a confined space, and it could be sawn accurately without risk of splitting.

To obtain a mould, the inner surface of the outer planking was cleaned away, and its curvature at that point transferred by scribing to the hard-board. A bevel-set was laid along the planking at selected points, and the change of bevel was transferred to the mould at corresponding points on its curvature. Other marks and instructions were noted on the mould as thought necessary.

The mould accurately cut to shape, was then laid on the new sawn oak slab which had already been cut to the siding — the width of its inner and outer faying surfaces — of the selected timber. If there was any grain curvature in the sawn oak slab it was used to advantage. Where the curvature was considerable, as at the turn of bilge, cutting across the grain was unavoidable. Care and skilled judgment was required in some parts of the hull, where salt water corrosion had eaten into iron plank fastenings, causing an accumulation of rust between plank and frame. The build up of rust had forced the plank off the outer faying surface of the frame in several places causing slight local distortion which had to be taken into account.

On 4 January 1975 work was begun on the restoration or rebuilding of frames starting on No. 14 frame, almost amidships. This particular frame although obviously too decayed for retention in the *Shamrock*, was of sufficient strength to be made up again after removal, for use as a museum exhibit, and it can now be seen in Gallery A in the West Wing of the National Maritime Museum at Greenwich. After moulds had been made of the floor and futtocks, the frame was carefully split apart with chisel ended bars and wedges and taken ashore ready for future assembly. This first attempt at removal and complete replacement with new timber, demonstrated the difficulties which lay ahead, especially with reard to handling the 12 ft × 6 in × 8 in floor timbers. The new oak for a floor of this size weighed about 3 cwt before cutting, and with its awkward shape it was as much as two men could safely handle on the band saw.

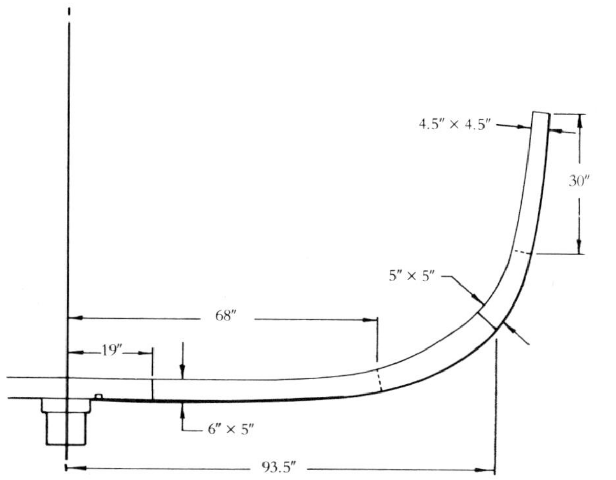


Sketch of frame 14 with dimensions.

Frame No. 13 was removed next, and like all the square frames it was made up of a floor, two first futtocks, two second futtocks, two third futtocks and two top timbers. The heads and heels of the floors and futtocks were simply butted one on top of the other without coaks; some of the short top-timbers were scarphed, however, with the scarph made to 'lock-in' the back of the frame so as to resist pressure from lying on quay walls, or from being squeezed between other vessels. The square heads and heels, or butt end joints of the separate timbers were given good shift to each other for maximum strength, and arranged in the usual manner *i.e.* side by side with their faying surfaces close jointed throughout their length, and tied with galvanised steel bars.

The closed joint frame is particularly susceptible to rot in the faying surfaces due to lack of ventilation between the timbers. The timbers of *Shamrock*'s frames were too large for specialised pickling treatment, and it was decided that all faying surfaces would be liberally soaked in creosote, not only some time before assembly, and immediately before, but also after assembly as a constant exercise, so that any 'opening up' of the timbers would allow fresh creosote to seep in.

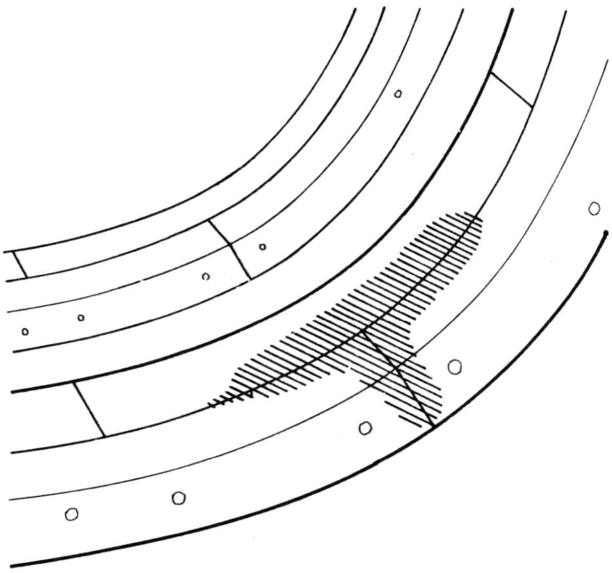

The butts between the heads and heels of the timbers and the closed joint of the frame are very liable to rot as the hull works and allows water to penetrate.

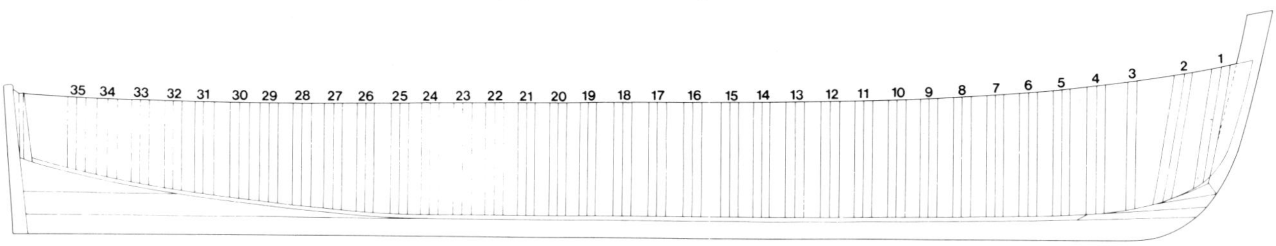


Disposition of the frames compiled from measurements taken over a period as sections of the ceiling were removed. Some timbers had obviously been removed from No. 3 frame. As restored No. 3 is a complete frame of doubled timber.

In January 1975 the first attempts at breaking out and replacing the vessel's timbers allowed a rough estimate to be made of the time required partially to restore, or completely to rebuild all of the vessel's 35 frames. To make the moulds, split out the original frame, remove and stack unserviceable timber ashore; cut new oak floors and futtocks, trim them, manhandle them aboard, fasten them together, and then temporarily secure the complete frame to the shell of the original outer planking, was taking three men up to 15 working days to accomplish. The band-saw in the shed was used to convert the sawn timber, but otherwise handsaws and the adze were used to trim and bevel to the mould line, and finishing work of this kind needed all the skill of traditional shipwrighting.

A meeting was held between The National Trust, the Museum and the shipwright-in-charge to see what could be done to speed up this particular job, since it was obviously going to take well over a year to complete at this rate. It was agreed that wherever possible original timbers should be left in the vessel, and that some cracked floors which, ideally, should have been removed, should in fact, be strengthened by doubling; that is, by having additional new floors secured alongside them. In this way the time taken to remove the original floor would be saved.

This attempt to keep the time needed for restoration within realistic limits was, to a certain extent, offset by the loss of two shipwrights. For various reasons, they had to be replaced by National Trust men who, although skilled in the use of woodworking tools, were not professional shipwrights. However, at this stage, it was confirmed by the vessel's owners that the restoration should be as good a one as possible, provided that it could be done with the money available to the project and within a tolerable time. Other decisions made at this time by the Museum and the Trust were that natural fibre rope should be used for the running and standing rigging, and that the shipwright-in-charge should continue to photograph every significant part of the restoration as he had done to date. This photographic record was to be processed by the Museum for the archives, and also for use in displays at Greenwich and Cotehele Quay relating to the *Shamrock* restoration in particular, and wooden ship construction in general. A number of these photographs appear in this book.

Meanwhile, the Museum's research programme continued, and as a result of enquiries all over the West Country, several more photographs of *Shamrock* were discovered. The Maritime Trust, owners of the *Kathleen & May*, which at that time was lying fully restored to something approximating to her original rig at Sutton Harbour, Plymouth, informed the Museum that the vessel's original bowsprit was laying in a local shipyard, and although soft in some places, it could probably be cut down to provide a lighter spar. This, and all other offers of contemporary gear and equipment were very gratefully received and no time was lost in inspecting all offers first hand. Chatham Naval Barracks were also approached re the supply of flax canvas, and local sailmakers were advised that a suit of traditional sails would be required for *Shamrock* in due course.

Because of insufficient data, the initial intention had been to rig the vessel as a smack, as she had been in her later working life, but the increasing information relating to how she was rigged as a ketch during the 1920s, led to a final decision on this point to be delayed. However, a sailmaker was found who was willing to stand by until there was sufficient information, and, as the difference between the sail area of the smack and ketch rig was not too great, it was decided to purchase all the necessary canvas and bolt rope, twine, cringle irons etc. before they became too expensive.

The Museum and The National Trust received generous offers from various bodies, and private persons, as the interest in *Shamrock* grew, most notably from Mr Geoffrey Le Mare of Chelsworth, Suffolk with a substantial cheque, and The Ocean Transport and Trading Company offered to meet half the cost of the sails.

By the end of March 1975 research by the Museum had established the most probably position of the mizzen mast which had been removed after 1934. A previous inspection of the deck and keelson where the mast was thought to have been positioned had failed to reveal evidence of it ever being there at all. The hole in the deck beam for the mainsheet eyebolt, which practically decided the length of the main boom, was discovered easily enough, but the holes which would have been bored through the sides of the keelson for the iron bolts which secured the heels of the tabernacle side cheeks could not be located, and evidence that the cheeks had passed through the deck planks was also lacking. To obliterate such obvious signs the holes must have been well plugged, and at some period planks must have been renewed in that area.

However, further information from Mr Grosse of Truro, who had sailed in *Shamrock* during her last years, and who had known Mr Trebilcock, her Master during the 1930s, confirmed that the mizzen had indeed been set up in a tabernacle, just like the mainmast. At this date there were no photographs showing the ketch rigged vessel broadside on, but many others were coming to light, including three very significant prints from Mr Grosse himself, which justified the drawing of a 1:48 scale plan showing the *Shamrock* as she most probably appeared in 1926. The height of the mizzen remained unknown — it varied from between 20 and 37 ft, according to descriptions obtained from several visitors to the Quay who claimed that they had seen *Shamrock* as a ketch — but from more reliable evidence it was possible to make a fairly shrewd guess as to its real height and diameter.

An interesting sidelight on the pitfalls of research was revealed by a photograph of *Shamrock* taken at Truro in the late 30s from directly astern. This showed the vessel with what appeared to be the normal long boom of the typical smack rigged Tamar barge, with its sheet end almost directly over the taffrail. At first this photograph was accepted as proof that the vessel had been rigged with a typical long boom like the *Flora May* in this fashion, but when a scale size sail plan was drawn the exceptionally long-headed mast seen in the photograph (which compared exactly with the one removed from the vessel at Cotehele) produced a mainsail with an abnormally short luff for a boom of such length. It did not look right, but the photographic evidence seemed to justify it. It was not until Mr Bishop of St Budeaux (who some weeks later recognised himself in the photograph) confirmed that the boom seen in the photograh was in reality the boom of the original ketch rigged mainsail, and not, as an optical illusion made it appear, a long boom at all, that the puzzle was solved.

*Shamrock* at Truro during the late thirties.

Further drawings of the *Shamrock* were made in the light of information that had come available from various sources, and a final decision was made by the owners to have the vessel rigged as a ketch *circa* 1926. At this stage apart from actual confirmation of the height of the mizzen, sufficient data had been gathered for rigging the vessel in this manner, and everyone concerned with the restoration agreed that it was the most handsome of all the rigs which she had sailed under at various times.

It was now necessary to find a suitable mizzen mast, plus a bowsprit, main boom and gaff, mizzen boom and gaff and a club or forestaysail boom. A search for suitable spars was carried out by the Museum, and visits were made to many South Coast ship and yacht yards. Once the owner or shipyard manager had been acquainted with the facts of the restoration, shown photographs of the vessel, and was convinced of the historical significance of the work, their cooperation was readily forthcoming. Many fine spars were located, but so large as to make their transport and conversion to size totally uneconomic; others which had actually been barge masts and spars were found to be too far gone for use, but a lot of useful iron fittings were taken off them, such as saddle bolts for the throat and peak halliards.

Eventually, information regarding some Oregon pine sticks which were available in London, not far from the Museum itself, came from an anonymous rigger engaged in maintenance work on the Museum's 100 ft flagpole.

As a result, a visit to the premises of Mackney and Servis, in North London, revealed that they had several fine Oregon pine spars, one or two of which were practically of the length and diameter required for the mizzen mast and main boom. They could also provide the remainder of the spars to the size required, if need be.

This was to the advantage of the restoration because it meant that the expense of buying and transporting timber to Cotehele, and the further time and consequent expense of converting it into masts and spars, would be avoided. Also the timber was well seasoned, but not dried out, without shakes or objectionable knots, and of those inspected, the centre of the tree growth rings was located in the centre of the spar, as it should be, if warping and twisting are to be avoided.

On 28 May an order was placed for five spars —

- A mizzen 37 ft 6 in OA with a squared heel 8 in in diameter
- A main boom 26 ft OA and 6 in max: diameter
- A main gaff 24 ft 6 in OA and $5\frac{3}{4}$ in max: diameter
- A mizzen boom 15 ft 6 in OA and $5\frac{1}{2}$ in max: diameter
- A mizzen gaff 14 ft 6 in OA and $5\frac{1}{4}$ in max: diameter

Final shaping and finishing of the spars would be done at Cotehele. A bowsprit was to be made from the original *Kathleen & May* bowsprit, donated by The Maritime Trust, and a length of spruce had been put aside by Mr Eley at Cotehele, for the forestaysail boom. Thus the problem of providing masts and spars for *Shamrock* was solved.

A complete specification of rope required for the running rigging was supplied to British Ropes Limited of Charlton, who, after consultation with the Museum, agreed to supply 1st grade three stranded hawser laid manila rope, laid up

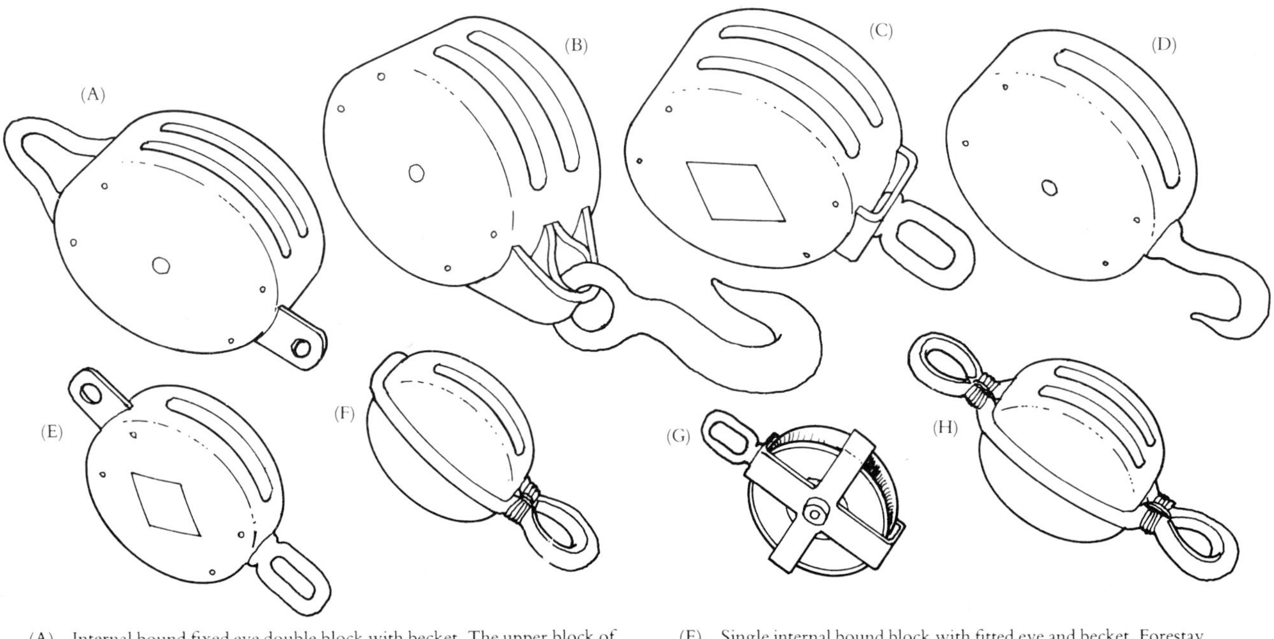


(A) Internal bound fixed eye double block with becket. The upper block of the main throat Halliard.

(B) Double block with free hook use to form part of a heavy duty purchase.

(C) Double block with swivel oval eye, lower block of main throat purchase.

(D) Single block with fitted hook. Main Peak Halliard span block.

(E) Single internal bound block with fitted eye and becket. Forestay Halliard block.

(F) Wire stropped single block with seized in eye Jib head Block.

(G) Small iron cargo gin-block with swivel oval eye.

(H) Wire stropped double block with two seized Thimble eyes. Used to form part of a purchase.

right or left handed as required, in 220 metre coils. On 29 May an order was placed for one coil of 3 in circumference left handed lay for the main sheet; one coil of 3 in circumference right handed lay for the main throat and peak halliards; one coil of $2\frac{1}{2}$ in circumference right handed lay for mizzen sheet, throat and peak halliards, and one coil of 2 in circumference right handed lay for jib and staysail sheets and halliards. A coil of 21 thread cordage was also ordered for head lashings, earrings, and other general rigging purposes.

By the end of May the 30 odd blocks of all descriptions which had been located at Belsize Shipyard, Southampton, together with shackles, iron wire stays and other fittings salved from local sailing barges, fishing boats, and yachts, had been gathered together, loaded on to the Museum van and delivered to the 'rigging loft' at Cotehele Mill. A mile or so down the road leading to the river at Cotehele Quay, work continued on the slow, methodical and laborious task of restoring or rebuilding the *Shamrock*'s frames. With the breaking out of each successive frame, the state of the original planking in way of the outer frame faces was revealed for the first time, and hopes that much of the planking could be used again were gradually dispelled. Gribble damage and rot had reduced the inner faying surfaces of some planks to one third of its original 2 in thickness. At other places an average of two thirds thickness remained and it was becoming obvious that these conditions would apply to practically all of the outer planking.

It was also discovered that additional treenail fastenings had been driven through plank, frame and ceiling at some time during *Shamrock*'s working life. The treenails (usually pronounced as 'trunnels') were some $9\frac{3}{4}$ in in length and $1\frac{1}{8}$ in diameter, all of oak, with their heads in way of the outside planking, wedged and caulked. Splitting across the end grain and inserting an oak wedge or punch to swell the outside head of the treenail helped to prevent the 'drawing' of the plank off the frame face. Ideally, the treenail, which should always be of the very best seasoned English oak, should be used to fix oak planks to oak frames, thereby ensuring that they all shrink and swell at the same rate. Treenails were successfully used for hull fastenings in men-o-war, when they were built entirely of oak; but as this timber became scarcer, especially after Trafalgar, and various other English and foreign timbers were used, their differing rates of shrinkage very often caused the oak treenail to lose its holding power, and this form of hull fastening fell out of favour in naval construction.

East Coast fishing smacks, built oak on oak, still continued to favour the treenail, and many builders preferred to use them throughout the 19th and early part of the 20th century. Many wooden trading vessels were treenail fastened between the light and loaded waterline, because it was in this area between wind and water that iron fastenings corroded most noticeably. Another point in favour of treenails was that the heads wore down at the same rate as the outer planking when subjected to abrasion from dock walls, pier fenders, other vessels alongside *etc*.

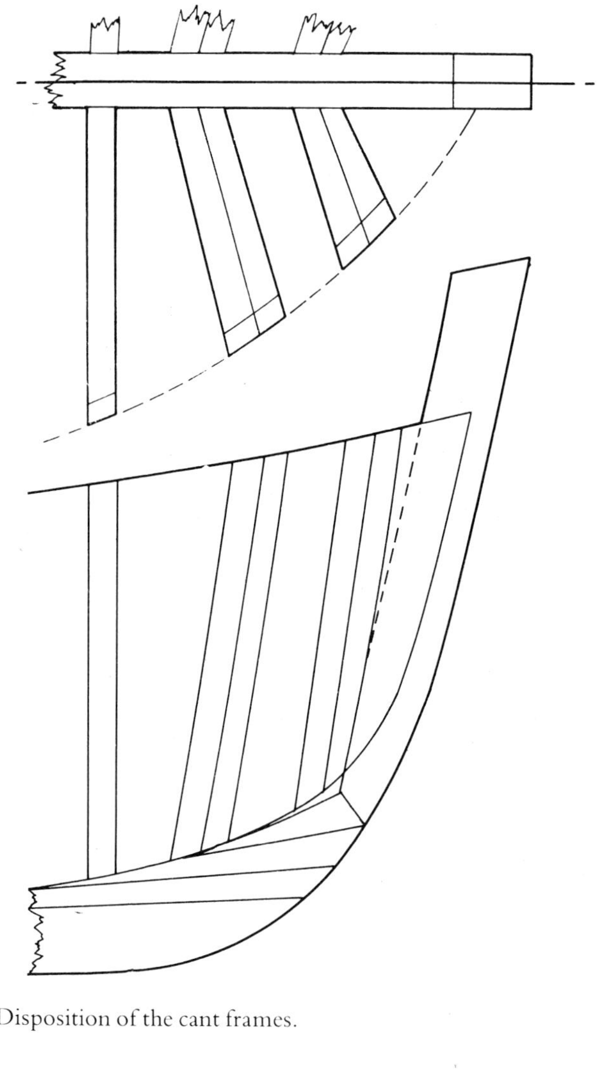

Disposition of the cant frames.

Most of the treenails in *Shamrock* were found to be loose, some were broken, and Mr Perkins was of the opinion that none of them were original fastenings. Treenails therefore, were not to be used for the restoration. A number of the treenails taken from the vessel were, nevertheless, kept for record and Museum display purposes.

By August 1975 15 frames had been either restored or fully replaced in the gutted hull, the average time to complete each frame having been reduced to ten working days. Another 18 square frames — those with floors which crossed the keel — and two cant frames in the bow had to be restored or renewed before any other structural work could be put in hand.

The timbers in the fore part of the hull were in a very poor state. Note the cant frames in the bow.

At the current rate of progress, with the same team, consisting of Mr Perkins, the shipwright-in-charge (who was acting in this capacity for some 19 working hours each week), Mr Warne and Mr Carter both full-time employees of The National Trust and Mr Eley, the Foreman of the Cotehele Estate, who was responsible for the day to day running of the site, it would take at least another 180 working days, or up to April 1976, to complete the framing of the hull.

Further estimates made at the time in consultation with the National Maritime Museum were:

For replacement or renewal of original keel, renewal of skeg and replacement of the 'planted' or false keel — 62 working days, completing by June 1976.

Removing the decayed and damaged sternpost, selecting and converting, moulding and fitting the new sternpost — 67 working days, completing by September 1976.

Removing the sternpost rudder and decayed transom, and building and fitting the new oak transom — 63 working days, completing by December 1976.

Removing outer planking and renewing as required — 64 working days, completing by April 1977.

Removing decayed beam shelves, beams and replacing by new and replacing ceiling — 121 working days, completing by October 1977.

Removing original decking and replacing with new where required, and renewal of bulwark structure — 64 working days, completing by end of December 1977.

Making and replacing new cargo hatch, deck fittings and caulking deck — 66 working days, completing by April 1978.

Caulking the hull planking — 65 working days, completing by July 1978.

Making mizzen mast gaffs booms and all the fittings and fixtures necessary to rig the vessel fully — 65 working days, completing by October 1978.

Rigging and fitting out by Spring 1979.

These estimates made no allowance for holidays, sickness of staff, delay in supplying of materials, or for weather conditions preventing outside work. They were provided at this early stage of the project to indicate the extent of the work which lay ahead, so that future decisions regarding the economics of the restoration could be made on a realistic basis.

# Chapter 3

*Finding contemporary materials; fitting new beamshelf beams and knees. August 1975–December 1976.*

On 30 July 1975 the first stage of the Museum's new Outstation at Cotehele Quay was opened to the public by Lord Morley and Ole Crumlin Pedersoln of the Danish Viking Ship Museum. The ceremony was attended by the Director and Deputy Director of The National Maritime Museum, Mr Trinick of the National Trust's local organisation, Mr and Mrs Le Mare, who had given generous donations to the project, Mr and Mrs Hoskings (the former Master of the vessel and his wife) and many guests who in some form or another had contributed to the *Shamrock* restoration.

This first display was mounted in the stone warehouse on Cotehele Quay which had been renovated by The National Trust. One room had been restored as a 19th century shipping office by the Trust; in the other, the National Maritime Museum had mounted a display illustrated with photographs and models of *Shamrock* as she appeared before and after structural alterations in 1920. The display also included other exhibits illustrating the importance of the river in the industrial and social life of the Tamar Valley a century before. A special section was devoted to the saving and restoration of *Shamrock*, and parts of her decayed structure and fastenings were displayed as an example of what was involved in the restoration of a wooden working sailing vessel.

Now that the extent and duration of the restoration had been realistically assessed, The National Trust and the National Maritime Museum combined their efforts to raise sufficient money for the project to continue. During the next few months negotiations for a Grant from the Government Fund for the Preservation of Technological and Scientific material, were successfully

The stone warehouse on Cotehele Quay.

concluded. The Maritime Trust donated sufficient money to cover the cost of the new mizzen mast and spars, and other donations in cash or in kind were received by The National Trust as a result of appeals.

The National Maritime Museum's programme of research and seeking out of contemporary materials, was to continue, together with a regular monitoring of the restoration, and for this purpose I was formally put on detached duty to deal solely with the *Shamrock* for three days each week. It was essential that the actual work of restoration should not be delayed by lack of technical information or the supply of contemporary materials or fittings. Such information and materials still existed if one knew where to look for them, but seeking them out required knowledge which could only be gained locally, and also the ability to make decisions regarding acquisitions *etc.* on the spot.

Thus, a telephone call from a contractor clearing a disused shipyard site near Plymouth, stating that a lot of old iron that they had dug up was going for scrap that day, resulted in a hurried visit to the site, and the salvaging of a contemporary anchor which proved to be sound enough and of a size suitable for *Shamrock*.

*Shamrock's* bower anchor.

In a like manner over a thousand 10 in × $\frac{1}{2}$ in diameter galvanised iron bolts were discovered in a Southampton shipyard, buried under tons of scrap. These could be purchased for less than a quarter of their current value provided they were removed by the time the scrap was cleared that coming week. A quick inspection to check their condition, and a weekend spent in extricating and bagging the bolts, and within 3 days they were ready for transportation to Cotehele. These bolts were ideal for through fastenings of heavy timbers, such as beam shelves and lodging knees, and many would be required as the restoration proceeded.

By October 18 frames were in position and by March 1976 24 frames had been replaced and the forward sections of the beam shelves had been made and cramped into position.

The original beamshelf was of pitch pine, some $2\frac{3}{4}$ in thick and 9 in wide. It was made up of three sections on each side of the hull, scarphed together to form a continuous ledge from stem post to transom on which the deck beams should rest. The lower outer edge of the shelf was chamfered along its entire length. This prevented what would otherwise have been sharp corner edges from being split by heavy cargo or cargo handling gear. It also improved the otherwise unfinished appearance, and allowed the bottom edge of the shelf to fit snugly into the iron hanging knees which were shaped to its contour at that point, thereby providing additional support from below.

Like most of the other timbers in the vessel, the true state of the beam shelf could not be gauged

Cramping in the beamshelf.

until its various sections had been removed. Here again, fresh water seepage had caused rot and decay which had reduced the scantling to levels which were unacceptable for the restoration.

Pitch pine of the size and quality required was very difficult to come by, and with the limited amount of money available for the project, prohibitively expensive.

Larch was eventually chosen as the most suitable substitute timber for this job. Provided care is used in its selection it is excellent for hull planking, fairly easy to bend, not prone to splitting, and holds fastenings well.

The fitting of a beam shelf can be an awkward and frustrating job if due consideration has not been given to the amount of curve inside the frames at the bows, and also the rise of sheer. The shelf timber had to be bent round cold, and if knots or curving grain are not carefully checked, the loss of longitudinal strength which they may cause, could lead to a fracturing of the timber at a critical point.

The method used to 'cramp home' the beamshelf.

The methods used for bending or 'cramping in' a beam shelf varies with the amount of stress required, available labour, and other factors peculiar to a particular vessel or shipyard. A slow deliberate bending allows even compression of the grain, and at the area of maximum curvature the placing of cramps close together lessen the risk of cracking the timber. For *Shamrock*, the shipwright-in-charge used a timber shore, placed upright with its heel 'G' clamped to a frame at the turn of the bilge close by a selected point of bending. A packing piece of soft timber was placed on the beam shelf to prevent the crushing of its surface, and a sash cramp, placed just above the same frame head, was used to force the timber shore against the packing piece, and thereafter, gradually to pull the beam shelf hard in against the inside face of the frame. Once it was 'cramped home' it was held in place there with very heavy metal plate 'hairpin' clamps, which were locked over the outside plank, the frame head, beam shelf and packing piece, then tightly wedged. The hairpin clamps remained in position until fastening off the beam shelf could begin, but before that could be done a decision regarding the removal and replacement of the original outer planking had to be made.

In most of the Tamar sailing barges pitch pine was generally used for the topside planking. English elm was mostly used below the turn of bilge, because elm endures well under totally immersed conditions. Elm planks of fairly large size could be obtained locally, but seasoned larch in sizes over 12 ft length 6 in wide and 2 in thick were proving difficult to come by. Kiln dried Douglas Fir was available and facilities for chemically impregnating the timber with preservatives against early decay existed in the area.

Having sought the advice of local timber merchants, and official timber publications relating to the availability of timber for outside planking of the required size, Larch was chosen as being the most suitable for the sheerstrake and topsides, and if larch was unobtainable locally in the quantity desired, then kiln-dried and tanalised Douglas Fir would be used down to turn of bilge, and English elm for the bottom.

Work on the frame replacements continued meanwhile, and when frame 27 was completed, it was decided to take advantage of the coming summer to work on the hull planking and other major outside work during fine weather, and to finish off work inside the vessel on wet days.

The rigidity of the hull would need to be maintained when the 'planted' false keel was eventually dropped to facilitate removal of the original keel. It was therefore decided to remove the original sheerstrake and two strakes of topside planking to port and starboard and permanently fasten off the clamped beamshelf so as to obtain the necessary stiffness.

The 'electrically fired' steel tube 'steam box'.

The removal of the planking was simply a question of chopping sufficient wood away from around the head of the cut nail fastening, which held it to the frame, then inserting a clawhead lever under the nailhead, and drawing it out. The old planks then served as moulds for the new ones. To facilitate the bending of new planks they were softened in an improvised 'steam box' made up of a metal pipe some 8 in in diameter, fitted with a flange cover at one end, with a slot in it of sufficient size for the insertion of the plank end. An electrically heated boiler was fitted at the other end of the pipe to provide the steam. This device was one of the very few departures from traditional practice during the entire restoration, but it worked on the same lines as the old steam chest except that they had boilers with fires which were usually fed by timber scraps.

The new planks were fastened to the frame timbers with 6 in spike nails, wedge-shaped along their length, and heavily galvanised. Plank and frame timbers were bored before the nail was driven and plenty of creosote was soaked into the holes, and on the frame faces and faying surface of the plank before fastening off began. The sequence of fastening was one nail just below the top edge of the plank, driven a little off centre one way into one timber of the frame — and another nail just above the lower edge of the plank driven a little off centre the other way into the adjacent timber of the same frame. By staggering the fastenings in this manner they are cast out of the line of grain of both plank and frame timber, thus being less liable to split either during the initial fastening off, or later, when planks and timbers swell or shrink at differing rates.

Pre-boring through plank and frame is required before any fastenings can be driven.

The oak for the new deck beams, which had been specially selected and ordered some weeks before, had been delivered and work now began to convert the timber. This was done in the shed as a wet weather job, and since rain had been plentiful during the past few weeks the work

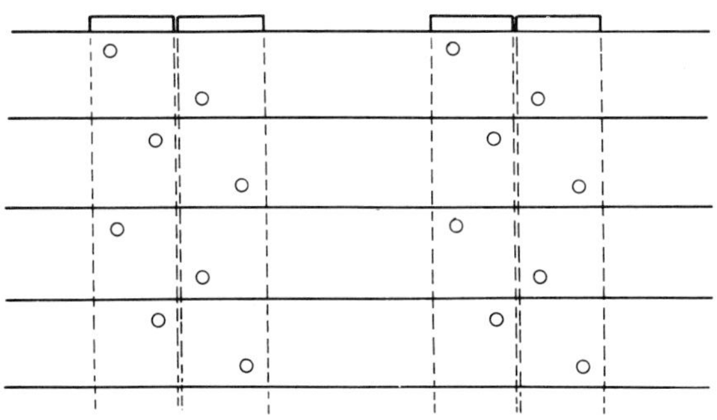

Sequence of fastenings.

had progressed satisfactorily. Apart from their bulk the beams presented no real difficulty in working. The curvature of the main beams was 3½ in at the centre, and this 'round up' as well as providing strength, produced a camber to the deck which allowed water to drain from its surface.

No. 5 beam was made first. This was the forward main beam upon which the head ledges of the cargo hatch were supported. When it was ready it had to be manhandled from shed to *Shamrock* since there were no derricks or cranes. First it was carted on a four wheel trolley to the site of the public viewing platform on the vessel's port side, where a differential chain block was used to hoist the beam to platform level. The starboard end of the beam was shoved inboard, a roller was placed under it, and also on to the old beam, which, acting as a bridge, allowed the new beam to be moved across it. The new beam was then lowered on to the beamshelf aft of the old one. Work then began on the breaking out of the original beam which in due course was moved sufficiently far forward to allow room for its replacement. The two end grains of the new beam had already been liberally soaked with creosote and the bear-

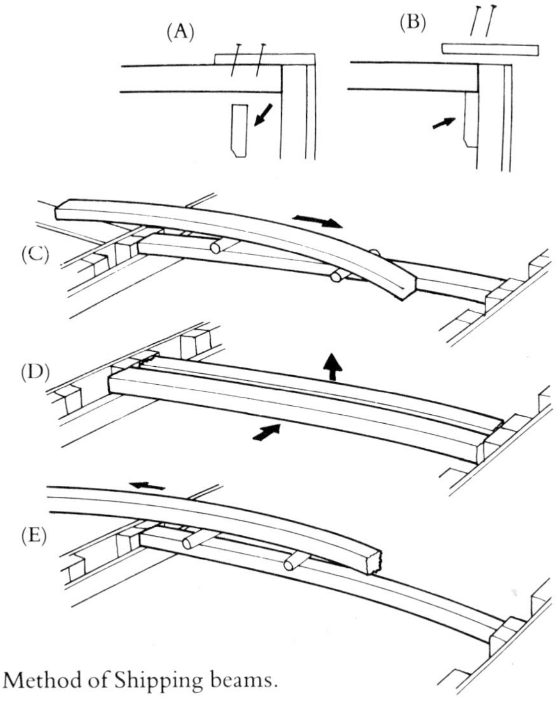


Method of Shipping beams.

(A) Old beam temporarily secured in position after original beam shelf removed.

(B) New beam shelf fitted beneath old beam.

(C) New beam rolled in on its side.

(D) New beam resting on beam shelf aft of old beam. Old beam broken out, and replaced by new beam.

(E) Old beam rolled out.

Horizontally disposed timber lodging knees and vertically disposed wrought iron hanging knee.

ing surface of the shelf and the timbers of the frame were treated likewise before the new beam was finally placed in position. The original beam was then removed from the vessel, using a roller as before, this time using the new beam as a bridge.

Beam No. 4 forward was made and fitted next, followed by beam No. 6, the other main cargo hatch beam, upon which the after head ledges of the hatch rested. The lower corner-edges of all beams and half-beams were chamfered to prevent splintering and also to give them a 'finished' appearance.

The beam ends are secured to the sides of a wooden vessel with horizontally laid lodging knees, and vertically disposed hanging knees. The 14 hanging knees in *Shamrock* were made of wrought iron and were in good enough condition to be used again. The 20 lodging knees, however, were badly affected by rot, some were split and only three or four were fit enough for further use. Ideally, all knees should be of grown or compass oak, since they are less liable to be shaken by stress or a collision than those shaped from relatively straight grained timber. In spite of enquiries covering a wide area of Cornwall, Devon and Hampshire compass oak of the size and of the quantity could not be found.

Oak with a twisted or suitably disturbed grain often gives good service in this capacity, and it was from this type of timber that most of the lodging knees had to be fashioned. As soon as the initial shaping and trimming was completed on the bench ashore, the knees were got aboard, and with moulds and handsaw, made to fit snugly in the angle between the beam and ships side. Once again, the holes bored for the galvanised through bolts were thoroughly soaked in creosote, as were all faying surfaces, before fastening off the knee began.

By the end of October 1976 29 frames had been fitted, nine new strakes of topside planking were fastened off, the beamshelf and beams were fitted as far aft as the new frames and work had commenced on the removal of the old stem assembly and the making of the new stempost.

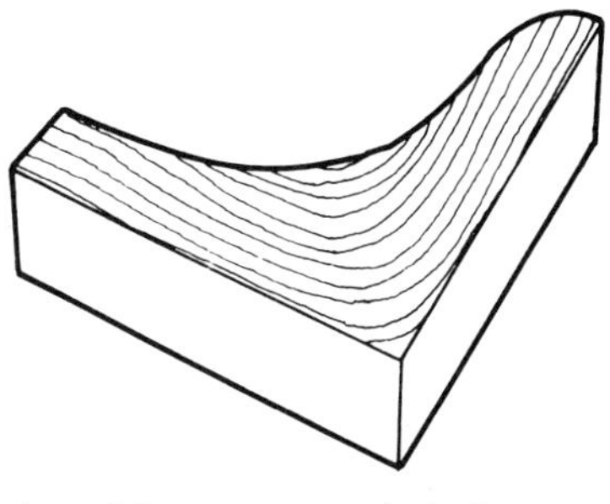

Lodging knee shaped from grown oak timber.

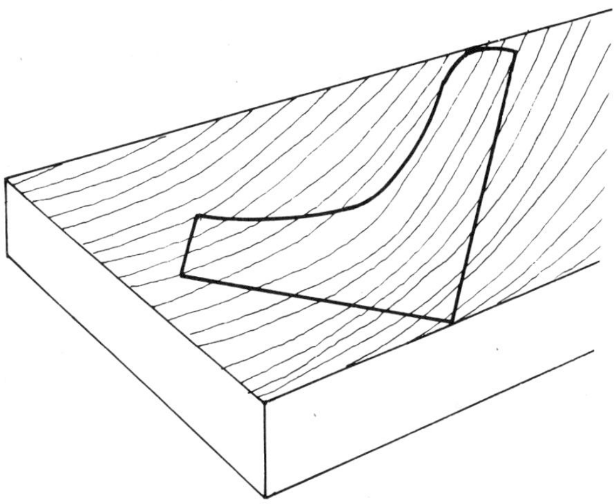

Lodging knee sawn from a slab of timber making maximum use of curved grain.

A selection of sailmakers tools.

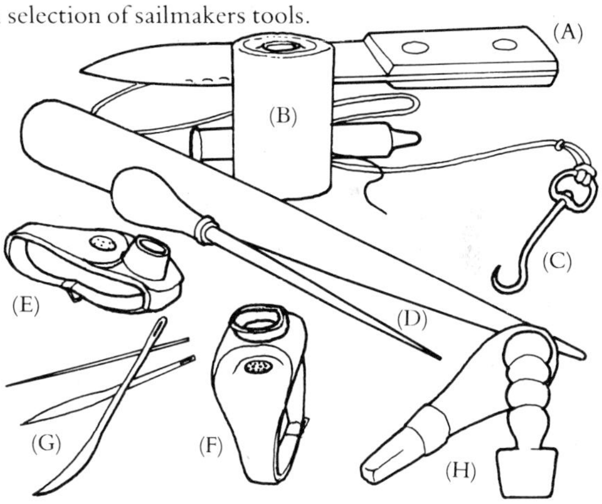


(A) Knife (B) Twine

(C) Hook (D) Fids

(E) Roping Palm (F) Seaming Palm

(G) Needles (H) Seam Rubber

The Museum had meanwhile continued its research programme. Mr Knight, a retired sailmaker who had formerly worked for Cory Barge Works at Charlton, visited the Museum to discuss the arrangements for making a suit of traditional sails for *Shamrock*. On the Museum's instructions, he had already purchased all the materials and flax canvas required for rigging the vessel as a ketch, and Corys had generously offered to keep it in their rigging-loft, free of charge, until it was needed.

The purpose of the sailmaker's visit was to confirm the arrangements whereby he agreed to make all the sails on the spot at Cotehele. Being retired he was free to spend time on the site, and be able to check at first hand all dimensions as the sails were made. He could measure off his spars at leisure and set himself up as required, rent one of the National Trust properties, and thereby make a working holiday of what he considered to be a very interesting and worthwhile job.

A visit to Cotehele was fixed for November and June or July 1977 was agreed as a possible time to commence work on the sails. The Museum had also received the new boat, which it had commissioned Alan Hinks of Appledore to build for the *Shamrock*.

*Shamrock's* workboat.

This was a straight-forward 13 ft clinker built workboat, entirely typical of those used by the Tamar sailing barges. In use it was usually towed astern in river and esturial waters, or stowed on, or to one side of, the cargo hatch on coastal passages. Some barges rigged a fish tackle for hoisting in and out, others rigged hoisting tackles as and when required.

The Museum had also established a liaison with Mr Woodley and Mr Rowse, Directors of the Torpoint Slipping Company. This firm specialised in the fitting out and restoration of wooden sailing vessels, among them the brigantine *Marques* of Spanish Mediterranean origin and then based at Charlestown, Cornwall. The Company had recently acquired the hulk of *Grazia* formerly a Danish working sailing vessel, and were planning to strip out her useable timber and iron fittings. After a meeting on board the hulk, Mr Woodley generously agreed to present the wrought iron chainplates, cargo hatch wedge cleats, shroud bottlescrews, 3 in circumference wire shrouds, a quantity of chain cable, wrought iron half round rubbing strips, and other items useful to the restoration, for the cost of their removal only; or, if the Museum could provide its own labour, for no cost at all, as a gesture of goodwill towards the *Shamrock* restoration.

Regular fortnightly visits were made to Cotehele, not only to monitor the progress of the restoration, but to deal with any problems relating to work on site. Drawings, sketches and photographs were received from Mr Perkins illustrating various stages of construction, all of which were listed and recorded in the Museum's log book of the restoration.

## Chapter 4

*Stempost, keel and transom; making new rigging. January–April 1977.*

By the end of 1976 work had begun on the making of the new stempost to replace the old one. The new stempost was fashioned from a single huge branch cut from an oak tree which had been felled some 2 years earlier on a nearby farm.

Perkins with Mould

Transporting over a ton of oak from farm to quay was as much as the small workforce of three men could handle, and the rough timber had to be cross cut and split with steel wedges to reduce its bulk to a workable size.

This particular branch had been selected because the curve of its grain was sufficient to encompass the line of the original stem. After the log had been sided and levelled, using three sighting battens to maintain straight and true surfaces on both sides, then the adze and plane, the stem mould was offered to it. The outline of the mould was then marked in, together with the lower scarph, and the rebate or rabbet line for the hood ends (the end grains) of the outer hull planks. The stem was trimmed to its finished shape with axe, adze and plane. It then weighed about 6 cwt.

Before the old stem could be removed it was necessary to hold the shape of the bow planking which remained, and that which had been recently renewed. This was achieved by the use of exterior wooden clamps placed on each side of the bows and held by through fastened tie-bars.

Removing the stempost structure proved to be a difficult job, and any lingering ideas that the 'original' stem should have been incorporated as part of the restoration were soon dispelled, as after much prying, cutting through fastenings, wedging and hammering apart, the stem came away in three separate pieces — each one signifying a repair at some stage — but with no indication as to when they had been effected.

When everything had been cleared away — a great deal more work than conveyed by this bald statement — over a quarter of a ton of oak stem was manhandled into position and hoisted by a differential chain purchase into its appointed place. The stem had already been rebated on each side ready for the hood ends of the outer hull planks, and after creosote had been liberally applied to all faying surfaces, they were offered up to each other and fastened off.

The next big job was the release of the original and false keels to allow removal of the skeg. It was estimated that this work would take three men some 3 months or some 60 working days to complete.

It was January 1977 and during a period of increasing unemployment throughout the country, and even more markedly so in Devon and Cornwall, the Government introduced the Job Creation Project. The National Trust considered that the *Shamrock* restoration might qualify for this form of non-profit making labour. After application by the Trust, and investigation on site by Government Inspectors, JCP labour was duly hired, with preference given to shipwrights or shipyard workers.

The extra manpower was a great asset in the handling of heavy timbers which the current work involved. First the frame floors in way of the middle line of the hull had to be faired to allow a straight and true seating for the keelson.

Job Creation Team

Next a pair of vertical timber plumb-guides, one on each side of the false keel were erected and secured to the cradle fore and aft. The guides were there to prevent the possibility of the false keel from turning over and fracturing whilst it was being lowered.

With the false keel held in position by two hydraulic jacks, the next job was the heavy work of punching down the $\frac{7}{8}$ in diameter wrought iron keel bolts. When all had been finally punched out the false keel was gradually lowered by the hydraulic jacks enough to allow removal and eventual replacement of the original keelplank

New Frames and Old

and the skeg. Meanwhile with an increased number of men available work was also able to continue inside the hull on the restoring or rebuilding of the remaining frames both forward and aft.

In the Museum, plans for the masting and rigging of the *Shamrock* had been prepared in order that work on that part of the restoration could begin in the Spring. The coils of manila rope, small cordage, marline, whipping twine, beeswax, seizing wire, fids, spikes, knives and measuring tapes, were all ready in the 'rigging loft' at Cotehole Mill, and several riggers had been interviewed, both in the West Country and in London. It was to prove impossible to find men who had the necessary skill available to do the job when and as required. The best men were already fully employed, or living so far away that it was economically impossible for them to do the job. Some submitted samples of traditional seamanship which did not reach the required standard, others who saw the size of the ropes, wire and blocks up at the Mill, did not come back to demonstrate their abilities.

It was therefore decided that the Museum would undertake to rig the vessel and that I would do the job. By extending by one whole day each week the existing arrangements made to monitor the restoration, no extra travelling between Greenwich and Cotehele would be necessary. Preparatory work commenced on 15 March 1977. The floor of the Mill was swept clean and measured, and 40 ft lines, marked at every foot, were chalked out, and lightly scribed in the wooden floorboards. The mizzen mast and spar timbers had been lightly varnished, and stowed in crutches at the Mill for over a year. They had been regularly turned and shifted, and as a result there were no signs of twisting or warping nor any indication of unacceptable shakes having developed.

The first job was to mark off the main dimensions of the mizzen, and mark in chalk the positions of topping-lift and peak halliard bolts, the crane for the throat halliards, approximate position of gaff-jaws, height of hoist and boom saddle. These positions were scaled up from the 1 : 24 sail and rigging plan which I had drawn from information received and the photographs which were available at this period.

Next, the gaffs and booms were measured and marked. The gaffs were marked for the lengths of their timber jaws, the position of the angled slot which houses the iron tumbler for the lower throat halliard block, and the thumb cleats which keep the eyes of the gaff spans in position; the booms for the positions of the sheet bands, the boom end bands; the sheave-holes for clew ropes; the clew rope cleats; the oak reef combs on each side for reef pendants; and the eye-bolts under and between the boom jaws, into which the reef-purchases were to be hooked.

On the next visit a fortnight later, the coils of manila rope which had been delivered by British Ropes some months before and stowed on slatted racks, were broken out. A turntable was improvised and hung off the roof beams of the Mill, in order that the rope could be reeled off, so avoiding kinks. With this method one man can handle new rope of any size in a restricted space without too much trouble. If kinks are allowed to develop, however, he will have a job on his hands getting them out.

The 1 : 24 rigging plan showed all the information relating to the lengths of the various sheets and halliards, and provided allowance was made for stretching and splicing, all that was necessary at this stage was to reel off the required lengths using the scribed-in 40 ft floor lines as a guide. The ropes were fleeted down so that in wet weather they could be easily set up for stretching in the Mill Loft itself, or in dry weather they could be hauled outside and stretched full length between two of the many trees which surround the Mill.

To stretch the rope it was planned to use the double block-purchase of the main throat halliard, which when rigged to advantage gives a 5 : 1 increase in power. Its fall, or hauling part, would be the double and single block luff-tackle purchase of the mizzen sheet, which when rove to advantage gives a 4 : 1 increase in power, *i.e.* the initial hauling power would be increased four times by the mizzen luff-purchase, and the power so gained would be increased five times by the double-block purchase. By first reeving off the main throat halliard and mizzen sheet purchases, then rigging them 'luff upon luff' in the manner described, both they and the rest of the rope would be stretched at the same time.

Before the purchases could be rove off however, the blocks had to be specially selected from those which had been obtained from the Southampton shipyard and sent to the Mill the previous May. Each block has its own particular function, and it is poor rigging practice to make a block perform work for which it is not suited.

Having laid out every block according to size, type and function, each internal-bound block was stripped down in turn by punching out the sheave pin, thereby releasing both sheave and the iron strop housed inside the wooden shell. External-bound blocks were stripped by cutting away the throat seizing which secured the wire strop around the shell and cringle eye, and punching the sheave pin out as before. The sheave pins were inspected for excessive wear, the sheaves themselves for chipped rims, rough edges and hairline cracks and, if fitted with roller bearings, for signs of strained or loose fitting rollers. The iron straps were checked for wear around the holes of the sheave pin, at the crown in way of the eye or hook, and if swivels were fitted, for signs of excessive strain at that point. The wire strops were stripped of the old serving and parcelling which had preserved them against corrosion, then wire brushed and coated with fish oil.

The block shells of elm and ash, were stripped of all old paint, in some cases layers of it and the wood exposed. If they proved soft, or too damaged for future use, they were discarded. Out of a total of 35 blocks, only six shells had to be totally rejected. Three cracked metal sheaves, two pins and one strained swivel-hook, all from 9 in blocks, were also rejected. Four iron straps were put aside for galvanising. All the rest were cleaned off, greased and laid out ready for assembly and the block shells were placed in a 40-gallon drum to soak up a mixture of paraffin (for penetration) and raw linseed oil, until they were required.

At the beginning of April the restoration project received one of the setbacks which must be expected in any undertaking where long term forward planning is involved. Mr Knight, the sailmaker who was to hand-sew the sails for *Shamrock*, wrote to say that as a result of illness and a change in his family circumstances, he would not now be able to do the job. As a result it was arranged that all the canvas and sailmaking equipment in store at the Cory Barge Works at Charlton in London, should be brought to the Mill, until alternative arrangements could be made.

The Torpoint Slipping Company also delivered, at this time, the ironwork from the *Grazia* which included five wrought-iron chainplates, two fisherman type anchors, two wrought-iron diaphragm pump bases, eight iron masthead saddle-bolts for peak halliard blocks, two throat halliard cranes, metal bands of all sizes, and 24 wrought-iron cargo hatch cleats.

While he was in the Mill, Mr Rowse measured the main and mizzen boom diameters for the making of their sheet-bands and collars, and the boom end hands for the topping lifts. A bowsprit end band was also ordered. If possible, these fittings were to be made of wrought iron or if the iron was unobtainable, then of mild steel of low carbon content which was to be also heavily galvanised.

On the restoration site, the Job Creation Scheme enabled Mr Eley and Mr Perkins, the shipwright-in-charge, to organise the increased labour force to maximum advantage. Work could now be continued on the vessel itself, as well as ashore, and this allowed for continuity of effort on two or three separate jobs. In the shed, work was proceeding with the construction of the cargo hatch. This is a heavy rectangular timber frame of Douglas Fir 22 ft in length, and 11 ft in width, composed of two athwartship head ledges, and two fore-and-aft coamings, each 4 in thick, 10 in above deck level and joined together by corner halvings. To enable the hatch to be covered it is sub-divided into nine sections by two 'drop in' hatch beams with their ends resting in wooden beam or shoe-cleats bolted inside the hatch coamings. The upper faces of the coamings are rebated along their inner edges to receive the hatch covers. The beams and head ledges are fitted with similar shoe cleats for the six fore and aft timbers which fit between the hatch beams. Each of these six tim-

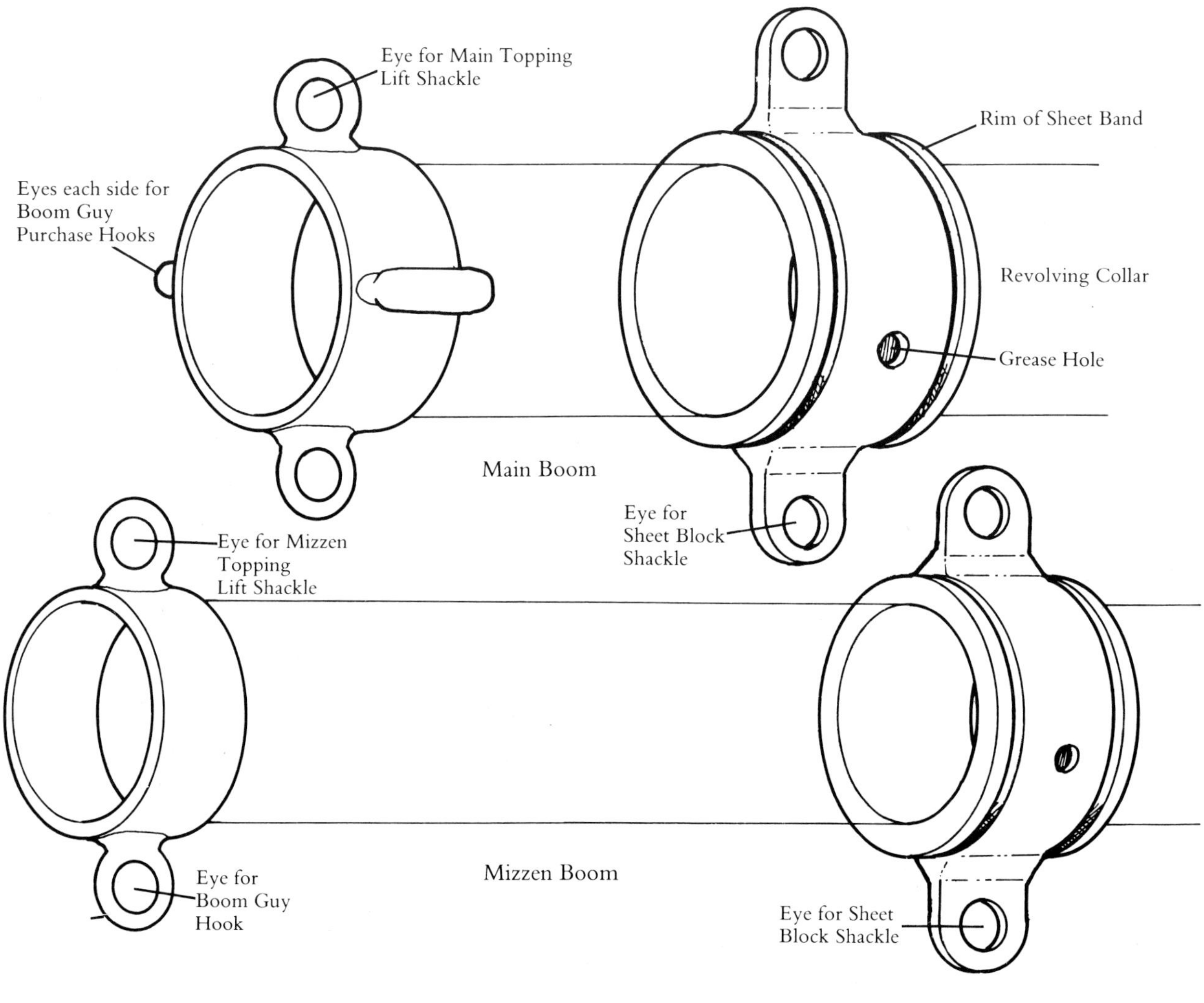

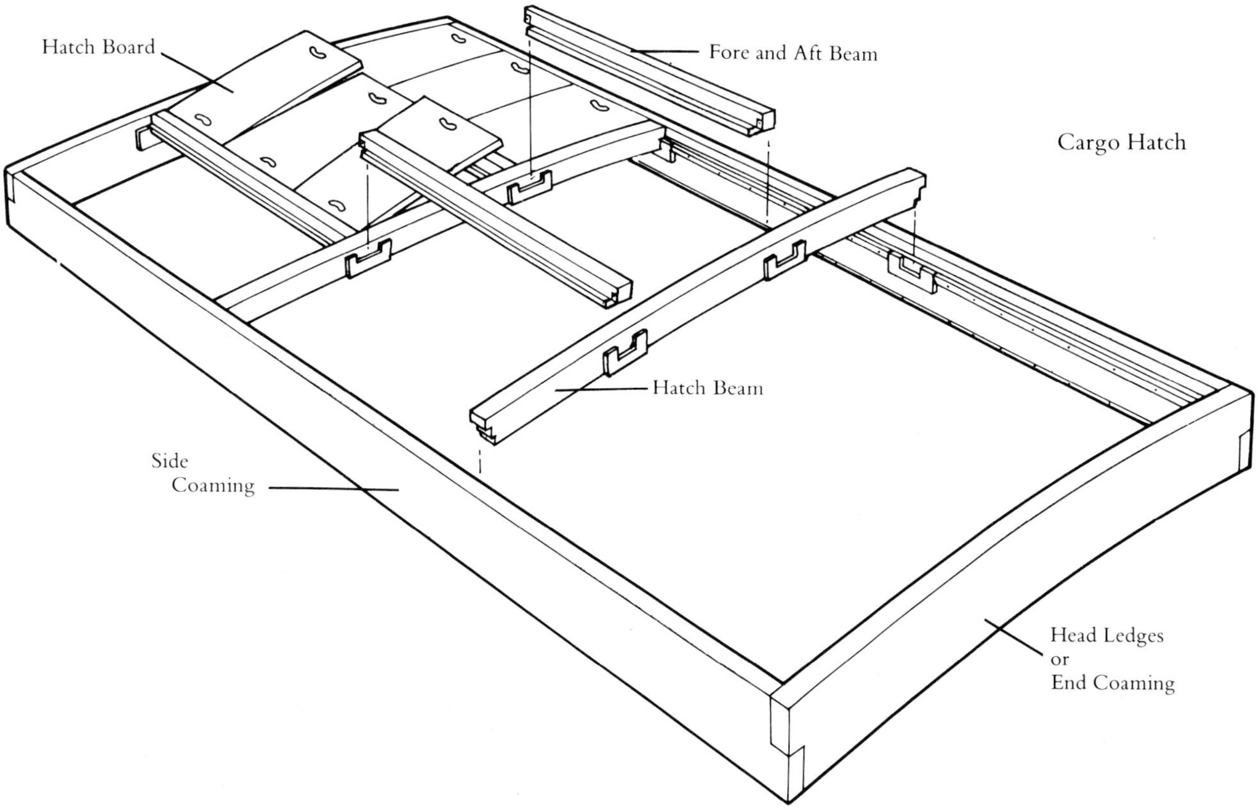


bers have rebates in their upper faces for the edges of the hatch-covers.

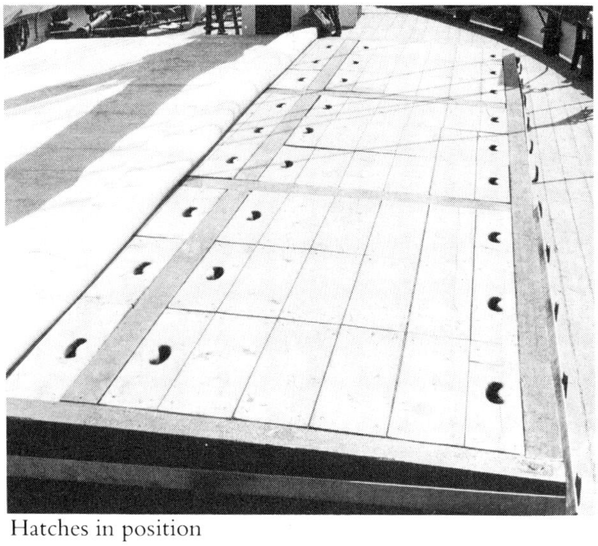
Hatches in position

The next heavy job was the removal of the transom skeg and the original keel. Before the transom could be removed a cradle had to be constructed and set up just forward of it to support and keep in place the after plank ends, which would tend to 'spring' when the fastenings securing them to the transom were cut. The cradle also ensured that there would be no hull distortion in way of the stern and to that end two parallel metal rods tied the upper port and starboard cradle arms together to maintain the shape.

As the work on removing the transom and clearing away the old fastenings began, it became clear that a new transom would have to be made. Overall the transom was 13 ft wide by 3 ft deep and 4 in thick, all of English Oak. There was no way of telling whether this was the original transom built into the *Shamrock* in 1899, but its general condition suggested that it

Transom from the stern

might well have endured nearly 78 years of hard service to have reached such an advanced state of decay.

An inspection of the lowered false keel however confirmed earlier hopes that it could be put back into the vessel. This was a relief to all concerned in the restoration, since to have to find suitable timber to replace it at this stage would have been a considerable set-back. This was the 8 in × 9 in keel that was 'planted' on to the original keel in 1920, when the drop keels were removed, and work now began on cleaning up its faying surface, plugging the bolt-holes, and generally preparing it for replacement.

The original elm keel or ram plank built into the vessel in 1899 had been badly affected by worm and rot, as expected, and once removed, it was obvious that it could not be replaced.

The slots for the drop-keels had been sealed during the 1920 rebuilding, but their positions were plainly visible, and care was taken to keep the keel intact as an object of considerable historical interest since very few wooden merchant sailing vessels in Britain had been fitted with drop keels.

The old keel was used as the mould for the new one, which was fashioned from English elm just under 1 ft wide, and 4 in thick. The awkward job of laying up the keel to the under faces of the frame floors, and then offering up the false keel to the new keel in turn, was accomplished by jacking, wedging and brute force. Jacks and wedges provide the most practical means of applying localised pressure when large surfaces such as these have to be fayed together. Once again, although the elm keel had already been treated with a chemical preservative, plenty of creosote was used to impregnate the faying surfaces before they were finally squeezed together.

Meanwhile, the new or restored frames inside the hull had been completed enough aft to allow the keelson to be lowered on to the upper face of the frame floors along the fore and aft centre line of the hull.

Once the keel and false keel were lined up true to the fore and aft centre line it was possible to line up the keelson, and after trimming the upper face of the floors with the adze where required, the keelson was set up ready for the boring of the keel bolt holes.

Auger-bits were to be used for this exacting job. They were of a length sufficient to bore down through the 15 in of Columbian pine keelson and 6 in of the frame floor, and to penetrate into the keel. This indent into the keel surface by the auger-bit was easily picked up later, when the keelson was eased over to port to facilitate the boring of the keel and false keel as a separate operation.

Work also continued inside the hull on the completion of the forward square frames. Once they were in position the fore deadwood could be fitted. The function of the deadwood is to strengthen the connection between the stem, keelson, keel and false keel. The deadwood knee

Stemson Knee

or stemson was a piece of grown oak some 12 in wide and over 3 ft in length. It had been put in the vessel during the 1920 reconstruction and was sound enough to be used again for the same purpose. The oak bow wedges which fill in the space between the false keel and the stem-post were also inserted into place at this time, and in the same manner as they had been fitted in 1920.

In traditional wooden shipbuilding practice, the rounding up of the fore end of the keel was continued up to the heel of the stem post by means of a gripe, an oak crook, specially selected to encompass the turn of the fore-foot. In *Shamrock* however, the bow wedges took the place of the gripe. A rounded forefoot is essential for vessels which, like *Shamrock*, worked in shoal and tidal waters and were constantly sailing on and off beaches, but in all classes of vessels the shape of the forefoot had some influence on sailing performance.

At the other end of the vessel, the replacing of the three large wedge shaped oak timbers which form the skeg were fitted into place between the false keel and the keel where it runs up to the transom. The skeg has the same 8 in siding as the false keel, and to ensure complete rigidity of the infill timbers the sequence of iron bolts through fastenings had to be very carefully considered. Before fastening off the skeg however, it was necessary to build up the new transom, and to secure the sterm post to the false keel.

Skeg Timbers

A mould was prepared from the old transom so that its shape and pitch could be transferred to the oak boards from which the new one was to be built. Three separate boards were required to build it — each of them 4 in thick. The lowest was 14 in wide, the middle one 16 in wide, and the top one 6 in wide. To ensure strength and watertight integrity, the top edge of the lowest board was rebated into the bottom edge of the middle board, and the top edge of the middle board was rebated into the bottom edge of the top board. Each rebated joint was bedded in a white lead compound and tightly secured by $\frac{5}{8}$ in diameter iron tie bars, spaced about 18 in apart.

The new transom was built to the 'pitch' or angle, taken off the old stern post, which was fitted in 1920, and now, like the stempost was too damaged and decayed for further service. It was wedge shaped, and set up so that its after face was almost at a right angle to the false keel, in order to allow the rudder to hang plumb. Its forward face was angled to accommodate the pitch, or 'laying back' of the transom and after end of the skeg.

The new sternpost 7 ft long 12 in at its broadest width, and 8 in thick, was fashioned from a fine baulk of oak, specially selected for the job. The bottom end of the post and the after end of the false keel were each cut to form a halving, so that locked and bolted together, they formed a secure frame work for the rudder and the timbers of the skeg. The stern post covered the end grain of the skeg timbers, and it was fastened to them by $\frac{5}{8}$ in iron ties. Six inch high draught figures, spaced 1 ft apart from the underside of the keel, were carved into the sternpost (and stempost) to indicate the vessel's draught.

With the transom in position work on the after frames continued until all were either restored or rebuilt. With the after framing complete the final sections of the beamshelf could be fitted ready for the after deck beams, which were being fashioned in the shed.

The oak deadwood timber which acts as a continuation of the keelson aft to the transom, was next placed in position, together with the sternknee connection to the transom. With the stern structure thus in place, the skeg was bored to take the 1 in diameter wrought iron bolts, some of them 4 ft in length, which, with the sternpost firmly bolted to the transom, would bind the whole assembly together.

# Chapter 5

*Progress on the rigging and planking up; decisions for the future. April 1977–April 1978.*

At Cotehele Mill, work on the running rigging was steadily going forward during my weekly 2 day visits from Greenwich. The 'luff on luff' procedure for initial stretching of the new rope between two trees, had proceeded well, until a spell of wet weather, which seemed to begin just as I arrived at the Mill Loft, and to end just as it was time to leave it on the second day, prevented all such work outside. Nevertheless, the same stretching procedure continued in the loft itself, although it was only possible in that confined space to stretch 80 ft of rope at a time. Before leaving the Mill, all the rope which had been stretched was hauled as taut as possible, and then a 160 lb anchor was hung in the bight, so that during a weeks absence, stretching slowly continued. On arrival at the loft the following week, the anchor which had been left hanging 3 ft clear of the floor, would generally be about an inch above it.

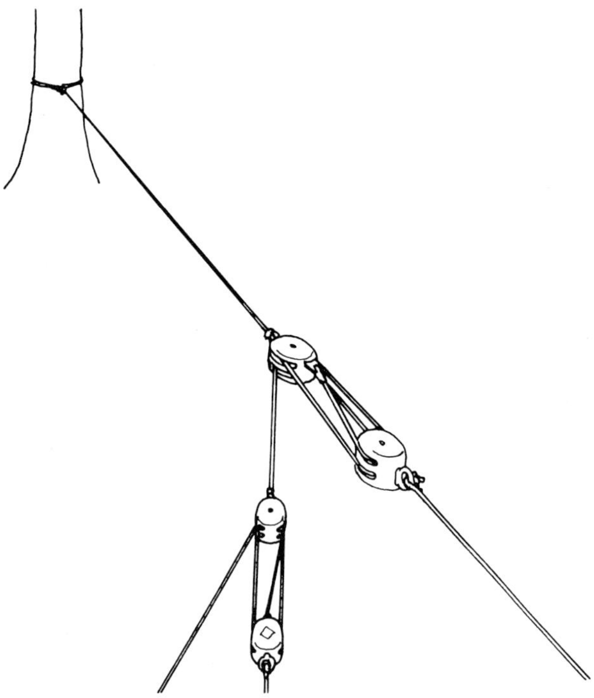

Luff on Luff Tackle

By the fifth visit on 20th April, all the ropes for the sheets and halliards had been well stretched, and cut to the required lengths; sailmakers whippings had been put on one end of each length; the other ends had been rove off through the two blocks of their respective purchases and spliced around the thimbles of the becket blocks, then overhauled several times to take out any half turns which might have developed.

Finally, all the purchases were individually set up taut between the roof beams of the Mill, the anchor was slung underneath them to keep them stretched, and the blocks were given a final coat of linseed oil. There they remained being regularly set up taut, until they were needed to rig the *Shamrock*.

Wet weather had also interfered with work on the *Shamrock* itself, but the completed cargo hatch frame had been got on board and bolted down to the hatch beams during a brief spell of fine weather. The wooden warping horse, which was always a characteristic feature of the Tamar barges, was also constructed and fitted.

Warping Horse

Consisting of two 6 in square uprights and a cross-piece of oak, double notched and through bolted for strength, the horse was bolted in place on the transom as soon as it was finished, since it provided some extra stiffening to the new transom boards.

Under the protection of the canvas cover the boring of the keel and keelson continued slowly and methodically, and the after beams No. 8 and 9 were laid in place on the beamshelf. Several of the original grown oak lodging knees were sound enough to be used again and when No. 10 beam had been made and brought aboard all the after beams and their knees were bolted into position.

During a spell of fine weather the job of cutting down the frame heads to the starboard sheer line was started and this work was continued as and when possible. This work was an essential preliminary to the fairing of the frame tops and sheer strake to the camber of the deck, allowing the combined waterway and covering board to be laid fair over them later:

As the summer approached visitors to the Quay were greatly interested in the work of restoration that was going on all around them. Most of them had never seen a traditional wooden sailing vessel, and some were astonished at the amount of timber required, and especially at the number of frames in the vessel. Most agreed that it was a worthwhile thing to do, one or two that were used to modern production methods were full of ideas as to how the job could be expedited by the use of modern machinery — regardless of cost. Others, older men who had worked with hand tools on wooden ships long ago, were quietly appreciative that the task had been attempted at all, and were well aware of the work that was being put into it.

As soon as possible after the boring of the keel and false keel was completed the keelson was shifted back into position over the frame centres and lined up ready for through-bolting to begin. The bolts were of 1 in diameter wrought iron, specially made for the restoration by Thomas Walmsley and Sons of Bolton, Lancs. On the advice of the shipwright Mr Perkins, and the Museum, Mr Eley had gone to great lengths to obtain this wrought-iron bar, since its resistance to corrosion made its use essential for securing the backbone of the vessel.

Each bolt, cold galvanised, and was over 30 in in length in order to penetrate through the keelson, frame floor, keel and false keel. The false keel was additionally bored on its underside in way of each bolt, to a width and depth sufficient to house a bottom nut and washer, with a grommet for watertightness, and an elm plug, sealed with white lead putty, which was driven in flush to a depth of $1\frac{1}{4}$ in. The upper surface of the keelson was likewise bored for the top bolt nuts which were tightened down to a bedplate, then sealed and plugged like the bottom nuts in the false keel.

All the bolts were staggered or alternately set off from the centre line of the keelson to ensure

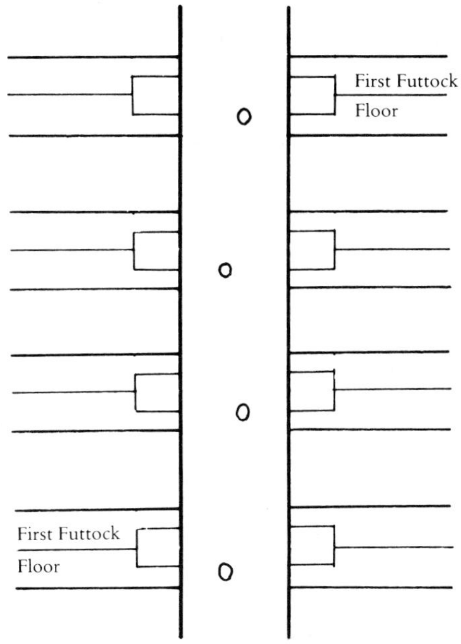


Staggered Keel Bolts

good holding of the whole assembly, and to lessen the chance of splitting the timber.

With the fore deadwood likewise bolted to the stem, the backbone and main strength of the vessel was restored. The wrought-iron breast hook was next brought aboard and bolted to the inner upper face of the stempost, and to the frames of the bow on each side. This knee provided a strong tie in that area and strengthened the stem post against heavy bumps or collisions.

The next jobs were the fitting of the forward beams, the planing of their centres to the middle line datum, and the fairing of their cambered surfaces to receive the deck planks. Although the actual laying of the deck was some way off, it was necessary at this time to complete any jobs which had to be done before decking commenced.

The base of the skylight/companion-way which

had been built in the shed as a wet weather job, was brought on board and laid on a bed of white lead putty was bolted to beams 8 and 9. This framework, with coamings 6 in high, was later fitted with the teak skylight/companion-way,

Fore Skylight

giving access to the cabin aft. A similar base, with dovetailed corners and with its top edges rebated in traditional style, was fitted some 6 ft aft of the stem over the foc'sle space. A curved hood, with sliding roof and weather boards, was later fitted on to this hatch.

Main Mast Tabernacle

The mast tabernacles were next brought from the shed and fitted in position. The main tabernacle unit consisted of two oak cheek boards $4\frac{1}{2}$ in thick and 10 in wide, of a length to stand some 3 ft 6 in above the deck, and to reach down some 5 ft to each side of the keelson, to which they were through bolted. The upper part of the boards were through-bolted to the forward main cargo hatch beam. An oak cross-piece, or cleat rail, was bolted on the fore edges of the cheeks 3 ft above deck level with an iron mast band above it. Both cheeks were bored through their sides for a 2 in diameter steel pin upon which the mast pivoted.

The mizzen tabernacle was of similar construction, with 4 in thick cheeks which stood 3 ft above the deck. The cheeks were bolted one each side of the keelson and to the fore side of beam No. 8, which also supported the fore end of the skylight/companionway. Right aft the wash strake of English oak was spiked on to the top board of the transom and through bolted to the uprights of the warping-horse. The wash-strake or fashion piece, later had the name of the vessel and port of registry carved into its outer face. Finally, the 8 in square pawl-post, or bowsprit bitt, was dropped into position 6 ft aft of the stempost, with its heel stepped into the fore deadwood, and its upper part bolted to an adjacent deck beam.

Meanwhile research had continued from Greenwich, and several sailmakers had been interviewed in London, Southampton and Plymouth, in an effort to obtain another craftsman. If possible, a retired but active man was required who had been trained in the traditional manner and who was familiar with sailmaking as applied to working sailing vessels. Once again, the difficulties of working on the spot at Cotehele were evidently the deciding factor. Apart from one man who was about to undertake a delivery voyage, but who was willing to take on the job on his return to England in 1978, and another who had worked exclusively on terylene sails, no one with the necessary experience had come forward to accept the challenge. Tenders were therefore sent out to established sailmaking firms who claimed that they still accepted orders for traditional work and three were submitted for consideration to The National Trust during the next few weeks.

More information concerning the *Shamrock* was still coming in, but the one photograph showing her broadside on with all sails set had not yet materialised. It was only a photograph of this description which could confirm or disprove the validity of the Museum's conjectural sailplan.

At the Mill, rigging loft, all the ironwork and rigging gear which had been collected since 1974 was now catalogued, cleaned, repaired or discarded. Apart from new rope, new sheet-bands, boom end and bowspritend bands, six bullseye fittings for the gaff-spans, and four mizzen shrouds, everything used to rig the *Shamrock* was contemporary material which had been made for wooden sailing vessels, or had actually seen service in them.

The National Trust, as part owners of the *Shamrock* and of her berth, and the National Maritime Museum, as part owners and historical and technical advisers to the restoration, had met officially on five occasions during the 3 years which had elapsed since the vessel had arrived at Cotehele Quay in 1974. Various problems relating to the money available for the restoration, availability of skilled labour, supply of materials, and so on, had been discussed, and now, in 1977, the question of *Shamrock*'s future as a restored vessel of local historic importance was becoming a pertinent one. Whatever the role she might be called upon to fulfill, one thing was certain — unless she was properly cared for and maintained in a responsible manner, whatever future was envisaged for her would be of relatively short duration.

A wooden vessel begins to deteriorate from the moment that her timbers are joined together. The degree and rate of deterioration is largely determined in the first instance by the quality of her materials, and the skill of her builders. Yet by skilled day to day maintenance, and the observance of a few basic rules, the life of a wooden vessel can be prolonged for many years beyond her initial classification. Wooden vessels rot internally from the effect of fresh water seepage and lack of ventilation, but they are preserved by a regular washing down with salt water and plenty of clean air circulation. The Falmouth oyster dredgers and Thames shrimp bawleys, mostly built of pitch pine on oak frames and iron fastened, had a great reputation for longevity. They sailed practically all the year round and by the nature of their work were constantly being washed down with salt water, which pickled their timbers. Vessels which lie in a dock or at moorings get only rain water on their decks which seeps below and that in time is ruinous.

Any wooden vessel at anchor, tied up alongside, or in a dock, should be washed down with salt water at dusk. That way the salt will have all night to seep down into all the crevices and also keep the timbers swollen tight. Washing down during the day helps as well, but the water generally evaporates too quickly to soak well in and do its work. This simple precaution and everyday routine upkeep of the hull, masting, rigging and sails, can ensure that no restored vessel ever reaches a state where major repairs are required, unless as the result of an accident.

In view of the escalating costs of repairing wooden sailing vessels, the Museum urged the Trust to agree to the employment of a permanent shipkeeper to maintain the *Shamrock* after she had been fully restored. The ideal type of man for the job would be a merchant service bo'sun, or former working yacht skipper used to the larger type of traditionally built cruising yacht; an ex Thames barge skipper, or any seaman used to heavy wooden working vessels. A first class seaman fully trained in fore and aft sail was eventually appointed and one who, moreover, can probably give perhaps twenty years to *Shamrock*. However, men of this sort of experience will become increasingly rare as the years go by. With this in mind we hope later to recruit a young man, perhaps as an apprentice, with the interest, determination and ability to learn the necessary skills. In this way the *Shamrock*, it is hoped, will serve as a true 'historian's ship' and keep alive in the consciousness of curators, conservators and historians, the complex processes of maintaining and using the wooden sailing vessel rigged with natural fibre rope and sails, afloat in her natural environment.

By August 1977, the half-beams which support the deck on each side of the cargo hatch had been fitted. Their outboard ends rested on the beam-shelf, and the inboard ends were bolted to the underside of the port and starboard hatch coamings. With the half-beams in place, and in due course faired in and cambered for drainage, all the main framing of the hull was complete except for the iron hanging knees, which could not be fitted until the ceiling planks from beamshelf to turn of bilge were in place. This job and the planking of the bottom from false keel to above the turn of bilge provided the main work during the coming weeks.

The work of stripping off the old outer planking and replacing with new followed the same procedure as had been used for the strakes of topside planking. The old plank provided the mould for the new, and all the heavily galvanised 6 in spike nails were driven in through drilled holes with the heads well below the plank surface to allow for plugging and planing off later on.

The garboard strakes to port and starboard were fitted first. Of English elm 11¾ in wide, and 2 in thick, the garboard is fitted with its inside edge faying straight on to the outer edge of the false keel and is not rebated into it. Like all the planking of the hull the garboards had been chemically pre-treated to preserve them, but plenty of creosote was also applied to all faying surfaces when they were fastened off. The plank butts landed on a frame timber and were double fastened.

Inside the hull, the frame faces were faired or dubbed out with adzes to ensure a good seating for the ceiling planks. In a wooden working vessel the ceiling is not only a protective cover for the frames, and a means of preventing cargoes

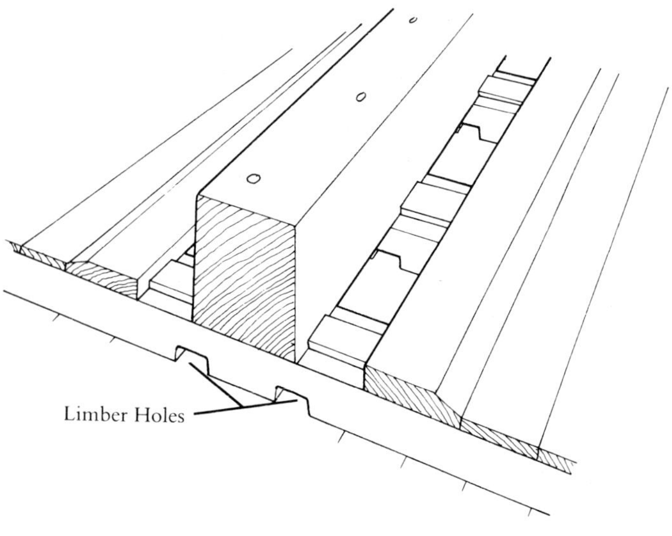


Position of Limber Holes

like coal, stone or china clay from choking the pumps: it is also a stressed surface without which the vessel would not be strong enough for her work.

To enable water to be pumped out of the vessel the frame floors have draining channels (limber holes) cut out of their under surfaces to port and starboard of the centre line, to enable water to flow freely on each side of the keelson to the pump well. Some vessels have a light chain running through the limber holes from forward to aft, which, pulled back and forth occasionally keeps them free of any blockage. To allow access to the limber holes in *Shamrock* the thick limber planks were bolted parallel to and 6 in out from the keelson, thus leaving a gap on each side of it. When the hold is empty it is a good policy to leave the gaps uncovererd to allow air to circulate and ventilate the frame spaces. When cargo is to be loaded, the gaps are covered with portable limber boards, which seat on to spacing blocks placed on the frames so that they lie flush with the surface of the limber planks.

The thick limber planks, like the beamshelf, provide extra longitudinal strength within the hull. In *Shamrock* the planks were of chemically impregnated Douglas Fir 4 in thick and just under 10 in wide. Their outer edges were bevelled along their length to match up with the ceiling planks in the bottom of the hold which were 2 in thick, except for those along the turn of the bilge where they increased to 2¼ in.

Most of the ceiling planks had to be properly lined off again to obtain the various plank widths required, and evenly tapered seam lines. The cheap deal planks which had been used for a quick repair job at some time or other were no use as moulds for the new planks. Lining off was done by measuring the curved length of all the inner faces of the frames between the outer bevelled edge of the limber plank and bottom edge of the beamshelf, less an allowance of some 2½ in for the air course gap. The air course is essential for ventilating the frame spaces and in conjunction with the open limber space provides a constant circulation of air where it is needed most.

The air course is also useful for injecting creosote or other preservative between the frames, or for replenishing salt boxes which in many vessels were placed between the frame-heads. The boxes had small holes in the bottom, and were filled with rock salt. Moisture collected by the salt constantly dripped through the holes and down between the frames to the bilges, gradually pickling the timbers in the process. This practice may be adopted in *Shamrock* at a later stage, but the main objection to it is the tendency to hasten the corrosion of iron fastenings. Cutting the new planks from the moulds, trimming them, steaming them if necessary, lugging them from the shed, offering them to the frames, clamping, marking off, boring for fastenings, then fastening off, all took time and good organisation, especially as many of the men engaged under the Job Creation Scheme were unfamiliar with the process.

Other jobs at this time included the fitting of the starboard hawse block right forward and the making and temporary fitting of the starboard bulwark stanchions. The hawse blocks were pre-bored at the required angle for the insertion of the original iron hawse pipes at a later date.

Bulwark stanchions are usually fastened into position between the frame spaces as required, and the waterways and covering boards are fitted afterwards. *Shamrock* has a combined waterway and covering board 9 in wide, to cover the top edge of the sheer strake, the frame-top and the beamshelf. In Mr Perkin's view it would be simpler in this case to make the stanchions first, fit them temporarily in place, make the necessary moulds for the waterway, cut out the stanchion slots from the moulds, fit the waterway in sections, and finally insert the stanchions in their appointed slots and fasten off. There were 18 oak stanchions on each side all 4 in square and 14 in high from the deck to the underside of the main rail.

Work continued on the vessel's inside and outside planking. The port side of the vessel was alternatively exposed to hot sun, and sudden rainstorms sweeping up the river, and this affected the rate of progress under the bottom from time to time. Inside, work was concentrated on fitting the ceiling, from the air course under the beam shelf down to the turn of the bilge, for as soon as those planks were in, the wrought-iron hanging knees could be fitted.

Spacing blocks of larch $2\frac{1}{2}$ in deep were spiked on to the frame faces below the bottom edge of the beamshelf for the top edge of the upper ceil-

Beamshelf and Air Course

ing plank to butt against. The ceiling planks were as long as it was possible to get and there were only two butts (*i.e.* three planks) in each strake from stem to stern. Each butt was double-fastened on to a frame timber and a good shift of butts was maintained throughout. As before, all faying surfaces were liberally soaked with creosote before fastening off.

Bulwark Stanchions

On the 15 November one of the three tenders which had been submitted for the making of a suit of sails for *Shamrock* was accepted. Four days later, Mr Tresidder, Managing Director of the selected firm, Penrose Sailmakers of Falmouth, Mr Eley of the National Trust, and I met at the Cotehele Estate Office on the Quay to talk about the aims of the *Shamrock* restoration, and the necessity for the sails to be hand made and truly representative of those used by the vessel during the 1920s. The actual making of the sails could not begin immediately, since it was the usual practice for the sailmaker to take his own measurements of the masts and spars, after they had been rigged and properly set up in the vessel. However, Mr Tresidder had already collected all the canvas and gear from the Mill, and a copy of the sailplan, which he had seen and approved in principle, was provided by the Museum.

Meanwhile the additional workforce provided by the Government's Job Creation project enabled the planking up of the vessel to continue at a steady rate, but the lack of men skilled in wooden shipbuilding made some delays inevitable. Although it looked deceptively simple for a shipwright to run in a strake of planking, it required years of experience in selecting and handling timber to achieve the skill to make it appear so.

On the advice of the Museum, The National Trust had already attempted through the Government's Job Creation Scheme to employ any local shipwrights who were temporarily out of work, and especially those with experience of caulking. When the planking programme was completed there would be a need for at least one man, in addition to the shipwright-in-charge, who was skilled in this particular job. Caulking looks simple, but unless it is done with the know-how gained by years in the trade, this operation can cause unseen damage to the planks and fastenings, the results of which will not become evident until the vessel has carried one or two cargoes, or experienced her first bad weather at sea.

In January 1978 the Trust made an application for an extension of its contract with the Job Creation Project in order to expedite the restoration work. This was eventually granted, and once again, it was hoped that shipwrights, or shipyard workers with caulking experience, would become available to work on *Shamrock*.

Work inside the hull was proceeding to the plan, and the planks of the ceiling had reached down beyond the turn of bilge. This meant that the wrought-iron hanging knees removed in 1974 and stored in the shed ever since, could be replaced in the hold. Before they could be fastened off however, it was necessary to try them in their former positions to check whether the shape of the inner hull at that point had appreciably altered during the restoring or rebuilding of the frames. If so, slight variations could be corrected by heating the knee at the local blacksmith's forge and resetting it on the anvil, but the careful cradling, blocking off, shoring, and girdling of the hull with wires, had ensured that *Shamrock* was pretty well the same shape as the vessel which had entered the cradle nearly 3 years before.

There were 14 wrought iron knees to be replaced — seven on each side — and a start was made on those to starboard first. Each knee weighed about 65 lb and all were of the same dimensions, except Nos. 4 port and starboard which were positioned in the centre of the hatch space, and their vertical arms were extended 1 ft to overlap the thicker ceiling plank at the turn of bilge.

The placing of the hanging knees was so arranged that if a knee was bolted to the centre of the timbers which composed the after side of a frame — for example, the first and third futtocks of frame No. 13 — then the next knee aft of that one, was bolted to the timbers which composed the foreside of its particular frame, which in this case, would be the top timber, second futtock, and part of the floor of frame No. 16. Placing the knees in this alternating pattern provided an even distribution of stress and allowed for a good shift of the bolt fastenings which passed through knee, ceiling, frame and outer planking.

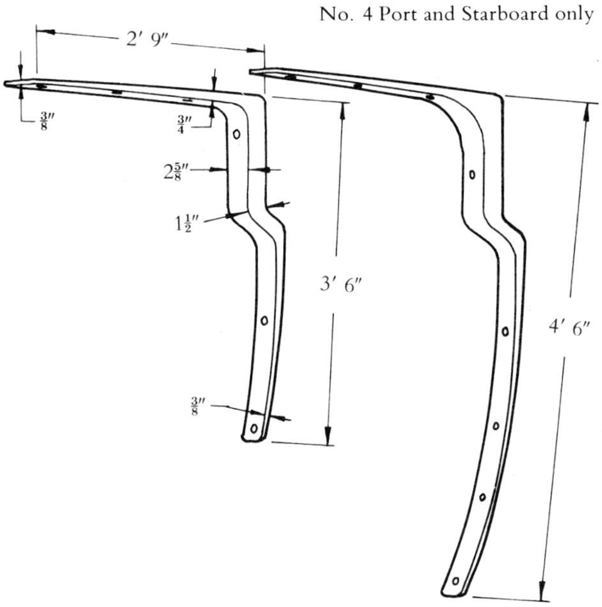


Shape and dimensions of Hanging Knees

The four wrought-iron bolts used to secure the hanging knee to the vessels sides were $\frac{3}{4}$ in diameter and 11 in in length. Great care had to be exercised when boring through from inside the hull, in order to avoid fouling outer plank fastenings, or piercing through plank seams or butts, thereby causing problems relating to watertightness in that area. The bolts were driven from outside and their heads were counter-sunk to allow for plugging. A grommet of oakum or boat cotton was fitted below the bolthead and bedded in white lead, so that when the bolt head was well driven home a watertight fastening was assured. The inner end of the bolts were threaded to a depth sufficient to allow the vertical limbs of the knee to be well tightened up by a nut seated on a round washer.

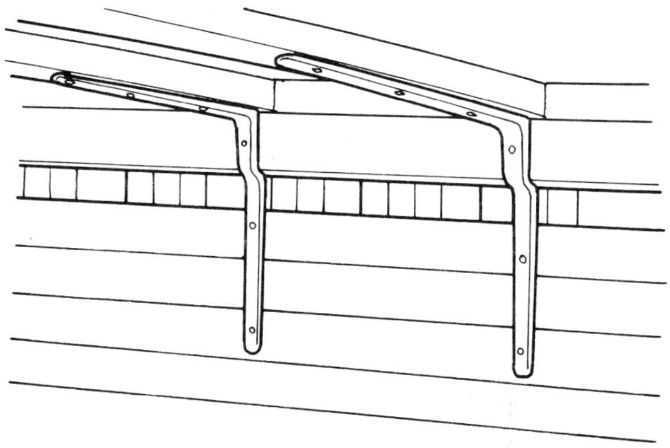

Disposition of Hanging Knees

The horizontal limbs of the hanging knees were fastened to the underside of their respective beams or half-beams with three snap or dome-headed dump bolts, of 6–9 in in length and of $\frac{5}{8}$ in diameter. Pre-boring was necessary before these bolts were driven home.

By the end of April 1978 the outer planking of *Shamrock*'s hull was complete. There were 16 strakes on each side, all fastened and stopped off ready for caulking which would be done after the deck had been laid. By this arrangement both the hull and the deck planks could be caulked at the same time.

Inside the hull, the hanging knees were all secured in position and the ceiling had been completely fastened off and faired. Below the turn of bilge two planks were coach-bolted in place instead of nailed, so that they could be easily lifted to allow additional ventilation, and also to facilitate the constant spraying of creosote on the underside of the ceiling planks and between the frames.

The cable locker bulkhead had also been built across the bows. It conforms to the original layout, being 'stepped' from frame No. 3 starboard across to the middle line, then fore and aft to pick up and cross along the line of frame No. 4 to port. The frame of the bulkhead is covered by $1\frac{1}{4}$ in tongued-and-grooved larch boards vertically disposed. Small doors to port and starboard provide access to the locker, which is fitted with a perforated galvanised steel cable tray to allow drainage of mud and water to the bilge when heaving up the anchor.

# Chapter 6

*Relaying the deck; making the sails, an essential clue discovered; caulking the hull planking. April–Autumn 1978.*

During a further meeting between The National Trust and the National Maritime Museum earlier in the year, the progress of the restoration had been discussed, and also the effect which the termination of the Job Creation contract would have on it. As a result, it was decided that if the reduction in the labour force prevented the full restoration of the vessel by the end of the year, the aim should be to achieve the completion of the hull at least, then launch and fit her out during the following spring. Meanwhile, the most essential requirement was to get the vessel decked over so that she would be a whole hull again, and no longer dependent on the canvas cover to prevent rain water getting below.

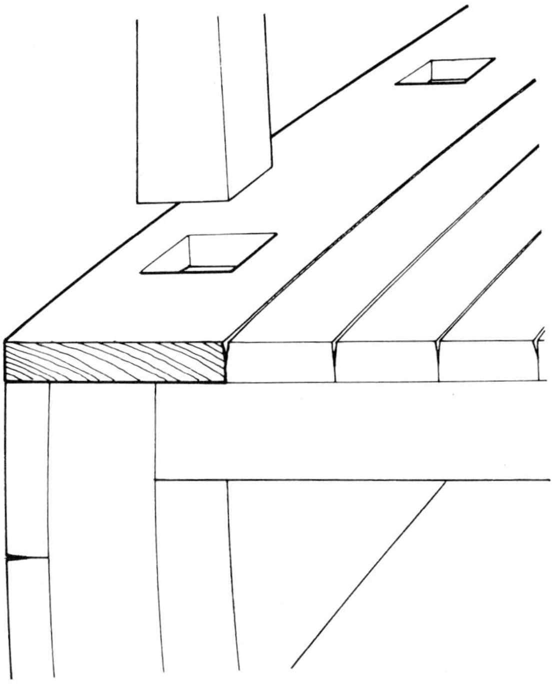

The combined covering board and waterway, showing slots for bulwark stanchions.

Before the deck planks could be laid the combined waterway and covering boards had to be fitted. These were elm boards 2 in thick and up to 9 in wide, it having proved impossible to obtain seasoned oak of the required dimensions. Like all the timber plank used in the *Shamrock* the elm boards had been treated with a chemical preservative before delivery, and were specially selected for their run of grain and freedom from objectional knots or shakes.

The moulds were made with the bulwark stanchions fixed temporarily in position as planned; they were then laid on the board and the outer and inner edges were marked out, and also the positions of the stanchion slots. The board was then cut to the required shape on the bandsaw. The slots for the stanchions had to be cut to allow them to stand plumb to the sheer line, and care was also taken to ensure a good all round fit.

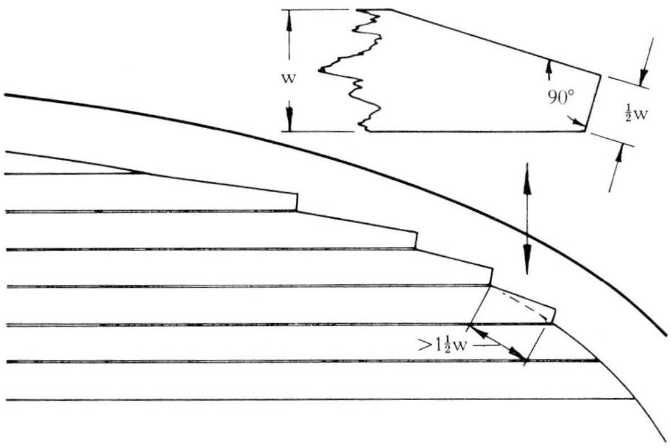


Deck plank ends joggled into the combined covering board and waterway.

In *Shamrock* there was no margin plank, or nib strake. Usually this plank is laid immediately against the inner edge of the waterway, and receives the fore and aft ends of the deck planks as they meet the in-curve of the bow and stern. Deck plank ends are never run off to a shim point; if the length of the cut across the deck plank exceeds one and a half times the width of the plank it is 'nibbed' or 'joggled' into the margin plank, the butt end of the joggled plank being usually one half its width. In a vessel with thick waterways, which stand proud of the deck plank, a margin plank, or else an inner waterway (which is bevelled so that its inner edge lies flush with the deck plank) must be fitted to receive the joggled ends. With a waterway of the same thickness of the deck plank as in *Shamrock* the plank ends are joggled directy into it.

The deck planks are laid from the king-plank which is fastened to the middle line of the vessel first. Some of *Shamrock*'s original Columbian Pine decking was used where possible, other-

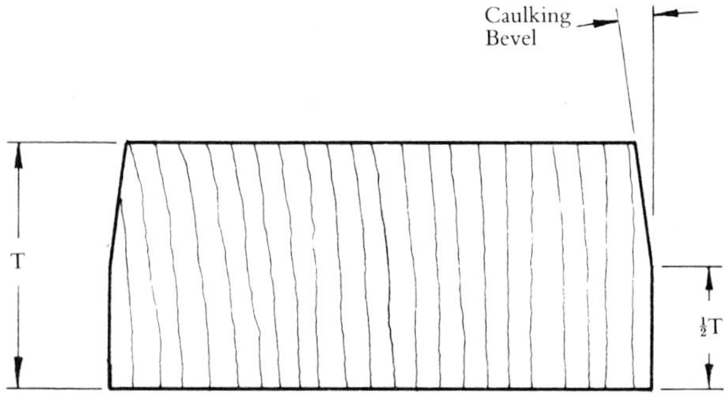


Deck plank with hard wearing edge grain showing. Note caulking bevels.

wise straight clear grained larch and Douglas Fir was selected for this purpose. To provide a good wearing surface all decking should be laid with a vertical or edge grain showing on the top face.

For the driving of spikes used in fastening the deck — holes must be bored in the deck plank but not necessarily in the beam. Opinions vary as to the size of the hole, many preferred it to be $\frac{1}{16}$ in less than the spike to provide for a slight drift or grip of the spike through the plank. Others like a hole the same size as the spike to avoid any possibility of splitting the plank, but

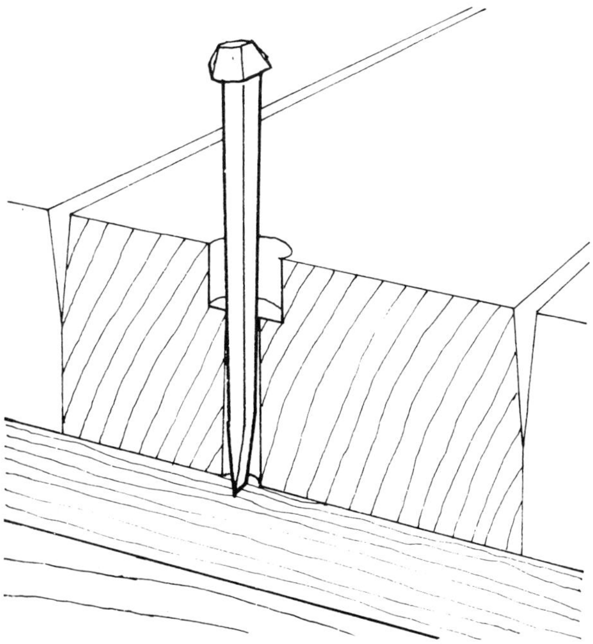

Counter bore and bore hole for the spike, set with chisel point across the grain.

splitting may also be caused by not wedging the plank tightly enough against its neighbour. If no hole is bored in the beam the deck spike must be so set that the chisel edge cuts the grain of the wood, and not the other way, which will tend to split it.

Deck planks are normally arranged to fill evenly the spaces between the deck hatches and the waterway and this practice was followed in *Shamrock*. Cutting a deck plank to fit around hatch corners weakens the plank, tends to cause splitting at that point and is troublesome to caulk.

Individual opinions differ as to the size of deck spikes in relation to thickness of plank. One old rule recommended a spike to be $\frac{1}{8}$ in square and 2 in long for every inch of plank thickness, *i.e.* $\frac{1}{4}$ in square and 4 in long for 2 in thick planking; $\frac{3}{8}$ in square and 6 in long for 3 in thick plank *etc.*

All spikes are set down in counterbores with plugs of the same timber as the plank. The plug is dipped in thick white lead and tapped down against the spike head with its grain in line with the plank grain. The counter-bores are generally bored with special bitts called plug bitts which

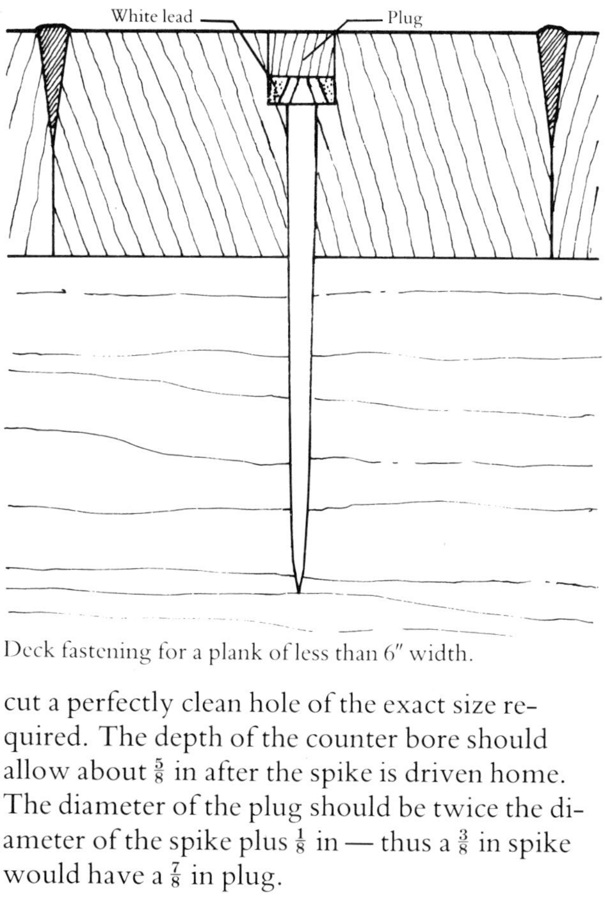


Deck fastening for a plank of less than 6″ width.

cut a perfectly clean hole of the exact size required. The depth of the counter bore should allow about $\frac{5}{8}$ in after the spike is driven home. The diameter of the plug should be twice the diameter of the spike plus $\frac{1}{8}$ in — thus a $\frac{3}{8}$ in spike would have a $\frac{7}{8}$ in plug.

Before a deck plank is laid, its upper face and edges are bevelled according to its width, and to a depth equal to half its thickness, so that a V shaped channel or caulking seam is formed by any two adjacent planks, when fastened to the deck beams. The bevel on *Shamrock*'s $4\frac{1}{2}$ in wide deck planks was $\frac{1}{8}$ in and 1 in in depth, thus the caulking seam between any two planks was $\frac{1}{4}$ in.

It has been said earlier that despite the many useful photographs of *Shamrock* that research had turned up, none provided the crucial view which would confirm her masting and sail plan between 1920 and 1934. We needed a broadside view of her rigged as a ketch. Such a photograph would demonstrate with reasonable accuracy the height and position of the mizzen mast and the general proportions of the sail plan. As it was, the sail plan drawn by the Museum for the guidance of the sailmaker was based on the inadequate (for this purpose) photographs available at the time, verbal descriptions from Richard Hoskings, her Master in 1926, other statements from local people who remembered the vessel, and the Museum's own knowledge of how a small merchant sailing vessel like *Shamrock* would be rigged at the period chosen for the restoration.

As time passed and it became necessary to go ahead with making the sails, it seemed that this sail plan would have to be used. If at a later date evidence were to be produced showing *Shamrock*'s mizzen to have been of a different size, or differently positioned, then a great deal of extra time and money would be required to put things right.

On 16 June 1978 the Museum received a letter from a Mr Bird of Falmouth, a friend of Mr Tresidder of Penrose Sailmakers. The letter simply stated that the enclosed photograph had been taken in 1934 just before the vessel's mizzen mast was removed.

As soon as the photograph was taken out of its cardboard cover, a glance was sufficient to establish that the moment of truth was at hand. There was *Shamrock* under full sail, almost completely broadside on with her mizzen mast fully revealed.

Copies were made of the photograph and a tracing was taken off it, enlarged to the 1 : 24 scale of the conjectural sail plan, and then laid over it. After an allowance had been made to compensate for the vessel being not quite broadside on

*Shamrock* 1934. This was the photograph which finally proved the Museum's conjectural sail plan.

to the camera, the position and height of the mizzen on the tracing was compared with the position and height of the mizzen on the sail plan. The only disparity between them was $\frac{1}{4}$ in (or 6 in in full scale) difference in height. The tracing showed a height of 30 ft, the sail plan a height of 30 ft 6 in. The two positions of the mast practically coincided and when the necessary adjustment of the height had been made, the sail plan was accepted as being as true a representation of how *Shamrock* appeared under sail in 1926 as it was possible to achieve.

Work on laying the deck was well underway by the middle of August, and provided the weather did not get any worse than that of the average English summer, it was hoped that all the deck would be completed by Autumn. Then Mr Perkins would be able to organise a caulking team from those men who were sufficiently experienced either to work on their own at this particular job, or able to do so under his supervision.

10 in, 13 double threads of oakum and 2 single threads of spun yarn; for 3 in, 4 double threads of oakum and 1 single thread of spun yarn. Below 3 in only oakum was used — for 2 in thickness (as in *Shamrock*'s planks) 2 double threads of oakum were specified.

Topside planking, waterways and deck planks also have their allotted amounts of caulking according to their thickness. The method advocated for finding the necessary seam for any thickness of plank is to draw two lines 10 in long so that they meet at one end and are $\frac{1}{2}$ in apart at the other; if the thickness of the plank is then set off from the point where the lines meet, the distance that the lines are apart at this place is the width of the seam that must be allowed.

The progressive manner of performing the caulking is by first caulking the treenails if there are any; then by driving large sharp wedge-like reaming irons into the seams that are under the standard width. This also closes any rents or

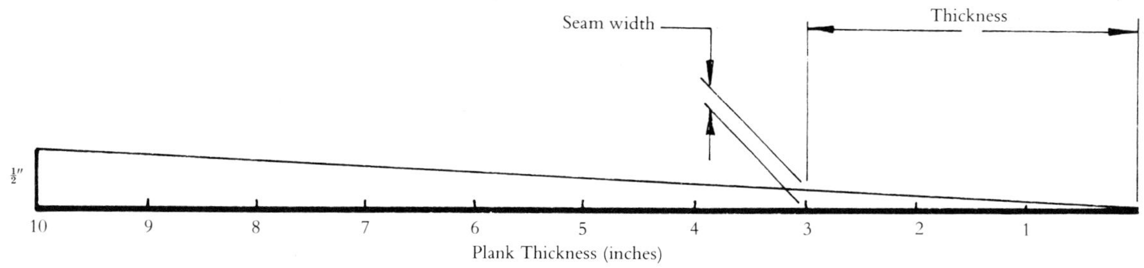


Scale to determine width of seams according to thickness of plank.

The importance of caulking has been alluded to earlier. It is an integral part of the restoration and maintenance of traditionally built wooden vessels. As such it demands as much knowledge, skill and application as any other technique of shipbuilding.

It is not just a question of stuffing the plank seams with oakum, willy nilly, then sealing them off with pitch, although it might appear to the casual observer that such is the case. There are quite definite rules for caulking the different thicknesses of planking so that the proper quantity of oakum may be got into the V shaped seams. Tables covering width of plank from 1 in to 10 in give the correct number of single threads of spunyarn and double threads of oakum to be used, *i.e.* for bottom planking of

shakes in the planks. The planking butts are also seamed to a depth of half their thickness like the longitudinal planks. In large vessels an older experienced man kept the butts caulked ahead of the gang that caulked the plank seams.

A reaming kit was composed of a heavy mallet and as many as five reaming irons. During the reaming operation, the skill of the caulker is demonstrated and the work of the shipwright is tested. The opening of the seams by such a powerful force as that formed by a range of wedges of acute or small angle struck with force by a heavy mallet also closes the seams above and below the one that is forced open, thus bringing a strain on the fastenings of both planks. This is why the caulker must be careful to caulk first those seams which are less than the

A selection of caulking tools.

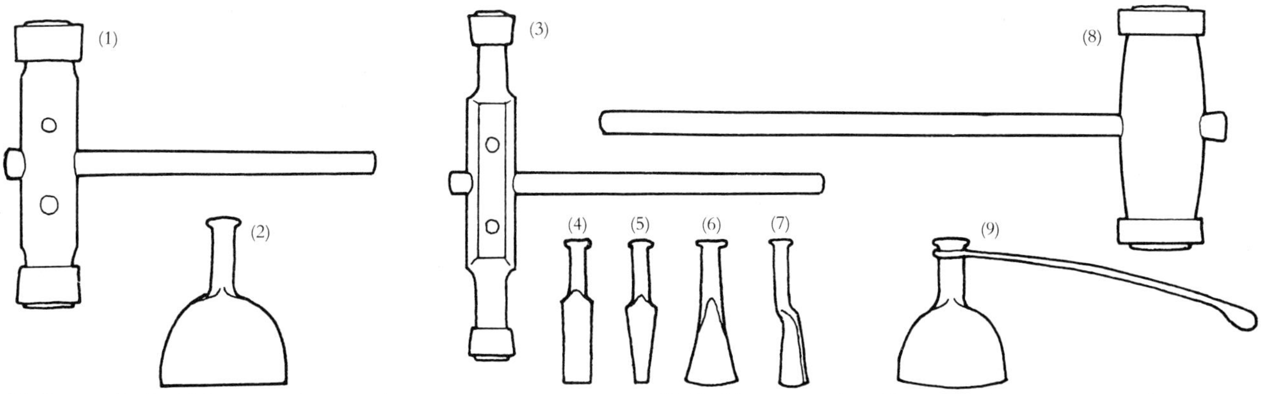


(1) Heavy mallet for driving the reaming or raming iron.
(2) One of the set of five reaming irons.
(3) Caulking mallet for driving caulking iron.
(4) Treenail iron for splitting treenail ends, prior to caulking.
(5) A spike iron for caulking in narrow spaces.
(6) Caulking or crease iron. They vary in blade thickness from $\frac{1}{32}''$ to $\frac{1}{4}''$.
(7) A bent or cranked for work in awkward corners.
(8) Caulking hammer, or Beetle, for driving the horsing iron.
(9) Long arm horsing iron with straight handle. Curved handles were also used.

standard width, and which are situated above or below seams that may be more than the standard width, thereby obtaining as many seams of even width as possible.

During this operation a shipwright should be in attendance (if he is not doing the actual caulking himself) to put in additional fastenings if the planking should be forced off the frame face. This can happen with inexperienced caulkers, especially if the seams or joints do not stand square to the timbers. If a shipwright is not standing by or supervising the work, unseen damage to the vessel's structure can result, which will only be revealed after she has been launched.

After reaming the seams, the spunyarn, if any, and then the stipulated number of threads of oakum are driven into the seams by the caulker, with his caulking mallet and range of caulking irons. The oakum is then hardened in and firmly bedded down into the seam (or 'horsed up') by two men — one holding a horse-iron in the seam upon the oakum; the other driving upon it with a large mallet called a beetle. It is essential at this stage of the caulking operation to give firmness to the oakum to prevent decay, and to

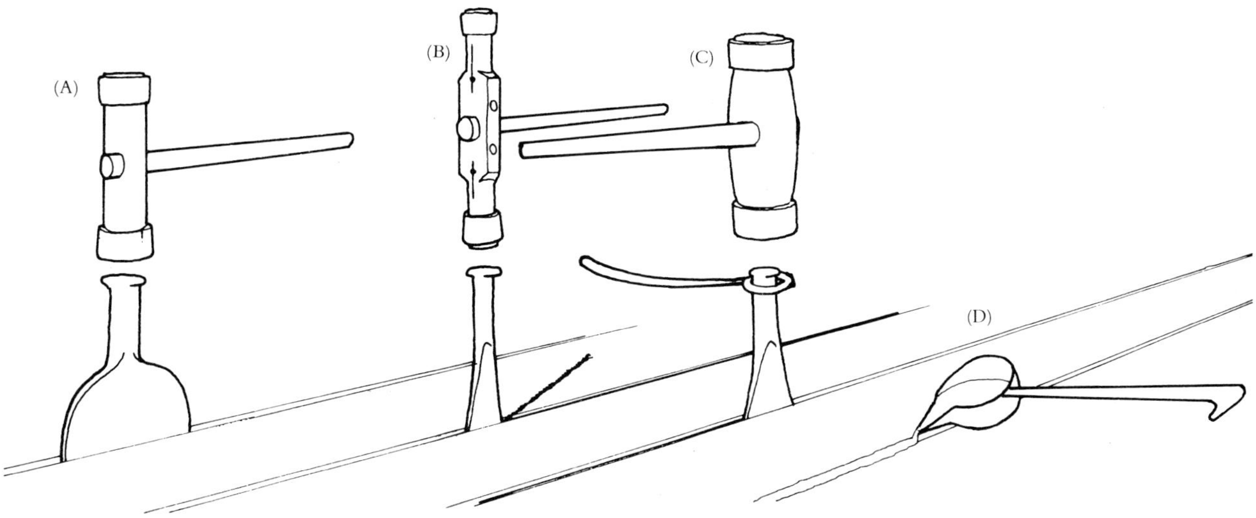


(A) Opening the seam with a reaming or raming iron and a heavy mallet.

(B) Driving the strand of oakum with a caulking iron and caulking mallet. It was customary to caulk from left to right.

(C) Compressing, 'hardening down' or 'horsing up' the oakum with a horsing iron and caulking hammer, or beetle. Working from right to left.

(D) Paying the seam with pitch from a ladle. A mop was used to pay the hull seams.

The Caulking process.

ensure that the threads, as they are driven into the seam, are forced in as far as possible. Thus the whole of the oakum is made to form a wedge to the bottom of the V seam, and to penetrate slightly into the back joint of the two planks, thus causing the oakum to be gripped by the timber as it swells. The outer surface of the oakum should be maintained at a constant depth of about $\frac{1}{8}$ in below the two surfaces of adjacent planks. Next, using small mops, melted pitch is payed over the horsed up oakum, the aim being to overfill the seam so that the pitch stands slightly proud of the planking surface.

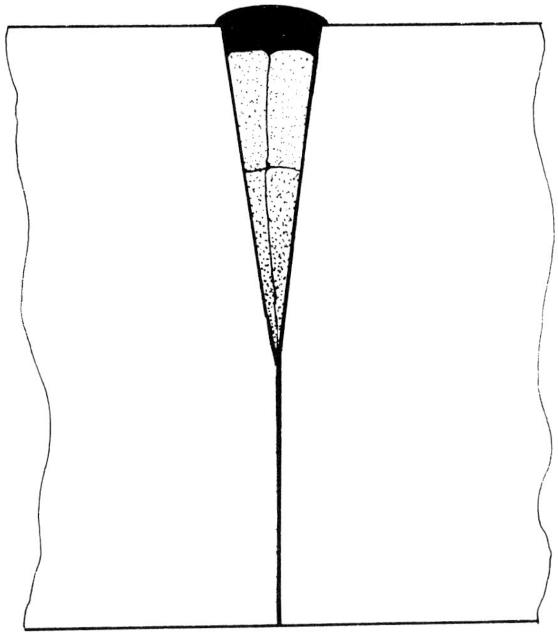

Section of caulking between deck planks.

Caulking a vessel tends to stiffen up the hull fabric, and when properly done does much to delay the racking and straining of fastenings which are inevitable in a working vessel. Indifferent or careless caulking will hasten this process, and be in itself a constant source of trouble through leakage, and the consequent necessity to rake out and recaulk the seams.

When *Shamrock* was built in 1899 shipyard hours were 6.30 am to 6 pm with a half an hour for breakfast, 1 hour for dinner for 5 days a week, and on Saturdays from 6.30 am to 2 pm — 10 hours a day actual working time, from Monday to Friday and 6 hours on Saturday — a total of 56 hours a week.

Many shipbuilders reckoned that one man could caulk from 90 to 100 ft of hull seam per working day, and from 100 to 120 ft of deck seams. The *Shamrock* has 32 strakes of outer planking, 16 on each side; and allowing for the curvature of the hull, the average length of each strake is some 60 ft, giving a total of some 1,920 ft of seams. Allowing a mean average of 95 ft of seam per man per day, it would have required some 20 working days to complete the job in 1899 — the equivalent of $3\frac{1}{2}$ working weeks in those days.

In 1978, assuming an 8-hour day and a 5-day week, 70 ft a day could be expected using the same reckoning, that is $27\frac{1}{2}$ working days or the equivalent of $5\frac{1}{2}$ working weeks. Add to that some 1,600 ft of deck seams, at a 100 ft per day, or 16 working days or roughly 3 working weeks; allow 2 weeks more for bad weather, hold-ups while other work is going on, and $2\frac{1}{2}$ months could be required for caulking.

The National Trust had continued to seek shipwrights or shipyard workers with necessary skills under the terms of their extended contract with the Job Creation Project, but suitable men were hard to find. When a man with caulking experience was eventually employed, the Trust declared that the hull should be caulked under his supervision, and completed as soon as possible with assistance from the men who were already employed under the terms of the Job Creation contract.

Although Mr Perkins was not to supervise the caulking, and was therefore not responsible for the work, as the shipwright-in-charge, he felt that the owners of the *Shamrock* should be made fully aware of the problems which could arise with hurried caulking, largely by men unskilled in the trade. The National Maritime Museum as technical advisors to the restoration recognised that it was necessary to complete the *Shamrock* as soon as possible and get her into the water, but since the caulking was critical to the vessel's future maintenance, it was our view that an independent surveyor should be called in to assess the work as it proceeded if possible, and completely to survey the hull when it had been fully caulked.

With the agreement of the Trust, the Museum made the necessary arrangements through Lloyd's Register of Shipping for one of their local surveyors to inspect the vessel as and when necessary. As the caulking of the hull proceeded, Mr Perkins carried on with the laying of the deck. This work could not proceed at its previous rate because some men were taken off it to work on the caulking of the hull planking but it continued slowly and steadily, and was only held up during prolonged bouts of rain.

When rain put a stop to all outside activities there was plenty of work to complete inside the hull. Of this, the chief was the building of the two bulkheads which separated the cargo hold from the crew's quarters or the foc'sle forward and the master's cabin aft.

The foc'sle bulkhead was lined through under the forward main cargo hatch beam. The framework of the bulkhead was of 4 in × 2 in which was clad on its after side with 7 in × $1\frac{1}{4}$ in thick tongued-and-grooved boards. A doorway was fitted in the port side of the bulkhead to allow access into the hold or foc'sle when the vessel was empty of cargo.

The after cabin bulkhead was lined through No. 8 beam just aft of the mizzen tabernacle. This bulkhead was of the same construction as that forward but without the door.

Other work below included the traditional screw-beading of the under faces of the deck planks along the line of one of their faying edges. A special beading plane was used for this job. This method of finishing off the deck planks inside was common to most 19th-century wooden sailing vessels, together with the bevelling of the lower edges of the deck beams. This not only prevented their being split, but also presented a nicely finished appearance, especially when they were painted white.

The new skylight/companionway was modelled on the remains of the one fitted in 1920.

In the shed, work had started on the cargo hatch covers, and also the construction of a skylight/ companionway for the master's cabin. This was 6 ft long and 3 ft wide built of teak, and panelled at the fore and after ends. There were three glasses, or windows, on each side each 6 in × 9 in and fitted with removable wooden shutters. Entrance to the cabin was through a 2 ft × 2 ft hatch fitted with a cambered sliding top at its after end, and two hinged doors.

# Chapter 7

*Making the sails; caulking and rigging; the* Shamrock *re-launched. Autumn 1978–April 1979.*

In the Autumn of 1978 Penrose Sailmakers of Falmouth had started work on the *Shamrock*'s sails. Since there was now no likelihood of the masts and spars being rigged in the vessel until the Spring of the next year, it had been agreed between all concerned that the sails would have to be made from measurements taken off the 1: 24 sail plan.

In this plan the sails were shown as they would appear after they had been naturally stretched. Therefore the sailmaker had to use his skill and experience to calculate the 'allowance' for stretching that each sail would require to make it fit the sail plan. Flax canvas had been used for all of *Shamrock*'s sails in 1926, and this was usually supplied in 40 yd bolts, made up of 24 in or 18 in widths. Flax canvas can be of any one of six or eight differing weights, known by numbers — No. 00 being the heaviest and strongest. Mr Knight the sailmaker originally chosen by the Museum to make the sails, had provided some first class No. 1 24 in flax canvas for the mainsail and staysail, and some equally fine No. 3 18 in flax canvas for the jib and mizzen.

It always paid the owner of a merchant sailing vessel to obtain the best canvas that was available. This was not only because the safety of the ship might one day depend on its quality, but also because a suit of sails of inferior material costs just as much to make as a suit made of the best canvas, which since it lasts much longer is by far the cheapest in the end.

In selecting canvas for making up into sails, considerable practice and close observation are required as well as a general acquaintance with the process of manufacture. The traditional sailmaker used to form his opinion of the strength and quality of the canvas from its evenly spun appearance, and by drawing an individual thread or two to see if they were composed of long flax, without a mixture of tow and were also of strong staple, fresh, sound and well cleansed. Sometimes he would force a fid, or wooden spike, through the canvas, causing the threads of poor quality canvas to be easily broken; or test them by hanging weights on the selected threads. There is a great deal of difference in the amount that the various grades and quality of canvas could be stretched, and it was the sailmaker who had mastered the art of making the right allowances for stretching whose sails were always recognised literally as a cut above the others.

Having studied the sailplan Mr Tresidder of Penrose Sailmakers drew up another plan of the sails as they were to be made and delivered to *Shamrock*. This showed some of the allowances that would be necessary in order to obtain the true shapes of the sails when they were stretched.

In the actual making of the sails the cloths of 24 or 18 in canvas are joined together by overlapped seams, sewn down each side. On some sails the seams vary in width between $1\frac{1}{4}$ in to $3\frac{1}{2}$ in at different places along their own length. This

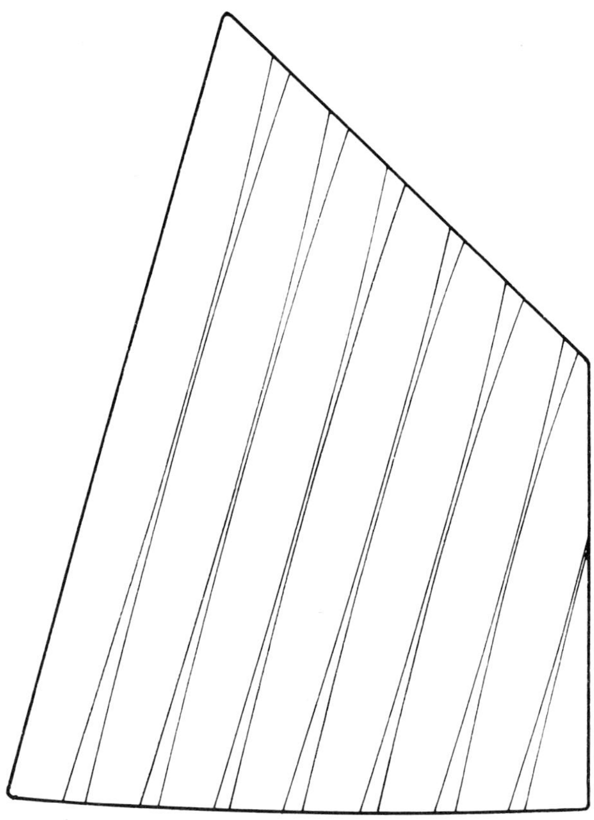

Exaggerated view of tapered seams in mainsail.

taper in the seams will not apply equally, throughout the whole sail, but will increase or decrease in adjoining seams and so mould the sail to the shape which the sailmaker requires. The average distance between seam centres in 24 in cloths is 22 in; and in 18 in cloths 16 in. The seams are sewn together with best flax seaming twine doubled and well coated in beeswax. There ought to be from 124 to 144 stitches in every yard of length, or three-and-a-half to four stitches to the inch.

The bolt ropes, which are sewn on around the port side perimeter of traditionally made fore-and-aft sails, should be of the very best quality hemp and tarred with the best Stockholm tar. The bolt ropes are sewn on to the sail with doubled roping twine through every strand of the rope, and if this is not done skilfully the bolt rope can spoil the look of a well-cut sail. For the bolt ropes of *Shamrock*'s sails Mr Knight had obtained some Italian hemp which was found to be of good quality and sufficient to do the job, with some to spare.

By the end of October the caulking of the outer planking was complete and 80% of the new deck had been laid. Mr G. R. May, surveyor to Lloyd's Registry, accordingly attended on the vessel and on the 7 and 18 November to examine and report on the condition of the work carried out to date, and the further work that was necessary to enable the vessel to be kept on a tidal berth as a museum type exhibit.

As expected, the surveyor found that many butts and seams of the bottom and topside planking would require their caulking oakum to be hardened or horsed up, or in some places completely raked out of some seams in order that new caulking could be properly put into them. His report also stated that shrinkage on the inside face of the bottom planking would 'take up' but that prior to launching, the vessel should be hauled back in the cradle to a half-tide position on the slipway for a 48-hour period, to enable the initial swelling to take place.

The new deck planking and all other work was found to be satisfactory. Work on the bulwark planking, wash strakes, chainplates, rudder, tiller, mast, spars and rigging which was outstanding on the 18 November was to be examined during two further visits, one while work was in progress and a final one when the vessel was launched and all work completed.

At a subsequent meeting between The National Trust and the Museum on 18 December the Trust announced that, as their contract with the Manpower Services Commission Job Creation Project had now expired, they would be applying for men to finish the work on *Shamrock* under the STEP Scheme — a Special Temporary Employment Programme Scheme — brought in by the Government to ease unemployment. Under the new contract they would employ eight men for a period of 6 months as soon as possible after 31 December 1978. Mr Perkins's contract with the Trust would be at an end by that time, but the Museum was considering his temporary employment as shipwright-in-charge to finish off the hull and to co-operate with Museum staff during the masting and rigging of the vessel for which they were entirely responsible. If the Trust failed in its application for STEP assistance it was their intention to provide a carpenter to assist Mr Perkins to complete the remaining work on the hull, and if possible, one other man as well.

The year ended with a telephone call from Penrose Sailmakers stating that a fire had destroyed part of their premises in Falmouth and as a result work on the *Shamrock*'s sails would be delayed until well into the New Year. Fortunately, the sails themselves had not been destroyed and as a small consolation for this new set-back Mr Tresidder said that when clearing up the mess he had found a draught of *Shamrock*'s mainsail which the Firm had made for her in the thirties. Out of curiosity he compared the draught with the Museum's conjectural sail plan from which he was cutting her new sails, and found them to be practically identical. Thus any doubts as to the authenticity of *Shamrock*'s sailplan were finally removed.

With the beginning of the new year the Museum made its plans for masting and rigging *Shamrock*. There was a considerable amount of preparatory work to be done before the actual work on the rigging could begin, and this could only be done with a close liaison between myself and the shipwright-in-charge. The mizzen mast, main and mizzen booms and gaffs, and the bowsprit, had to be cut and trimmed to their correct dimensions, and fitted with their various pieces of ironwork, and the timber jaws for the booms and gaffs would also have to be made and fitted by the shipwright.

The main and mizzen masts would need placing in their respective tabernacles, and raised to their correct position so that the chainplates could be aligned and through bolted to the vessel's sides.

Bowsprit clamps and fittings for the pawl post would be required and eyebolts for the standing and running rigging would have to be bored for and fitted about the deck on their correct positions. Cleats, cavil-rails and fairleads had to be positioned in accordance with the sail and rigging plan and a host of small shipwrighting jobs were necessary at this stage.

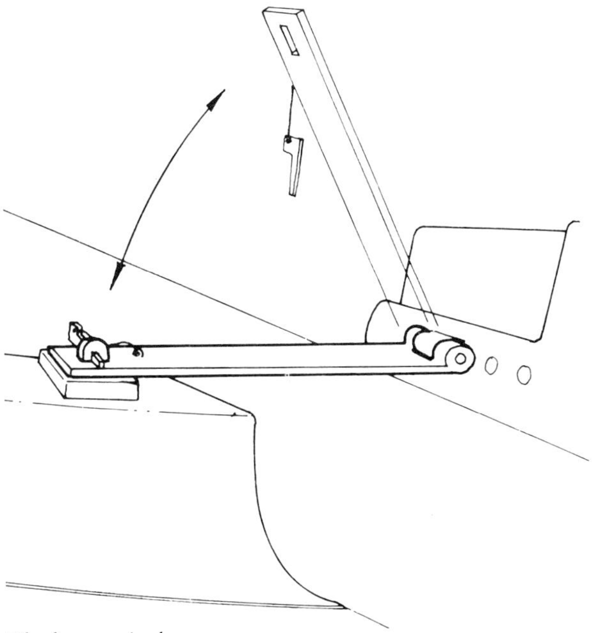

The bowsprit clamp.

Mr Perkins was thoroughly conversant with the sail and rigging plan, having gone over it point by point with me when I had drawn it. I was to make the remainder of the rigging at Cotehele Mill during my weekly visits to monitor and record the progress of the restoration work.

Owing to other Museum commitments it would be February before any work on the rigging could begin and another meeting between the Museum and National Trust was arranged for 2 February 1979 to clear up certain points relating to the completion of the hull. These included arrangements for the third examination of the vessel by Lloyd's Surveyor and the organisation of the masting and rigging programme. The meeting was also to confirm that Mr Perkins was to remain as shipwright-in-charge of the restoration until the completion of the restoration, now as an employee solely of the National Maritime Museum.

Work on the *Shamrock*'s standing rigging began on 16 February. First, the mainmast was thoroughly examined. It had been well clear of everything in the rack which had been specially made for it along one side of the shed since 1974, when it had been given an initial inspection to see if it was sound, and a coat of varnish to protect it.

It was a pitch pine mast, 41 ft from heel to truck, $10\frac{1}{2}$ in square for 36 in above the heel for housing within the tabernacle, then rounded above that to $10\frac{1}{2}$ in diameter for 25 ft to the 22 in oak bibbs, or cheeks, one on each side, which acted as a stop and a support for the shrouds. The top edge grains of the bibbs were protected by 2 in greenheart half-round bolsters for the shrouds to bear on without chafing, and above these, the mainmast-head measured 11 ft, and tapered to $6\frac{1}{2}$ in diameter at the truck.

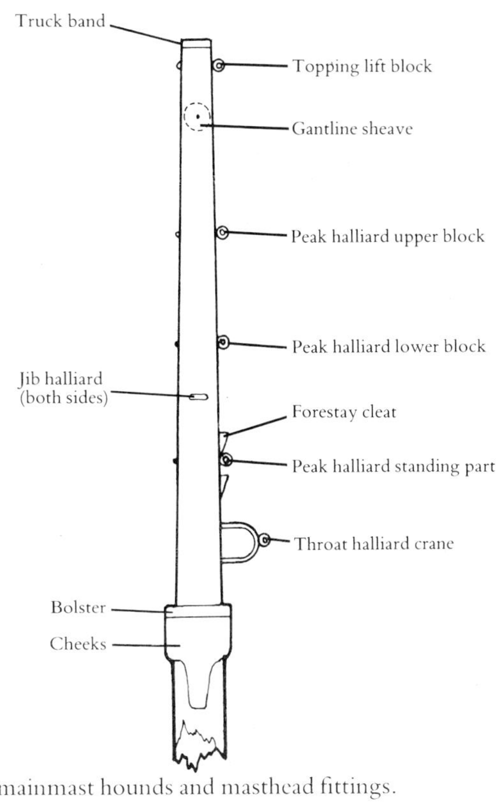


The mainmast hounds and masthead fittings.

Six inches below the truck on the after side of the masthead there was a vertically disposed iron eyebolt for the topping lift block, and 6 in below that a 7 in × $1\frac{1}{4}$ in sheave hole and sheave. A similarly disposed iron eye for the upper block of the peak halliard was fixed 2 ft below the sheave hole; the eye for the lower block of the peak halliard was 30 in lower and the eye for the standing part of the halliard 30 in below that. Midway between them there were two horizontally disposed eyes for the jib halliards, one on each side of the masthead. Immediately above the eyebolt for the standing part of the peak halliard there was a 6 in × 2 in wedge shaped oak chock for the eye or collar of the forestay to rest on, and a similar chock some 6 in below it.

A 'D' shaped crane of 1 in diameter round iron, $9\frac{1}{4}$ in in depth and 9 in proud of the masthead was fixed 10 in above the shroud bolsters. The crane had a 2 in inside diameter eye for the shackle of the upper double block of the throat halliard purchase.

It had been said that the mainmast was the original one placed in the vessel in 1899. There was no reason why it should not be, but proof had not been found. Photographs proved beyond all doubt, however, that it was certainly the same mast which was in the vessel in 1926.

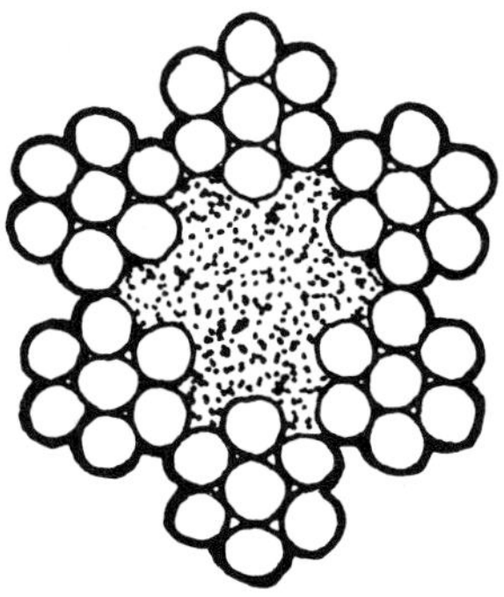

End elevation of 6 × 7 standing rigging wire rope.

The shrouds and forestay were still on the mast. These were of 1 in diameter iron wire made up of six strands formed round a hemp heart, the strands themselves being made up of six wires formed round a wire heart.

*Shamrock*'s shrouds had been set up by means of rigging, or bottlescrews, instead of the dead-eye blocks and rope lanyards, usually associated with wooden working sailing vessels. Bottlescrews were necessary in her case, since they could be easily slackened off and tightened up, when lowering or raising the masts. The ends of the shrouds were spliced round thimble eyes which were shackled to the upper threaded shank and eyes of their bottlescrews. Splices always slightly weaken a wire and for this reason *Shamrock*'s shrouds were of extra size to compensate for the splices at each of their ends. Most shroud thimbles were of the solid type with a hole for the shackle pin, but *Shamrock*'s were all open.

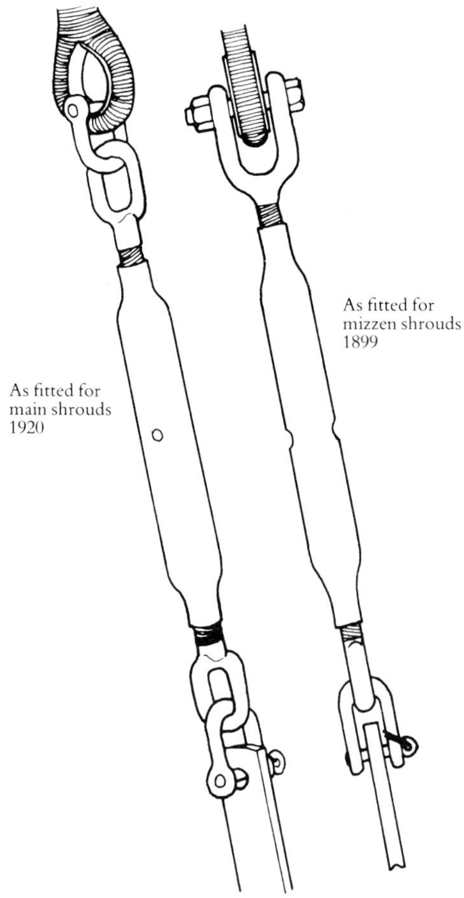


Main and mizzen shrouds. The bottlescrews and shroud plate connections.

The total lengths of the shroud wires were 80 ft and 80 ft 2 in. They were formed into port and starboard pairs by middling each length to form two legs. The legs were secured together with a round seizing of special heavy gauge seizing wire to form a bight, or collar, just large enough to be put over the mast head and worked down to the bolsters on the mast-bibbs. Traditionally the starboard shroud collar was placed first, and then the port collar on top of it. Because of this order of placing, it was necessary to make the legs of the port shroud 2 in longer to ensure that both pairs of shrouds reached down equally to the bottlescrews on each side of the hull. To obtain a neat appearance it was also traditional practice to have the round seizings just a little below the bolsters.

in the same manner and their round seizings had been put on over strips of canvas to prevent the seizing wire from cutting the service.

The forestay was also of 1 in diameter iron wire,

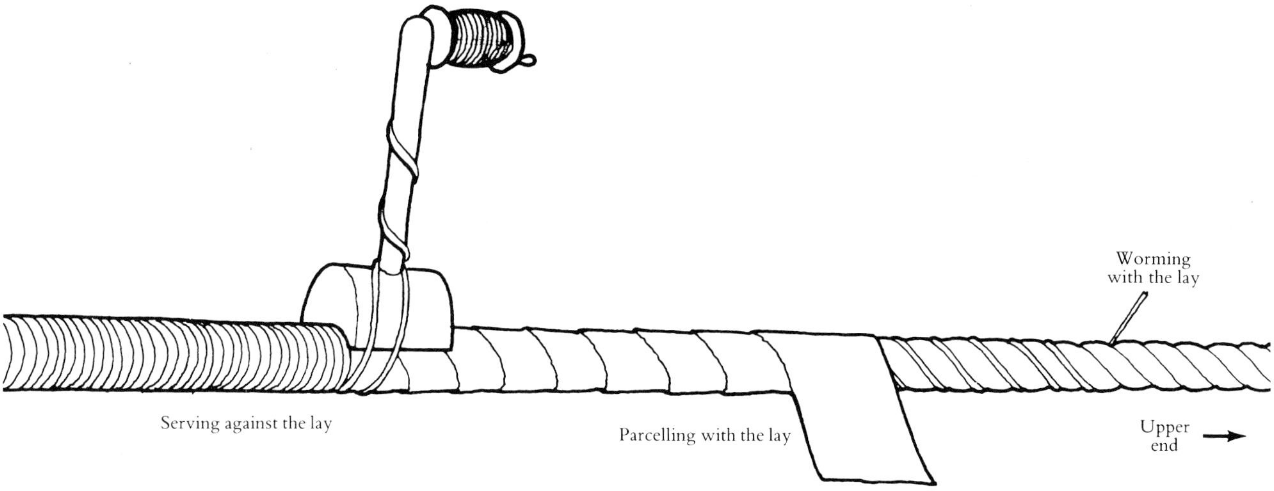


Worming, parcelling and serving in the traditional manner.

Before splicing the ends of the shrouds the part which formed the eye round the thimbles had been wormed, parcelled, and served to protect it from wet and chafe. Worming is done to fill up the space between the strands of the wire with spunyarn or small rope, in order to render the surface smooth and round for parcelling and serving. Parcelling is the passing round with the lay of the wire of strips of old canvas soaked in Stockholm tar, from 2 to 3 in wide, according to the size of the shroud so that the lower edges of the parcelling always overlaps the upper edge of the turn below it. This is done prior to serving the wire with marline. Serving is put on by laying the marline around the head and handle of a serving mallet for the number of turns required to produce the tension necessary to bind the marline tightly around the wire as the mallet is rotated against the lay. The head of the mallet is grooved to fit the round of the wire, which is set up bar taut for this operation. After the served wire had been bent round the shroud thimble it had been spliced with a 3½ in tuck locking splice, which had been tapered down by halving the strands cutting them off close, then lightly hammering it to make a neat tight job.

All the original splices in *Shamrock*'s shrouds had been well finished off and protected with tallow before being parcelled and served. The mast-head shroud collars had also been well protected

30 ft 6 in in length, with a collar 6 ft from crown to splice at its upper end, and a thimble splice at the lower end to take the shackle either of its stemhead bottlescrew, or the upper double block of the forestay-purchase, which was used to raise and lower the mast.

The forestay had been protected from wet and chafe in the same manner as the shrouds and whoever had put on the last parcelling and serving on all these wires had done his job well. All would now have to be renewed, of course, but they had certainly kept the splices in very good condition.

The first job of rigging would be to strip the shrouds and forestay and get them up to the Mill prior to setting them up ready for cleaning off with a stiff wire brush.

The National Trust's application for suitably skilled men under the STEP Scheme had not yet been granted, hence there was no additional labour available to help the shipwright to lay the remainder of the deck planks, or to rake out and recaulk defective hull seams. It was therefore decided to fit the chain-plates, the wrought iron straps, which are bolted to the vessel's sides abreast and aft of each mast and to which the bottlescrews which shackle on to the lower ends of their shrouds are secured.

The first thing to do was to mark out the position of the chain-plates on the outer planking of the hull. Ideally, the masts would have been set up in their tabernacles to ensure that the chain-plates and shrouds were in alignment by rigging mock-up shrouds of seizing wire from the hounds, or mast-head bibbs and bolsters, down to the vessel's sides in way of the chain-plates.

As the masts were not in position, the lead of the shrouds was obtained from measurements taken off the sail plan and transferred on to the hull planking. Frame timbers were then located within the hull to establish their position relative to the chain-plates, in order that their securing bolts should pass through the timbers, and not just the outer and inner planking.

Twenty-four 1 in diameter holes had to be bored for the wrought iron chainplate bolts, most of them through the 10 in of outer planking, timbers and ceiling plank abreast of the masts. Two of the upper bolt holes in the main port and starboard after shrouds had to be bored through 16 in of solid timber, where the bolts passed through the filling pieces above the beamshelf, and the side limbs of the oak lodging knees on each side of the hull. To facilitate the boring of these holes it was necessary to erect local scaffolding for the job, since the original scaffolding and staging had been removed once the outer planking had been fastened and stopped off.

While the shipwright concentrated on boring out the chain-plate bolt holes, I began work on the rigging in the Mill loft a mile away up the road from the quay.

All the tools required for the job — steel tape, chalk, lignum vitae fids for splicing rope, steel spikes for splicing wire, hammers and chisels of various sizes, pliers, pincers, a hacksaw, rigging-screws, serving mallets of several sizes, and two well sharpened knives, were placed in a allotted rack ready to hand. Balls of marline, hanks of twine, codline, point-line, and seizing wire were hung on handy pegs. Strips of canvas for parcelling were made up and placed in a wooden box. Shackles, hooks, eyebolts, cringle-irons, thimbles, bullseyes, bottlescrews, and small chains were hung off a wire line where they could be easily reached, and pots of grease, tallow, red lead, linseed oil, paraffin, turpentine

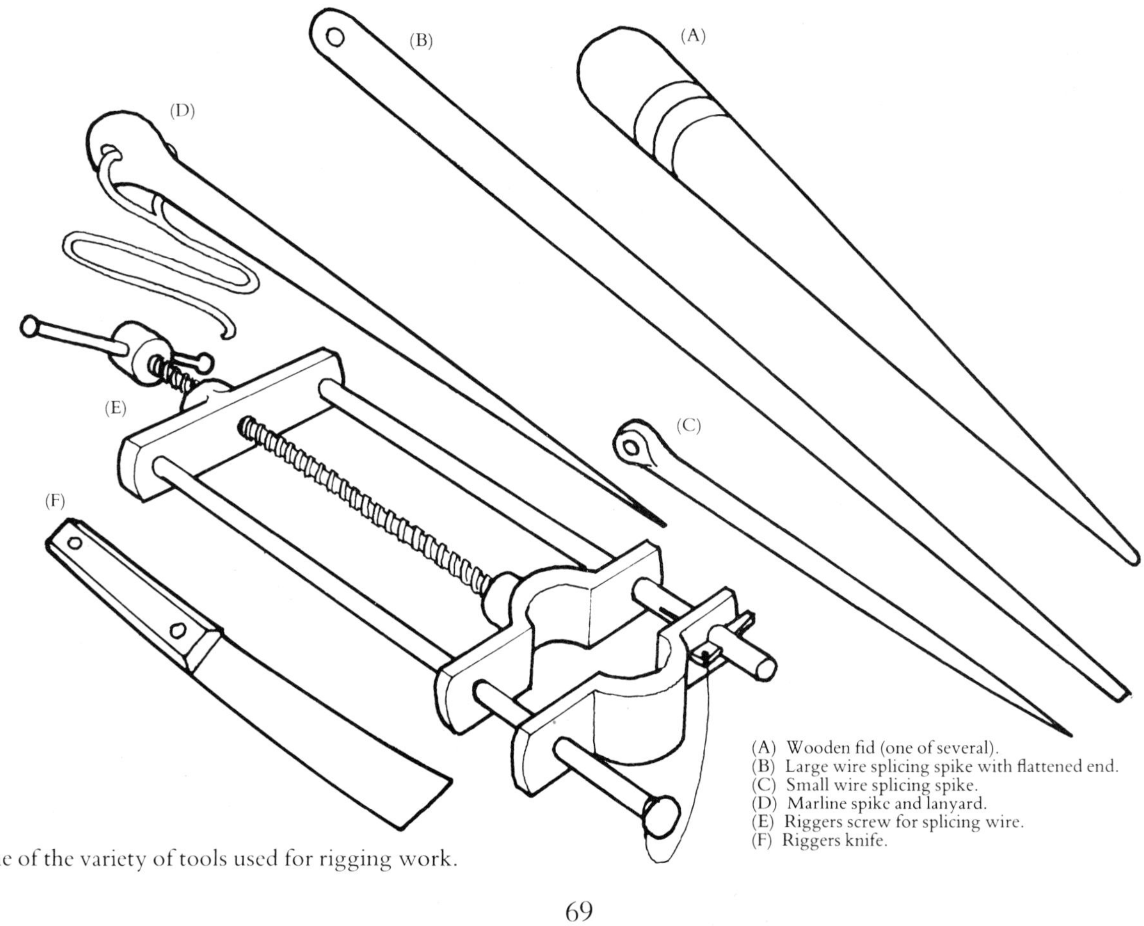


(A) Wooden fid (one of several).
(B) Large wire splicing spike with flattened end.
(C) Small wire splicing spike.
(D) Marline spike and lanyard.
(E) Riggers screw for splicing wire.
(F) Riggers knife.

Some of the variety of tools used for rigging work.

and Stockholm tar were placed in a corner out of the way of everything. All blocks not made up into purchases were laid out in size order, together with their sheaves and pins ready for replacement.

A space, 40 ft long and some 10 ft wide, was cleared for the setting up of the shrouds, stays, or other wires that were to be spliced or served; small handy billy tackles were made up and hung at each end of the loft and from the roof beams, together with strops and lashings and short lines with hooks, and everything necessary to facilitate the rigging work which would have to be carried out during a series of short weekly visits from London until the job was finished.

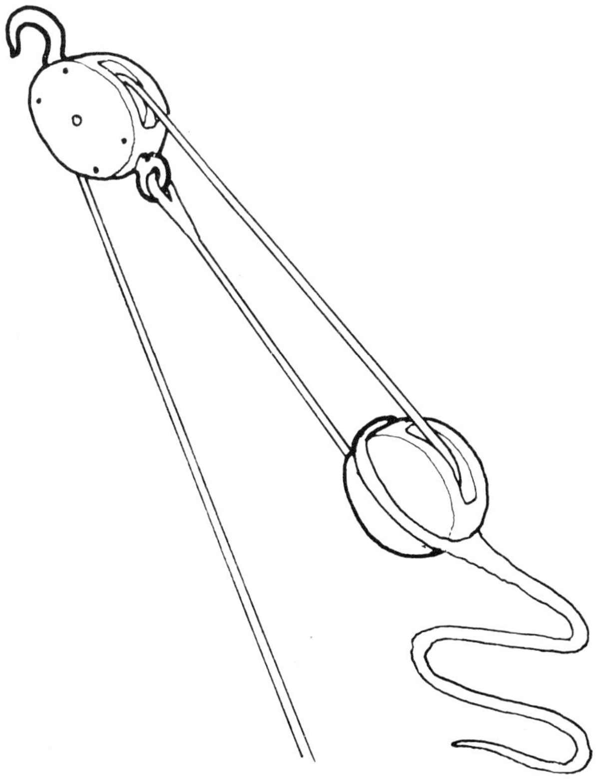

Watch tackle, tail tackle or 'Handy Billy'.

During the first week of March, it was confirmed that The National Trust's application for additional labour under the STEP Scheme had not been granted.

Since January Mr Perkins had continued to work on the *Shamrock*'s hull, and had bored out the boltholes for the chain-plates, raked out and recaulked several seams of defective caulking and assisted in the stripping of the mainmast shrouds and forestay and the cleaning off and refurbishing of the mainmast.

At a meeting between the Museum, Mr Perkins and Mr Eley of The National Trust, it was agreed that as it was impossible without additional labour to finish off the decks, rake out and re-caulk all of the defective hull seams, plank the bulwark stanchions and cap them, shape the mizzen mast, gaffs and booms and to generally complete the hull, the Trust would provide two carpenters and one general helper. Mr Perkins would remain responsible for the restoration of the hull. Mr Eley would be in day to day charge of the workforce, and I would be responsible for the vessel's masting, rigging and sails, with Mr Perkins assistance, and for continued monitoring and recording.

With the additional skilled men now available work began on the laying of the deck planks, and the raking out and re-caulking of the defective hull seams could proceed under the shipwright's supervision. The larch planking for the bulwarks and the elm for the capping, or main rail, was carefully selected and work began on this job from the port quarter to the midship cargo gate as soon as the deck in that area had been laid.

There were three strakes of bulwark planking of 1 in thickness, the upper one 5 in wide and scored with a beading line an inch above its low-

The washstrake, mainrail and bulwark planking. Note gap between lower plank and covering board.

er edge, the middle one 5 in wide with a slightly concave rounding of its outer surface, and the lowest strake, 4 in wide, also beaded 1 in below its upper edge. This strake was scored along its whole length with a 2 in groove for the white sheer line which was traditional to most of the small merchant sailing vessels of the 19th and early 20th century.

The bottom plank edge was 1 in clear of the covering board to allow water to flow freely off the cambered deck, and to prevent any accumulation of dirt, and particularly leaves under them; the quickest and surest way to rot both bulwark plank and covering board. Daily maintenance should prevent this happening, of course, but nevertheless, it always pays to let the lowest bulwark strake have plenty of air circulating under its bottom edge.

The elm capping, or rail, was 5 in wide and 2 in thick. Each section was tenoned and spiked to a stanchion, the head of the spike being countersunk and stopped off with an elm plug in whitelead putty. The cargo gates, moveable sections of bulwark to facilitate loading or discharging cargo, situated on each side of the cargo hatch, were also fitted with capping rails to maintain an unbroken line of sheer from bow to stern, when they were placed in position. Plans were also made for the cleaning and preparing of

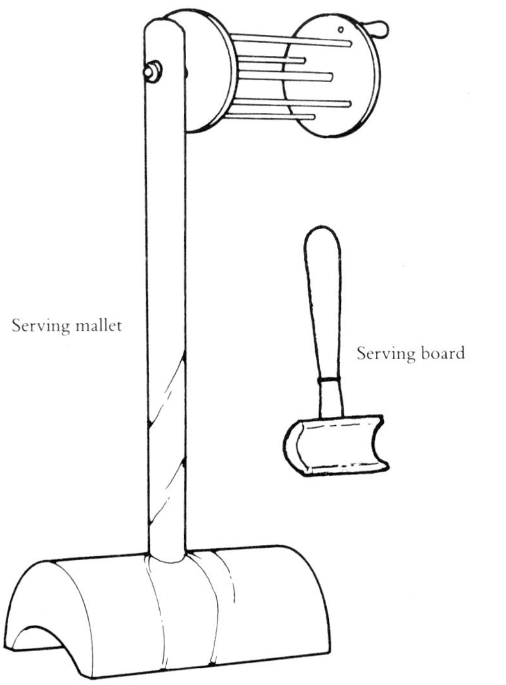

Serving mallet with spool for large ropes. A serving board is commonly used for eyes.

the slipway area in preparation for the launching of the hull, and by the end of the month Mr Perkins had commenced the re-caulking of the seams along the starboard bilge.

During April work on the rigging proceeded according to plan. As the parcelling and serving of the shrouds and forestay had to be done single-handed, the serving mallet was fitted with a spool on the end of its handle, on to which the marline used for the service was firmly wound. Thus, as the mallet was rotated around the shroud or stay — set up bar taut by block and tackle for the purpose — there was no need for an extra hand to pass the ball of marline round. In this manner, the forestay was first parcelled and double served around the collar, then tallow was squeezed well into the strands of its two splices, and they too, were parcelled and served. The ends of the marline were tucked through the last five turns, flattened out, and hauled through them, until snugly buried; then the ends were cut off.

The thimble eye splices at the end of each leg of the port and starboard shrouds was also served in the same way. The 6 ft lengths at the middling of each of the shrouds were double served, since they would become the shroud collars when the legs were seized together later, and once in place on the bolsters the serving could not be repaired or renewed. Some vessels had their shroud collars covered with leather as an additional protection against chafing and penetration of water into the wire.

The next job was the splicing of the main and mizzen topping lift wires. These were both made of galvanised $1\frac{1}{2}$ in circumference $6 \times 12$ wire, *i.e.* 6 strands with 12 wires in each strand made up around a jute heart. The main topping-lift wire was 33 ft in length and required two thimble eyes — one for the shackle which secured its lower end to the eye in boom end-band — the other for the shackle which joined it to the lower of the two single blocks which formed a double whip-purchase, the upper block of which was shackled to the topping lift eyebolt in the mainmast head.

The mizzen topping-lift was 39 ft in length and also required two thimble eye splices. On was for the shackle which secured it to the boom end-band, and one for the shackle of the double block of a luff-purchase which was shackled after the topping-lift wire had been rove through a single block at the mizzen masthead. The single block of the purchase was hooked into a deck eyebolt either to port or starboard abreast of the mizzen tabernacle.

All splices were the standard tapered locking splice each of three full tucks, then one tuck of two-thirds of a strand, and a final tuck with one-third of a strand. All were tallowed, parcelled and served in traditional fashion.

A 16 ft length of extra flexible $2\frac{1}{2}$ in circumference 6 × 37 galvanised wire rope was also made up, with a thimble-eye spliced in each end. This was for the main fish tackle which would be hung off an eye bolt in the centre of the port mast bibb, with its lower end shackled to a luff purchase. This wire had to be extra flexible because it would sometimes be required to be used on the starboard forward side when hoisting anchor inboard, or to lead aft if it was used in conjunction with a similar purchase from the mizzen mast hounds band to hoist the 13 ft clinker built workboat inboard.

Three $1\frac{1}{2}$ in circumference 6 × 12 galvanised wire gaff spans, each 5 ft 6 in in length and with soft eyes in each end were also made, and given a double parcelling and serving. These spans were later fitted with bullseyes, *i.e.* $2\frac{1}{2}$ in inside diameter cringles made of elm or lignum vitae, bound with $\frac{3}{8}$ in round wrought iron straps. When in place on the span the cringle could move freely along it when the gaffs were hoisted, thus allowing the weight to be evenly distributed through the legs of the spans and spreading the load along a length of the gaff. When rigged the spans were held in position by oak thumb cleats secured underneath the gaffs. The bullseyes were specially made by the Torpoint Slipping Company, from a pattern taken off an original one.

This company also made the hinged steel bowsprit clamp which fitted over the hole in the wash strake on the starboard side of the stem post, through which the bowsprit passed. Mr Hoskings, *Shamrock*'s master in the 1920s had such a fitting made in order to get the bowsprit out of the way when coming alongside, or laying in a crowded berth in Plymouth or elsewhere. The clamp pin was knocked out, the hinged clamp bar was thrown back, and the bowsprit, which was secured at its heel by a pivot-bolt which passed through it and the pawl post, was hoisted well clear of everything by the jib halliards.

In spite of wet weather and high winds, work on the quay site continued steadily. The hardening up and caulking of butts and bottom seams continued, and the laying of the port side deck planks was almost complete by the end of March.

The completion of *Shamrock*'s sails by Penrose Sailmakers had been much delayed by the Firm's removal to new premises after the fire which destroyed their old loft in November 1978, but at this time they reported that they were roping the mainsail and hoped to deliver all the sails within the next two or three weeks.

At the Mill loft the mizzen mast was cut to its 30 ft overall length, its 6 ft head tapered to $4\frac{3}{4}$ in diameter at the truck, and all its measurements for fittings and those of the gaffs and booms were checked against the sail and rigging plan once again, to ensure that when work began on

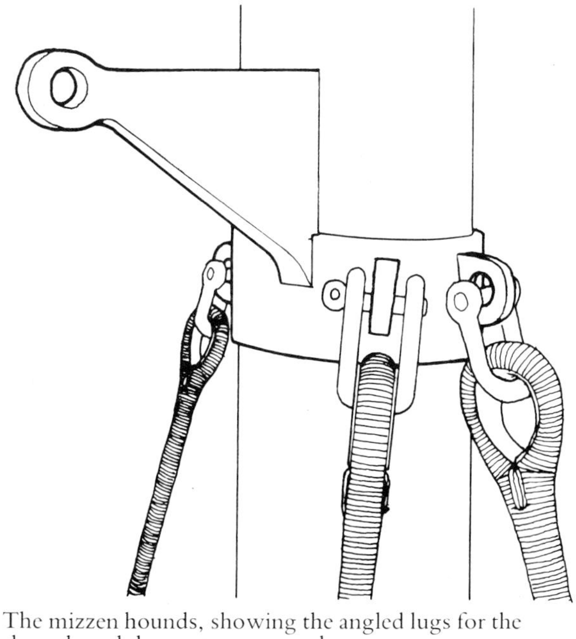

The mizzen hounds, showing the angled lugs for the shrouds and the contemporary throat crane.

the fixing of their eye bolts and all their ironwork, everything would be found to be in its correct position when the vessel was rigged. The four mizzen shrouds were to be of 2 in circumference 6 × 7 plough steel wire, and unlike the main shrouds, they were to be shackled independently of each other, direct to the mizzen hounds band which had to be specially made with slightly angled eyes to align with the shrouds. This band was also fitted with an eye on its foreside into which the upper block of the mizzen fish tackle could be shackled.

The lower ends of the mizzen shrouds also required a thimble eye spliced in them for the shackles which secured them to the chain-plate bottlescrews, making a total of eight wire splices altogether. The wire for the shrouds was obtained from the Southampton branch of Spencers Rigging of Cowes, Isle of Wight, who also put in an upper thimble eye splice into each of the four shrouds, leaving a sufficient length of wire for the lower eye splices to be put in at Cotehele after the mizzen mast had been set up in its tabernacle and the necessary measurements taken.

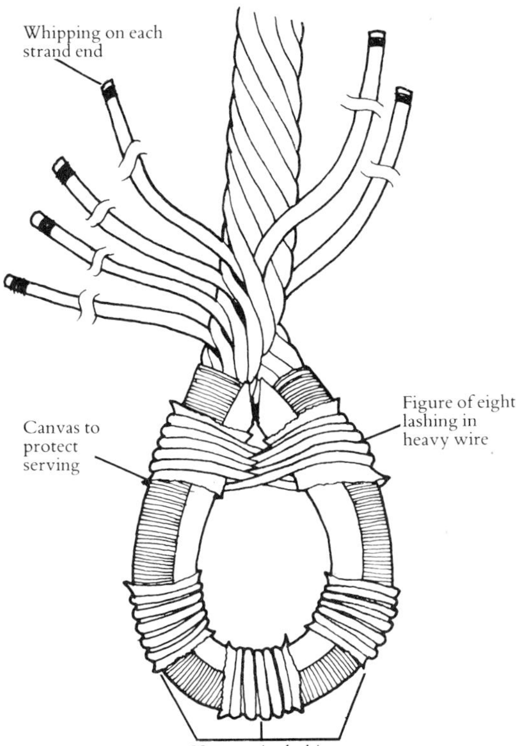


Thimble eye splice as made for the mizzen shrouds, showing one series of tucks put in.

Mr Perkins continued to supervise the planking of the bulwarks, capping and wash strake, and the laying of deck planks. Additional labour was also provided by the Trust for the clearing of the slipway and preparations for launching, which would take place as soon as the re-caulking of the bottom seams had been accepted as up to the standard required by the Lloyd's Surveyor.

All the running rigging which had been rove off and hung from the roof beams of the Mill since 1977 was now taken down for inspection prior to a final stretching before the rigging of the vessel commenced. It was necessary to do all this in order to avoid the troublesome twisting of the new purchases when the vessel was rigged, which will always occur unless the rope has been thoroughly stretched beforehand.

The sheet and halliard purchases were overhauled until they were 'block and block' and then made fast to a tree on the roadside adjacent to the Mill. Their falls, or hauling parts, were then laid out full length on the road, and taking care not to let them chafe on the gravel, each rope in turn was made fast to the Cotehele Estate lorry hauled taut and gradually stretched, as judgement thought fit.

Each purchase was then made up again ready for transport to the quay, together with the forestay, shrouds and all the other items of cordage and wire which had been completed. Later they were taken down to the Quay shed ready for rigging in the vessel.

The remainder of the rigging work to be done at the Mill loft was the putting in of a thimble-eye in each of the four mizzen shrouds which would be done as soon as the length of the shroud had been verified with the mizzen in position, and the checking of 240 ft of $1\frac{1}{2}$ in circumference 6 × 24 galvanised steel rope which would be used principally for raising and lowering masts, and other jobs requiring wire of such length and flexibility. The breaking strain of this wire was 6.1 tons, which allowed for a working strain of about 1.2 tons. One of the interesting tests to which steel rope of this quality is subjected consists of it being wrapped eight times around its own part, then unwrapped and straightened out again without breaking or splitting. This particular wire required a thimble-eye in one end only — the other end was whipped with light gauge seizing wire, so that it could be easily inserted through masthead sheave holes, or locked swiftly and securely into the staples of a wooden winch drum.

The re-caulking of the bottom planks was complete by the middle of April, and after an inspection by Mr May, Lloyd's Surveyor, the vessel was certified as fit to enter the water. The hull was then thoroughly coated with pitch.

of getting it off the vessel. However, the yard foreman had promised that as soon as the plates and scrap were shipped out he would break the pump out of its seating and put it aside for the Museum.

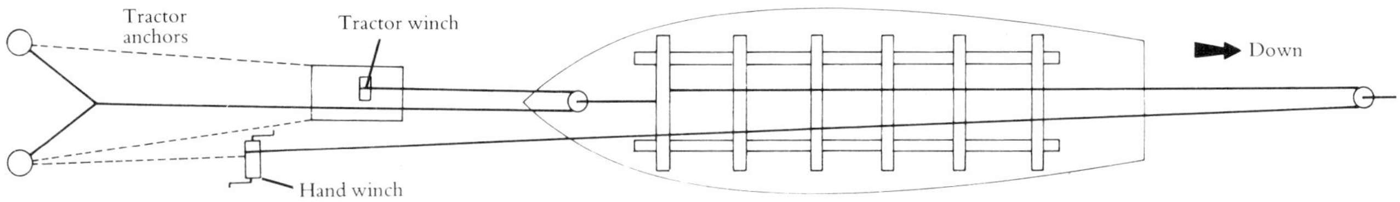


The plan for hauling *Shamrock* down the slipway, prepared by Mr George Eley.

The shipwright-in-charge and Mr Eley then worked out their method for hauling *Shamrock* in her cradle some 30 or 40 ft down the slipway to the low water level, and Mr Eley engaged one of the local mine rescue teams to set up the necessary gear. On 26 April after an entirely understandable initial reluctance to leave the berth in which she had been so completely restored, *Shamrock* floated off her cradle on the evening tide, 4 years 10 months after she had entered it on 22 July 1974.

*Shamrock* floated on an even keel 1 ft by the stern drawing 2 ft 1 in forward and 3 ft aft, and over the next 24 hours she took in some 2 in of water. Rotary pumps had been rigged to cope with any emergency but these were not necessary. A traditional cast iron sluice or diaphram pump of a size suitable for *Shamrock* had been located on a barge in a Southampton shipyard, but as it was buried under scrapped steel plates, and other gear from broken up vessels, there was no way

The traditional cast iron sluice pump.

# Chapter 8

*Caulking the deck; fitting masts and rudder. April–Autumn 1979.*

Now that the vessel was in the water the next jobs were to caulk the deck, which was already fastened and stopped off, get the masts aboard, then rig and raise them; make and fit oak jaws, wooden tumblers, iron tumblers, gaff span cleats, boom end-bands, sheet-bands, reef pendant clamps, eyes for the reef tackles, and the sheaves and cleats for the main and mizzen clewlines; taper off the gaff ends, fashion the bowsprit and forestaysail boom; make and fit the rudder and tiller; finish off the hatch covers; fit out the foc'sle and cabin aft, and generally to complete the vessel.

The caulking of the deck seams followed the same basic pattern as that used for the hull seams, apart from the use of a long curved handled reaming iron (sometimes called a battle-axe because of its shape), which was driven by a large wooden maul or beetle. The horsing and making in irons for deck work were also fitted with long curved handles, and there were a variety of crooked and double crooked caulking irons used for the seams adjacent to hatch coamings, deckhouses, stanchions, sampson posts, pawl posts and windlass bitts, and spike irons for caulking very short seams, such as those of the joggled or nibbed plank ends. Deck boxes were used as seats when caulking on deck; these were made with oval shaped or oblong openings at the front, so that the assortment of tools carried in them could be easily got at.

The melted pitch which sealed the oakum in the seams was poured into them with a pitch ladle, and it was good practice to use the pitch at the proper temperature, otherwise it tended to bubble and leave air pockets if too hot; and if not hot enough the pitch would conjeal before it properly filled the seam. By the first week in June the deck was caulked and payed and preparations were made to get the masts in the vessel. The mainmast had been cleaned off and oiled with a mixture of raw linseed oil and paraffin, coat after coat being applied to soak well into it. The head had been stopped filled and painted with the traditional buff colour favoured by the Tamar barges, or as near a shade as it was possible to obtain. A new steel sheave was placed at the mast head to take the 3 in circumference manilla gantline which would be permanently rigged aloft to facilitate going aloft in a bosun's chair, and a copper shim cover was fitted over the end grain of the mast truck and suitably insulated to prevent corrosion of the iron truck band.

The next job was to 'dress' the mast, or to place its standing and running rigging in position. But before this could be done the mast had to be manhandled out of the shed on to the quay adjacent to the deck. This was an 'all hands' job since the mast weighed almost half a ton.

Once outside it was placed on evenly spaced wooden blocks and wedged off to prevent any sagging or twisting, and more linseed oil was worked into its grain.

The two pairs of shrouds and the forestay were laid alongside the mast. The starboard shroud, middled and temporarily seized to form a collar was placed in position on the hounds bolsters. A piece of tarred canvas was wrapped around the strands just below the temporary seizing. This was to prevent the wire of the permanent round seizing from cutting into the new marline serving on the shroud collar. The heavy gauge seizing wire was then passed ten times around both legs of the shroud, each turn being heaved tight. Nine riding turns were then passed, which fitted on top of, and between the lower turns. These

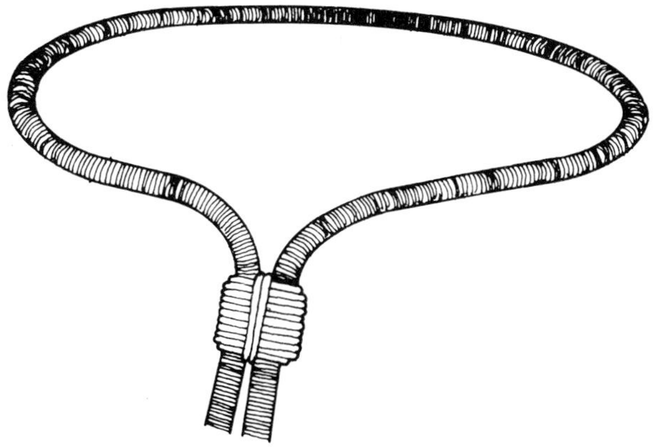

The throat seizing on the main shrouds.

were tightened by hand. The end of the seizing wire was then passed down between the last turn of the lower turns, heaved hand taut, and then two complete turns were taken around all parts, hove taut and finished off with a clove hitch. The temporary seizing was then cut away.

A similar throat seizing was put on the port shroud and both collars were then given a liberal coating of Stockholm tar, and bedded down on to the bolsters where they were temporarily lashed. Next, the forestay collar was placed over the masthead, tarred and bedded on to its cleat. Shrouds and forestay were then stretched along the length of the mast and lashed there.

The mainmast was then manhandled on board *Shamrock* with its square heel was inserted between the tabernacle chocks and its head raised about 4 ft above the deck on wooden blocks. It was also chocked along its length to prevent sagging or twisting.

The topping lift, peak halliard, throat halliard and fish tackle purchases were then humped on board, overhauled and laid out along the length of the mast.

The upper single 6 in block for the 2 in circumference staysail halliard was shackled and seized to the throat of the forestay halliard collar, and the two 6 in hook blocks for the jib halliards were hooked into their respective eyes, on each side of the mast-head. Each hook was moused with marline to prevent it being jumped out of the eye. Next the 8 in single upper block of the main topping lift purchase was shackled on to its mast-head eyebolt, then the two 9 in upper and lower peak blocks, and the standing part of the 3 in circumference manilla peak halliard, were each shackled on to their respective eyebolts in turn. The 9 in upper double block of the throat purchase was shackled on to the throat halliard crane, and finally the $2\frac{1}{2}$ in flexible wire pendant for the fish tackle was secured to the eye bolt in the port mast bibb. All shackle pins were moused with two turns of seizing around the shackle above its eye, and through the eye of the pin, and finished off with a clove hitch around both parts of the mousing.

Finally, the whipped end of the $1\frac{1}{2}$ in circumference flexible hoisting wire was passed from aft to forward through the mast-head sheave, and the wire was overhauled. Its thimble eye was shackled to its own part just below the mast bibbs, and after being parcelled with canvas to prevent damage to the mast, it was hove taut by belaying the other end of the wire around the cross piece of the main tabernacle, thus forming a span from the hounds to the mast-head sheave. With the mast fully dressed and rigged for rais-

The mainmast, fully dressed on deck.

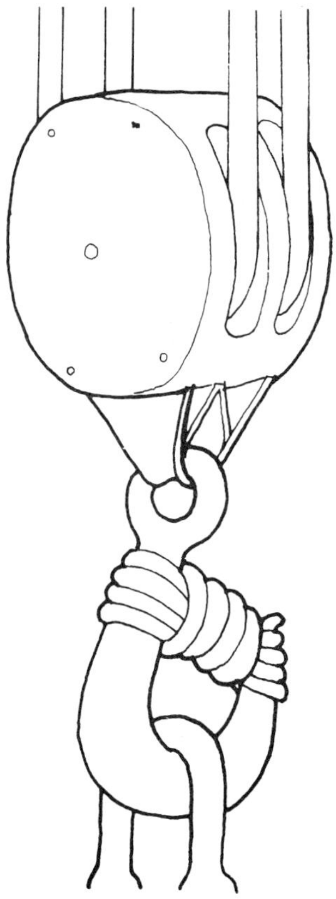

The moused hook on the main throat halliard block.

ing everything was squared away on deck in order that nothing would foul up the process when raising the mast.

Before the mast could be hauled in position by its own forestay purchase, it was necessary to raise its head some 20 ft above the deck. This initial lift was obtained by bolting a $7\frac{1}{2}$ in diameter pole 25 ft long into the mizzen mast tabernacle, rigged with a 'forestay' 'back stay' and a 'shroud' on each side to steady it. A single 6 in metal snatch-block was slung just below the head of the pole, the wire pendant of the mizzen topping-lift was inserted into it, and its thimble eye end was shackled to the temporary wire span on the mainmast head. The topping lift purchase was shackled to the port eye bolt abreast of the mizzen tabernacle to counteract the weight of the main mast which was to be hoisted to starboard of the pole.

To obtain more purchase for the second stage of raising the mast, the fall of the forestay purchase was led through a stemhead snatch-block to the mizzen throat purchase which was made fast ashore. It was the policy to use all the ship's gear throughout this operation both to test it and give it its final stretching.

Having checked that all was clear, three men tailed on to the shore purchase and the mast was slowly and evenly raised to 80 degrees. At this stage the forestay purchase was 'two blocks'. The Fish tackle purchase was taken to the stem head and hauled taut to act as a preventer, and for the final hoist both it and the $1\frac{1}{2}$ in flexible wire which had been rove through the mast head sheave were used to fully raise the mast.

Mr Perkins lined up the holes in the tabernacle cheeks and the heel of the mast and put in a tem-

Raising the mainmast.

porary bearing pin and then the holding bolt was passed through the after bolt holes of the iron binding band above the tabernacle cross-piece, thus firmly fixing the mast in place. It was now 20 June 1979.

With everything cleared, the fall of the topping lift purchase was led forward through a snatch-block at the stem-head, its end was made fast to the luff tackle purchase with its single block secured to the wooden horse right aft, and by these means the mainmast head was hoisted by its wire span to about 20 ft above the deck, and the slack of the forestay purchase was taken in at the same time. As soon as the forestay had the weight, the mast was blocked off to prevent accidents, and the starboard 'shroud' of the temporary pole was slacked right off to allow the main mast head to gain more height.

During the following week the 1 in diameter wrought iron chainplate bolts were delivered, and all the chain plates were through fastened to the vessel's sides.

Meanwhile, in the shed work was continuing on the mizzen mast and spars. The rudder was also being made of oak sections tongued-and-grooved together and through bolted in the traditional manner. The metal braces for the rudder were made by outside contractors and the whole assembly was put together exactly as it appeared in the photographs of *Shamrock*'s rudder in the Quay museum. The metal tiller was also made on site, again from photographs which clearly depicted it as it was in 1926.

The new rudder nears completion.

While the temporary pole was in position in the mizzen tabernacle it was rigged in the same manner as the mizzen mast. At a point 24 ft 4 in above the deck, or at the same height as the mizzen hounds band would be, a length of seizing wire was made fast and its lower end was then brought to the ship's side in way of the chain-plate positions. After allowing for the length of the two shackles which would join the bottle-screws to the chain plate and to the shroud, the bottlescrew itself, and the shackle which secured the shroud to the hounds band, a length of 21 ft $10\frac{3}{4}$ in was obtained for the four mizzen shrouds. With the shroud measurements known, all the lower thimble eyes were spliced in, parcelled and served during the following week.

By 27 June the mizzen mast was ready for hoisting and after a final oiling it was manhandled on board.

There it was dressed, with its four shrouds shackled to the angled eyes on the sides of the hounds band and a $1\frac{1}{2}$ in circumference manilla luff purchase fish tackle shackled on to the eye on its foreside. The topping lift, peak blocks and throat halliard purchase blocks were shackled on to their respective eye bolts (which were slightly staggered at the centre line of the mast to prevent splitting along the grain) and all shackle pins were moused in the same manner as those on the main mast.

The mizzen mast, fully dressed on deck.

In order to insert the heel of the mizzen into its tabernacle, its head had to be launched out some 12 ft clear of the stern over the crosspiece of the timber warping horse, which was well padded with old canvas to prevent damage to the mast. Before this was done, the thimble eye of the $1\frac{1}{2}$ in wire which was still rove off through the main mast-head sheave was shackled to a 3 in manilla strop placed at the mizzen hounds. This was the wire which would hoist the mizzen once its heel was inserted in the mizzen tabernacle, and secured with a temporary pivot pin. Meanwhile, the wire took the weight of the mizzen-head as it hung out clear from the stern.

With the heel in the tabernacle and the pivot pin inserted everything was cleared away ready for hoisting. The $1\frac{1}{2}$ in mainmast hoisting wire was led through a stemhead snatch and a temporary eye was formed in it with a large thimble held in position with two bulldog-grips. The eye was shackled to the double block of the mainsheet purchase which was overhauled until its single block could be made fast to the cavil-rail inside the port bulwark abreast of the mizzen tabernacle.

Raising the mizzen mast.

With this arrangement two men only were required to obtain the initial hoist and after an angle of 45 degrees had been reached, one man continued the hauling until the mizzen was upright and safely bolted into the tabernacle.

One week later the main boom, main gaff, mizzen book and mizzen gaff were completed. Traditionally boom and gaff jaws were made from grown oak crooks where the grain followed the curve of each half jaw as truly as possible. Such timber could not be obtained in the sizes required, and therefore, sawn timber had to be carefully selected to that whatever curve there was in the grain could be used to advantage.

The oak jaws were through rivetted to the spars, and the elm tumbler which takes the thrust of the gaff or boom against the mast, and remains vertically disposed against it when the gaffs are peaked up to some 40 degrees, was pivoted between the jaws on a $\frac{3}{4}$ in headed drift bolt. Eventually, both jaws and tumblers will be covered

Main boom saddle, main boom and gaff jaws, parrels and mast hoops.

with leather to reduce the chafe of wood on wood, when the vessel is sailing.

Meanwhile the forestay had been shackled directly on to the iron stem band (which in *Shamrock* was bent to the angle of the stay and bored for the pin of the large forestay shackle) — the main and mizzen shrouds were shackled to their chainplate bottlescrews and the boom saddles had been fitted to both masts at the required height from the deck.

The booms were brought on board by hooking on their topping lifts and throat purchases as they lay on the trestle at the dock side, and rigging a restraining line to a nearby bollard. Then by a simultaneous hoisting of lift and throat purchases each boom in turn was floated off the trestles, the restraining line was eased off gently as their weight swung them inboard, and with a heave and a shove forward the boom jaws were landed on to their respective boom saddles.

The same drill was used for the gaffs, which were gently lowered on to the booms; the gaff spans with their bullseyes were then placed in position, two on the main gaff and one on the mizzen. The hook-blocks of their peak halliards were hooked into the bullseye straps and moused with marline; the gaffs were then lightly lashed to the booms, sheet purchases were shackled on to their boom sheet bands and deck eyebolts, then set up and belayed, topping lifts were overhauled until they took the weight of booms and gaffs, the peak and throat halliards were overhauled and belayed, and, suddenly *Shamrock* looked like a working sailing vessel again.

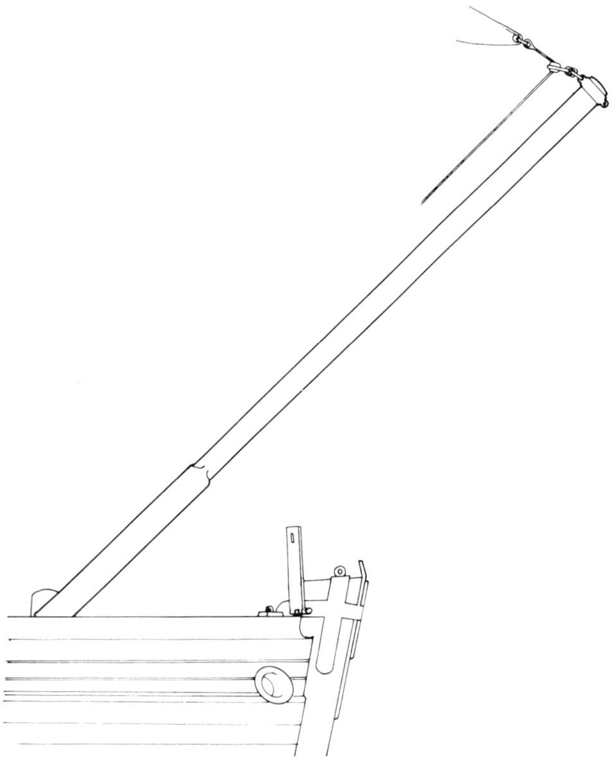

The method of topping the bowsprit.

and perhaps this was the most gratifying comment of all for those who had worked on her to hear, since it meant that one of the principal aims of the restoration had been achieved.

The 18 ft bowsprit was next shipped aboard. Its 8 in squared heel was bolted to the starboard side of the pawl post in such a manner as to allow it to be raised or lowered by the jib halliards which were temporarily hooked on to the eye of the bowsprit end-band 12 ft outboard from the stempost.

Next, the 14 ft 6 in, 4 in diameter staysail boom was shackled by an eye in its forward end to an oval iron link attached to the forestay shackle at the stem head, which allowed it to swing from side to side, or to be raised up by a $1\frac{1}{2}$ in circumference manilla topping lift, shackled to the upper eye on its after end-band. The lower eye of the after end-band was shackled to a chain sheet fitted with a roller link which was designed to travel along the length of a $1\frac{1}{4}$ in diameter staysail horse 12 ft long, fitted into ball stanchions some 2 in above deck level.

Now that the vessel was fully rigged, the next heavy job was to hang the rudder. For this, scaf-

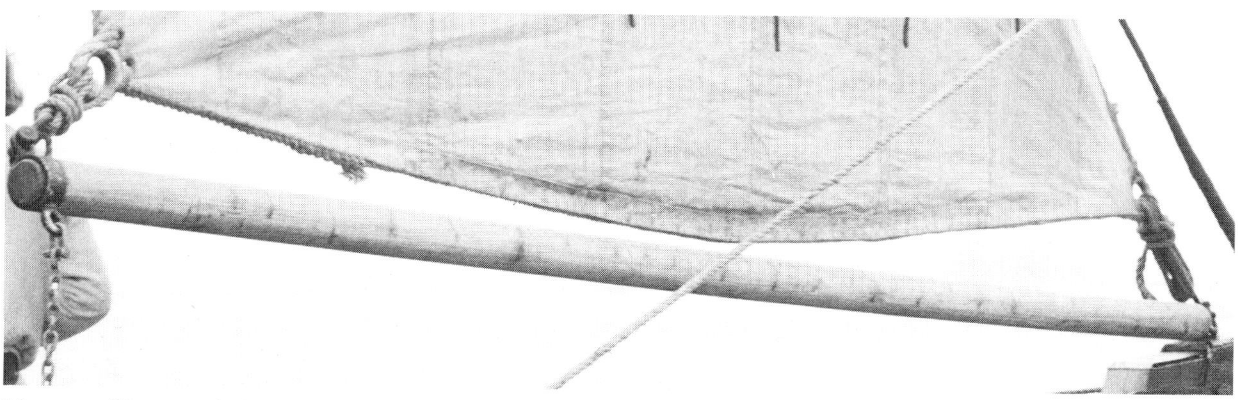

The staysail boom. The lower end of the chain sheet is shackled to a traveller on the staysail horse.

Visitors to the Quay who had watched her restoration over the two years during their annual holidays in the West Country were astonished that the seemingly immovable mass of timber of a few years ago could indeed be the same vessel. Others, completely unaware that any restoration had taken place at all, thought that she was a local sailing vessel still working in the Tamar —
folding was built up and over the sternpost

which was already fitted with its three iron gudgeons. The rudder was slung and lowered into position so that its three pintle eyes were over and in line with the gudgeon eyes. The pintle bar was then dropped down through the eyes and secured. This arrangement prevented the rudder from being accidentally unshipped when grounding.

The rudder is shipped in position.

The iron tiller was also fitted to the head of the stern post. The inner end of the tiller is fitted with a 3 in diameter elm drum. This is to allow two or three turns to be taken by tiller-ropes rigged from each quarter so that the helm can be controlled more easily by the helmsman when the vessel is sailing hard.

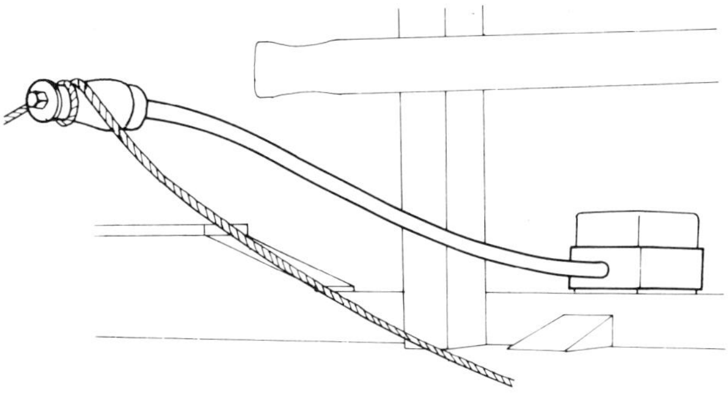

The tiller, showing the tiller-line rigged on the bight.

# Chapter 9

*Final fitting out and completion. Autumn 1979–May 1980.*

The fitting out of the vessel was then put in hand.

The iron patent windlass which replaced the original timber log windlass during the major reconstruction of the vessel in 1920, was thoroughly overhauled, oiled, greased and bolted in position in the bows forward of the pawl post.

The patent windlass allowed the anchor cable to be continuously hove in by its two handles which turned geared wheels and the gypsy, a wheel or drum, specially shaped to lock round and grip the individual links of chain as it turned. The cable stowed itself down a navel pipe directly under the gypsy, which led to the chain locker right in the eyes of the vessel. The 160 lb Admiralty or Fisherman type anchor which had been recovered from a South Coast scrapyard in 1974, was refurbished and placed on board at this time.

The iron cargo winch was also taken aboard and bolted into position forward and to port of the main-mast tabernacle. This winch was presented to the *Shamrock* by Peter Herbert of Herb Ship Ltd., Bude in 1976. It had been completely overhauled and found to be in very good condition, apart from the 8 in diameter elm barrel which was renewed. Winch handles to fit the winch were eventually found at Belsize Shipyard, Southampton, after a long search through tons of scrap.

*Shamrock's* iron cargo winch.

The hatch cover, hatch or wedge battens, wedge cleats and wedges.

Foredeck details, note bowsprit clamp, hawse pipe and cavil rails.

The cargo hatch covers which had been made ashore in the shed during heavy and often prolonged periods of rain, were finished off, brought on board and fitted into place over the hatch.

Iron fairlead bollards or chocks were fitted on both bows and at the port and starboard quarters. 4 ft by 3 in square curved oak cavil rails were bolted to the bulwark stanchions abreast of the foc'stle scuttle forward. Cavil rails aft were also bolted in position with ½ in diameter wrought iron bolts.

Owing to the problems of reorganisation following the fire at their premises in 1978, Penrose Sailmakers had not been able to deliver the sails in March 1979 as hoped. They were delivered by Mr Tresidder on 9 July and it was hoped to

Fitting the sails – Mizzen.

Fitting the sails, main and headsails.

Fitting the sails – The full suit. *Shamrock* was rigged in this fashion between 1920–1934.

spread them out on an area of grass behind the shed to inspect them, then to bend them on, temporarily and hoist them to see if they fitted and stood well. If satisfactory the sails would then be taken ashore again, laid out on the grass, and thoroughly proofed with Kanvo, a solution to prevent mildew and rot in canvas. This operation was expected to take a week, during which time it was planned to place the mast-hoops on the masts and to make the head lashings, earring lashings, tack lines, clew lines, reef pendants, jib sheets, staysail sheets, and all the other cordage required for setting and stowing the sails.

Heavy rain during the rest of the week prevented the laying out of the sails or any trial fitting, since in their unproofed state it would

Final fitting out as the restoration of *Shamrock* nears completion.

have been detrimental to get them wet. Mr Tresidder measured the spars for the sail covers, which would be essential, not only to keep the sails dry, but to prevent the ingress of dust, dirt and grit from the quay penetrating into the folds of furled canvas.

The following week the weather cleared just sufficiently to lay the sails out, and to compare their measurements against the sail plan from which they had been made, and measurements taken off the masts and spars, now that they were all set up in the vessel. The jib and staysail dimensions were in agreement, but those of the main sail and mizzen were not. Mr Tresidder therefore took them back to Falmouth for the necessary adjustments to be made.

On board *Shamrock* the foc'sle and after cabin were painted white and also the inside of the bulwark planking. The white cove line was painted in, and the name was carved on both bows and in the fashion piece across the transom, together with the Port of Registry, and painted white.

Alongside Cotehele Quay shortly before the ceremony marking the completion of the restoration.

The actual task of restoration was now complete, apart from the fitting of the traditional iron pump which was still buried under tons of scrap at a Southampton shipyard. All other jobs were concerned with fitting out and equipping the vessel with another bow anchor, anchor cable, a kedge anchor, stands and screens for the red and green sidelights, tow-lines, mooring-ropes, lifebelts, quant-poles, cargo gaff and associated gear, hatch tarpaulins, the sails, and all the other equipment that would have normally been carried by a vessel of *Shamrock*'s description in 1926.

Alan Viner of the National Maritime Museum (left) and Geoffrey Le Mare, one of the principal benefactors of the *Shamrock* project.

On 15 August 1979 *Shamrock* was moored on the outer face of Cotehele Quay and at 1230 hours a commemorative plaque on the foreside of the mizzen tabernacle was unveiled by Mrs Jennifer Collyer, daughter of Mr Geoffrey Le Mare who was one of the benefactors who made the restoration of *Shamrock* possible. Speeches were made by Dr Basil Greenhill, Director of the National Maritime Museum, and Mr Michael Holland-Hibbert, Chairman of the National Trust, Devon and Cornwall Regional Committee, and *Shamrock* was blessed by The Reverend David Peyton Jones, the Honorary Chaplain to the Missions to Seamen, Plymouth.

After the ceremony *Shamrock* was taken back to the dock and in the Autumn the running rigging was stripped off her, her masts were lowered, the main mast and bowsprit were set up to form a strongback for a specially made cover which would protect her during the winter months.

Mr Perkins was appointed by the National Maritime Museum as a temporary shipkeeper until a permanent man could be employed by them to keep the vessel in first-class condition. During this period he fitted the diaphram pump which by this time had been recovered from the Southampton shipyard, refurbished, and restored to a fully working condition.

On 24 October *Shamrock* sails and sail covers were delivered to Cotehele by Penrose Sailmakers.

Once again, they were spread on the grass, their measurements were checked, and being found satisfactory, they were accepted. The proofed cotton canvas sail covers were also accepted, after a trial fitting on the spars.

Rain prevented the bending on of the sails themselves, because they were unproofed at this time. They were therefore taken up to the Mill, where they would be hung under the rafters. The Mill had proved to be dry, airy, and altogether satisfactory for the stowage of ropes and canvas.

In Spring 1980 the *Shamrock* was re-rigged and preparations were made for proofing the sails prior to bending them on. Before proofing began, the sails were laid on the grass and aired. Kanvo was selected as the proofing material, since this solution for preserving natural fibre sails has proved its worth over many years at sea. One side of each sail was proofed in turn, then all were hung up in the shed to dry for 48 hours. Another coat was then applied with long handled medium soft brushes, dipped directly into the five-gallon drum, care having been taken to keep the mixture well stirred. After a further 48 hours drying the sails were taken on board and bent on. All fitted well, and all had sufficient allowance for stretching to their final dimensions.

On 14 May 1980 the sails were hoisted, formally signifying the completion of the restoration to the standard required by the National Maritime Museum.

15 August 1979. Mrs Jennifer Collyer, daughter of Mr Geoffrey Le Mare, after the unveiling of the commemorative plaque on the mizzen tabernacle.

# Glossary

## A

ABAFT Behind. Nearer to the stern or further aft than other parts of the vessel.

AMIDSHIPS Properly the middle of the vessel's length and breadth. More generally used to describe the middle body of the hull and to indicate the position of the tiller, the steering spoke of the wheel, and the rudder when they are in line with the keel.

APRON A strengthening timber shaped and bolted to the after face of the stem-post.

## B

BAULK The roughly squared tree trunk before conversion.

BEAM A cambered timber which crosses the hull transversely to support the deck. The breadth of the vessel.

BEAMSHELF A line of thick timbers scarphed together and bolted to the upper futtock and top timbers of the frames to form a hoop inside the hull for the beams to rest on.

BEVEL-BOARD A piece of wood used by shipwrights on which the various angles of the bevels for timbers are marked in lines.

BEVELLING The angles formed between one timber surface and another, such as the sides and outer faces of the frame timbers. An obtuse angle is called a standing bevelling — an acute angle is called an under-bevelling.

BIBBS Pieces of timber shaped to fit the sides of the mast at the hounds [*q.v.*] to act as a stop for the eyes of the shrouds.

BILGE The round up in a vessels' frame timbers where they begin to approach a vertical direction.

BLOCK A pulley designed to perform a particular duty either singly or in combination with other blocks to form a purchase or tackle.

BOLSTER Pieces of hardwood fixed on the top edges of the bibbs to take the weight and chafe of the shroud collars.

BOLTROPE A loosely laid up, high quality tarred rope hand sewn to the tabling edges of the sails to strengthen them and prevent rending under stress. In British sailing vessels, fore and aft sails are roped on the port side, square sails on the after side. Known as head-ropes, foot-ropes, leech and luff-ropes, and varying in size according to the position on the sails.

BREASTHOOK A grown timber crook or wrought-iron knee used either as a tie to bind the stempost, beamshelf, hawse or frame timbers of the bow together.

BULKHEADS The athwartships partitions which separate the hull into compartments, cabins, storeplaces etc.

Fore and aft partitions are also referred to as bulkheads in some wooden vessels.

BULWARK The raised assembly of stanchions, rail, topgallant rail or washstrake which runs right round the hull above the weather deck.

BULLSEYE An elm or lignum vitae block without a sheave, with a single circular hole in it, and grooved around its outer edge to receive an iron, wire or rope strap or strop. Used as fair leads for the running rigging, i.e. on gaff spans and for the jib sheets.

BUTT The joint where the ends of the hull and deck planks meet, or the heads and heels of the floors, futtocks, and top-timbers which make up a frame of single or double timbers. The butt end is the biggest end of a spar.

## C

CABLE A rope or chain by which a vessel is held to its anchor. The length of a cable according to the Admiralty was 120 fathoms (at 6 feet to the fathom). A wooden sailing vessel of *Shamrock*'s size would require at least one 50 fathom length of chain cable.

CAMBER The round-up or arching upwards of the deckbeams to facilitate the drainage of water from the deck via the waterways and scupper-pipes.

CANT FRAME Those frames without floors which are canted to present a faying surface square to the round in at bow and stern.

CARLING Timber of rectangular form not less than $4\frac{1}{2}$ inches thick.

CARLINGS. Timbers placed between the deck-beams to support the inner ends of the half-beams and the coamings of the hatch companion and ladder ways.

CAULKING The operation of forcing cotton and/or oakum into the treenail fastenings, butt ends and plank seams, with a variety of wedge-like caulking irons of suitable shape and size using a caulking mallet specially designed for the purpose. This operation renders the hull water-tight and stiffens the hull structure. After 'horsing-up' with a horsing iron and beetle mallet to harden in the oakum, the seams are sealed with pitch. Deck planks are also payed with marine glue.

CEILING The inner strakes of hull planking between the beamshelf and the limber-strakes on each side of the keelson. The ceiling prevents cargo or dirt clogging the pumps and spreads the weight of cargo or ballast evenly over the frames. It is also a stressed surface without which a wooden merchant vessel would not be strong enough.

COAMINGS A raised frame bolted to the carlings for the hatches, companion way, scuttle and laddder-ways.

COVERING BOARD The outermost deckplank which covers the timberheads of the frames. Also known as the planksheer.

## D

DEADWOOD A range of timbers bolted on the upper face of the keel and to the stem and stern post. In small craft, a large knee is used to effect the same purpose.

DEPTH OF HOLD In a single decked vessel the depth of hold is the vertical amidships between the upper side of the deck beam and the upper face of the limber strake adjacent to the keelson.

DUBBING OUT Reducing to size and shaping the inner faces of the vessel's frames in order to present a fair faying surface for the beamshelf, ceiling plank and limbers.

## E

EARRINGS Small ropes used to secure the upper corners (or peak and throat) of a fore and aft sail to its gaff.

EVEN KEEL Said of a vessel which is not heeled to port or starboard, and which draws the same depth of water at bow and stern.

EYES OF THE RIGGING The bights, or loops, formed by splicing or seizing the shrouds or stays which go over the masthead.

## F

FALSE KEEL An additional timber 'planted' on to the main keel to provide protection when grounding, or, as in *Shamrock*'s case, to provide more lateral resistance for an exceptionally shallow hull.

FAY To fit close. (see below)

FAYING SURFACES Two surfaces that are made to conform to each other, so that there may not be any perceptible space between them.

FILLINGS OR FILLING TIMBERS Pieces of timber used to fill unwanted spaces which occur in wooden shipbuilding.

FLAT FLOORS Used to describe the bottom timbers of a vessel when they project from the keel in a more or less horizontal direction.

FRAMES The bends of timbers which constitute a 'frame of single or doubled timbers' — i.e. one frame consisting of a floor, 2 first futtocks, 2 second futtocks, 2 third futtocks, and 2 top-timbers.

FUTTOCK Originally foothook. One of the several curved timbers which make up a complete frame of timbers.

## G

GAFF The spar to which the head of the gaff sail is bent by earrings and head lashings.

GAFF JAWS The timber horns bolted to the inner ends of booms and gaffs, which half encircle the mast.

GAFF JAW PARREL A rope spliced and seized to holes in the horns of the gaff jaws, which passes across the fore side of the mast and confines the spar in position. The rope has elm parrel-beads, or rollers, threaded on to it to assist in hoisting the gaff and boom if required. The parrel is kept well greased.

GAFF SPANS Lengths of rope or flexible wire well parcelled, served, and coated with Stockholm tar, either doubled, and seized to form eyes at each end, or with eyes spliced in a single part. The spans fit against cleats on the gaff and are provided with a sliding bullseye into which the peak halliards are hooked or shackled.

GARBOARD STRAKE The strake of bottom planking on each side of the keel into which its inner edge is rebated and fastened.

GUDGEONS Formerly goodgeons. Bands of iron, steel or mixed metal which terminate in eyes, bolted to the sternpost to receive the pintle bolts of the rudder.

## H

HALLIARDS The ropes rigged through blocks to form purchases for hoisting the sails, or singly through the mast sheaves with a purchase on its hauling part if required.

HATCHES The portable wooden coverings of the cargo hatchways.

HATCHWAYS A square or oblong opening in the deck which allows access to the vessel's hold.

HAWSEPIPES The flanged iron pipes which line the hawse-holes through which the anchor cables pass out and inboard.

HEAD The fore part of the vessel. 'By the head' means trimmed, pressed down, or immersed at the bow. Also refers to the upper ends of the frames — timber-heads, or the mast — masthead.

HEEL The lower end of the keel aft, a mast or a frame timber. Also the amount of list a vessel develops when sailing.

HOLD The interior of the vessel. Generally understood as the space below deck where cargo etc., is stowed.

HOOD ENDS The grain ends of the hull planks which are fitted into the rabbets of the stem and stern posts. Also a covering for skylights, sails etc.

HOUNDS The projections on a mast, principally the bibbs and bolsters, which act as a bed for the eyes of the rigging to rest on — normally the shrouds.

## I

IN AND OUT BOLTS Those bolts which pass right through the stempost, sternpost, outer planking, keel, frames, keelson, limbers, beamshelf and knees. Also known as 'through and through' bolts or simply 'through bolts'.

INBOARD Inside the vessel's bulwarks.

## J

JAWS See Gaff jaws.

JIB A triangular sail of light canvas. In *Shamrock* the jib is set standing from the outer end-band of the bowsprit.

## K

KEEL The fore and aft timber in the middle line of the hull upon which the vessel framework is erected, and to which the garboard strakes are fastened. As built, *Shamrock* was fitted with a ram or keel plank with two slots for drop-keels. In 1920 a deep false keel was 'planted' on to the original keel plank.

KEEL-FALSE See False keel.

KEELSON A heavy, fore-and-aft centre line timber fitted inside the hull, seated on top of the floors with bolts which pass through the false keel, keelplank and keelson.

KNEES Crooks of grown or sawn timber, generally oak and/or wrought-iron, with arms shaped to connect the deck beams to the vessel's framework, or to act as any other form of tie, such as floor knees and breasthooks. Lodging-knees are disposed horizontally between beam and frames — hanging-knees are disposed vertically under beams and to the frames — dagger knees cross the frames diagonally.

## L

LIMBER BOARDS Short lengths of portable planking used to cover the spaces between the keelson and the inner edges of the limber strakes, which are bevelled to receive them.

LIMBER CHAIN A small chain rove through the limber holes in the floors on each side of the keelson, through which the bilge water flows to the pumps. The chain is 'worked' regularly to keep the limber holes from blockages.

LIMBER STRAKES The thick strakes placed at about a plank's width from each side of the keelson to form a watercourse to carry the bilge water to the pumps.

## M

MIZZEN MAST The smaller mast of a ketch-rigged vessel, stepped before the tiller. The sail which is set from it is called the mizzen.

MOULD A thin piece of deal or board used by the shipwright as a pattern for the curved timbers of a vessel's frame.

MOULDED Formed to the mould. The depth or thickness of any timber between its curved surfaces.

MOULDED BREADTH The greatest beam of the vessel to the outside face of the frame timbers at that point.

MOUSING Rope yarns wound tightly round the jaws of hooks to prevent them from becoming detached. Wire strands passed round the lug of a shackle and the eye of its pin, to prevent it from unscrewing.

## N

NAILS
*Deck nails* have small heads which can be countersunk in the deck plank and plugged with a wooden dowel dipped in whitelead.
Doubles are from six to twelve inches long.
Singles are from four to five inches long.
*Weight nails* — similar to deck nails, but with large square heads — used for temporary fastenings.
*Timber nails* — four to seven inches long for fastening planks edgewise.
*Clamp nails* — short, stout nails with large heads for fastening iron clamps.
Also *Port nails* for fastening ironwork, rudder nails, copper or yellow metal sheathing nails, lead nails, scupper nails, float heads for tarred paper and copper nails 1 to 12, from $\frac{7}{8}$ inches to $3\frac{1}{2}$ inches long.

## O

OAKUM Strands of old rope untwisted and with the yarns teased out. The fibres are rolled into threads of suitable thickness for caulking the vessel's seams. (see Caulking.)

## P

PARCELLING To cover a rope with strips of tarred canvas (with the lay of its strands), prior to its being stitched and served over with marline.

PAY To run hot pitch or tar into plank butts and seams after they have been caulked with oakum.

PEAK The upper after corner of a gaff sail.

PEAK HALLIARDS See halliards.

PINTLE The metal bolts which are attached to the rudder braces with their points down. The pintles are dropped into the gudgeon-holes on the stern-post to form the hinge necessary to work the rudder.

PORT The left hand side of a vessel when looking towards the bows.

PURCHASE An arrangements of blocks and rope to increase mechanical power in order to hoist or control spars, etc.

## Q

QUANT A long timber pole used for pushing the vessel along in relatively shallow water, or for bearing her off from the bank or shoals.

## R

RABBET An angular groove or channel cut into the keel, stempost and sternpost, to receive the garboard edges and ends of outer planking.

REEF To shorten sail by reefing it or temporarily reducing its area in strong winds.

REEF CRINGLES Large cringles in the luff and leech of a sail through which the reef-pendants are rove, and tacks and sheets hooked into when reefed.

REEF KNOT The knot used to tie reef points.

REEF PENDANT — MAINSAIL A short strong rope, sometimes served overall with a stopper-knot at one end which butts against a hole in the reefing-comb or cleat, on one side of the boom. The other end is led up through its reef-cringle, down through a sheave-hole on the other side of the boom. A bowline is put into it for the node of the reef-tackle, which hauls the sail down ready for reefing.

REEF POINTS Lengths of light cordage, or pointline, sewn in a line at each seam in the sail from luff to leech at the heights above its foot designated as the first, second or third reefing positions.

RUDDER BRACES Metal straps through-bolted to the timbers of the rudder, with eyes at their fore parts for the pintles, which are hinged on the gudgeon eyes of the braces on the stem post to form a hinge.

RUDDER HEAD Upper end of the rudder post to which the tiller is secured.

## S

SHEAVE A solid wheel of lignum vitae, phosphor bronze, steel or iron, with or without roller bearings, with a grooved outer edge over which the rope or wire runs. Fitted into mortices of masts, spars, blocks, and parts of the vessel's structure where necessary.

SHORES Wooden props placed at various points about the vessel's frame and under the bottom to provide temporary support during building or when laying in a dry dock.

SHROUDS Properly, the standing rigging that supports the mast sideways which are made up in pairs, i.e. one length of wire is middled and seized so that an eye is formed to enshroud the mast at the hounds.

SKEG The after end of the keel, or that part of it upon which the heel of the sternpost is secured.

SPANS Lengths of rope or flexible steel wire, well parcelled, served over and tarred. In *Shamrock*, the gaff-spans have a soft spliced eye at each end which slip over the gaff and butt against thumb-cleats. The span is fitted with an iron bound elm cringle, oval or circular bullseye (into which the peak block hooks), that travels along the span as the gaff is peaked up. The two legs of the span spread the weight along the spar.

STARBOARD The right hand side of a vessel when looking towards the bows.

STROP A loop of rope yarns, rope or wire, used to put round blocks and spars to hook tackles to.

## T

TABERNACLE A strong upright casing or trunk used in barges to step the heel of the mast in on deck, so that it can be lowered for passing under bridges.

TACK The lower fore corner of a fore and aft sail. Also used to describe "beating to windward", i.e. to tack, tacking.

TACKLE (Pronounced tay-kel). An arrangement of ropes and pulley blocks for increasing hauling power.

THIMBLE EYES Eyes spliced or seized into rigging round a pear-shaped or circular ring of solid metal with a groove for the rope or wire to fit into.

THROAT Upper fore corner of a gaff sail, hoisted by the throat halliards. Hollow of a V-shaped knee.

THUMB CLEAT Pieces of wood fixed on spars to prevent ropes, strops or spans etc. from slipping.

TILLER A piece of timber or iron, shaped as convenient, fitted to control the rudder and so to steer the vessel. Also known as the helm.

TIMBER-HEADS The heads or upper grain ends of the frame timbers.

TONNAGE The ton register = 100 cubic feet capacity.
*Gross tonnage* = The total volume of a vessel divided by 100.
*Net Registered tonnage* = From the gross tonnage certain deductions are made on account of crew spaces, engine room, or any space not used for passengers and cargo. Lights, Pilot and Harbour dues are assessed on the Net Tonnage.
*Displacement tonnage* = Total weight of vessel and contents, or the number of tons of sea water displaced when floating at her load water line.

TREENAILS Generally pronounced as "trunnels". Cylindrical pins, principally made of well seasoned best quality oak, and used for fastening the outer and inner planking to the vessel's frames. They vary in diameter from $\frac{3}{4}$ inch to $1\frac{3}{4}$ inch, and were formerly distinguished by marks denoting their size, i.e. one, two, three, four and five edlars cross, cross, broad arrow, round o, round o and spot.

## W

WASHSTRAKE Or washboard. A wide board fitted on top of the bulwark rail to provide extra height and protection from the sea. In some vessels the washstrake is removable in way of hatches to facilitate cargo work.

WINCH, HAND For cargo and general purposes. An iron framework supporting a wooden drum with an iron spindle turned by winch handles through a system of gears fitted with one or more pawls to prevent the drum "working back" under load.

WINDLASS A special form of winch fitted in the bows to haul in the anchor-cable. *Shamrock* has a patent reefing windlass, heavily geared, with a 'gypsy' wheel patterned to fit the studded chain cable, which stows itself as it is heaved in.

# ÍNDICE

# EL ESPECTÁCULO MÁS GRANDE DEL MUNDO

▲ *Durante la ceremonia de inauguración de cada olimpiada se sueltan palomas, símbolo de la paz. El objetivo de los juegos es promover la amistad y el entendimiento entre los pueblos.*

Cada cuatro años, en uno de los continentes del mundo, miles de los mejores deportistas del planeta, decenas de miles de trabajadores, entrenadores y periodistas, y cientos de miles de espectadores se reúnen en una ciudad. Su objetivo es sencillo: organizar, presenciar, participar e informar acerca del mayor espectáculo del mundo: los juegos olímpicos de verano.

### El gran premio

Diseñadas como un acontecimiento global donde los mejores atletas pueden competir entre sí, las olimpiadas modernas se crearon como una manera de promover la unidad mundial y de encontrar vías para que el deporte traspase las fronteras políticas y culturales. Desde sus comienzos relativamente humildes en 1890, el movimiento olímpico ha crecido más y más. En la actualidad, para muchos de los mejores deportistas del mundo, el premio último por el que luchan en su carrera deportiva es una codiciada medalla de oro.

▲ *En la ceremonia de inauguración de los juegos olímpicos, los equipos nacionales entran al estadio y desfilan por orden alfabético, con las únicas excepciones del equipo de Grecia, que siempre va el primero, y el de la nación anfitriona, que cierra el desfile.*

### A cargo de los juegos

El COI es el organismo que vela por las olimpiadas. Tras un largo proceso en el que ciudades de todo el mundo presentan su candidatura, el COI decide dónde se celebrarán las olimpiadas (consulta la página 12). Los juegos de verano se celebran cada cuatro años. Desde 1924, se han celebrado también unos juegos de invierno, independientes y más reducidos, para deportes como esquí, patinaje artístico, patinaje de velocidad y hockey sobre hielo. Los juegos de verano comienzan con una espectacular ceremonia de apertura, en la que todos los participantes desfilan por el estadio, por equipos, con su bandera nacional. Personas de todo el mundo siguen atentamente las olimpiadas. La página web oficial de Sydney 2000, por ejemplo, atrajo 9.000 millones de visitas, mientras que la audiencia televisiva se mide en cientos de millones.

▼▶ *Tres palabras* –Citius, Altius, Fortius– *componen el lema olímpico, que está grabado en el pebetero que mantiene la llama olímpica. El lema, que significa "Más rápido, más alto, más fuerte", fue ideado por Henri Didon, un amigo del fundador de los juegos, el barón Pierre de Coubertin.*

IUS ALTIUS FORTIUS

▲ *El estadio olímpico es el escenario de las ceremonias de apertura y clausura. Al final de cada olimpiada, se entrega la bandera olímpica a la siguiente ciudad anfitriona, se extingue la llama olímpica y el presidente del COI declara clausurados los juegos.*

◀ *Las mercadería olímpica es un gran negocio. Casi todos los artículos muestran la mascota oficial de los juegos. Estas son las dos mascotas de las Olimpiadas de Atenas 2004, Phevos y Athena, que tienen el nombre de dos dioses de la antigua Grecia.*

### Un escenario global

Las primeras olimpiadas modernas, celebradas en 1896, reunieron a menos de 250 atletas de unas cuantas naciones. Hoy, más de 10.000 participantes de cerca de 200 países acuden a los juegos de verano. Ningún otro acontecimiento mundial despierta tal interés en tantas personas de tantos países. Pocos eventos internacionales pueden igualar la gran variedad de deportes que ofrece. En un calendario de competiciones que dura un máximo de 16 días, más de 300 pruebas distintas de diversos deportes ofrecen acción y emoción mientras los deportistas olímpicos luchan por ser los mejores. Aunque el atletismo (con más de 2.000 participantes) y la natación (con unos 1.000) son las competiciones olímpicas más populares, un total de casi 30 deportes diferentes están representados en los juegos. Las olimpiadas ofrecen un escenario global a deportes menos conocidos como el arco, la lucha y el levantamiento de peso.

### Amenazadas pero afianzadas

Dada la importancia actual de las olimpiadas, resulta difícil creer que los juegos modernos se han visto amenazados en varias ocasiones. En los primeros años, la falta de organización y un gran desinterés amenazaron los juegos, hasta que Estocolmo 1912 fue todo un éxito. Las dos guerras mundiales obligaron a la cancelación de tres olimpiadas. Desde entonces, la mayor amenaza ha procedido de la negativa de un gran número de naciones a acudir a las olimpiadas de 1976, 1980 y 1984 por cuestiones políticas. Estos boicots debilitaron el estatus de las olimpiadas como celebración global. Pero desde los Juegos de Seúl en 1988, los boicots han sido mínimos y podemos afirmar que las olimpiadas son la gran competición deportiva global.

# JUEGOS ANTIGUOS Y MODERNOS

El deseo humano de rivalizar ha originado competiciones de fuerza, velocidad y habilidad desde hace miles de años. Los primeros juegos de la antigua Grecia tuvieron lugar en Olimpia en el 776 a.C. Durante más de mil años, los juegos se celebraron cada cuatro años, antes de ser prohibidos por un emperador romano. A finales del siglo XIX, cuando el deporte se iba organizando cada vez más, surgió un movimiento para revivir la gloria de los juegos antiguos. Esto llevó a la creación de las primeras olimpiadas de invierno y de verano.

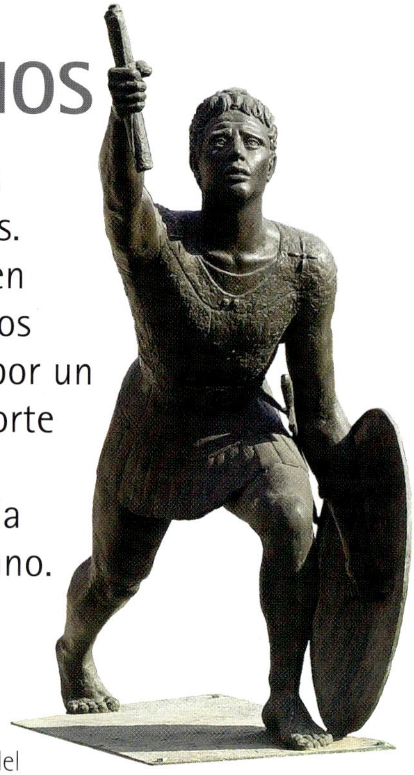

▲ *El maratón de Atenas 2004 seguirá un recorrido casi idéntico al de Filípides, el corredor de la antigua Grecia que inspiró la prueba (consulta la página 27).*

▲ *Los atletas de la antigua grecia competían desnudos en la mayoría de las pruebas, y no se admitía a mujeres, ni como participantes ni como público. Esta vasija, que data del siglo V a.C., muestra a unos atletas corriendo.*

**Las antiguas olimpiadas**

Según los escritos antiguos, el primer campeón olímpico fue un joven cocinero llamado Coroebus, que ganó la única prueba de los juegos del 776 a.C., una carrera de unos 192 metros llamada *stade*. Poco a poco se fueron añadiendo más pruebas, como el *dialus* (dos vueltas al estadio de Olimpia; unos 384 metros) y el *dolichus* (24 largos del estadio; unos 4,6 kilómetros), además de disco y jabalina. También se incluyeron el boxeo, la lucha, el salto de longitud y las carreras de carros. Las antiguas olimpiadas eran un festival religioso además de una celebración deportiva. Durante los juegos, se declaraban treguas, se detenían las batallas y estaba prohibido portar armas. Los ganadores obtenían una corona de hojas y la fama.

◀ *El barón Pierre de Coubertin, el padre del movimiento olímpico moderno, creía en el poder de los eventos internacionales para promover la armonía entre las naciones. En 1928 recibió el Premio Nobel de la Paz.*

**Los juegos modernos**

En la década de 1880, un noble francés, el barón Pierre de Coubertin, tuvo la idea de revivir las antiguas olimpiadas como una forma de promover el deporte y la actividad física. En 1894, después de varios años de incesantes presiones, de Courbetin fundó el Comité Olímpico Internacional (COI). Tras adjudicar los primeros juegos de la era moderna a Francia en 1900, el COI decidió que deberían celebrarse cuatro años antes en Atenas, la capital de Grecia. Únicamente 14 naciones participaron en los Juegos de 1896, en los que los ganadores recibieron una medalla de plata y una corona de ramas de olivo. Las primeras olimpiadas no lograron captar la atención mundial, pero poco a poco despertaron la pasión que las ha convertido en el espectáculo deportivo global que hoy conocemos.

▲ *Esta postal del estadio Panatenaico de Atenas muestra a una gran multitud presenciando las primeras olimpiadas modernas. Spiridon Louis (izquierda), un pastor griego, ganó el maratón y fue elegido para encabezar el desfile de la ceremonia de clausura de los juegos.*

### Tradiciones olímpicas

Con el paso del tiempo, las olimpiadas han desarrollado una serie de símbolos y costumbres que han dado a los juegos una identidad propia. En 1913, Pierre de Coubertin desveló el símbolo olímpico: una serie de cinco aros enlazados, que representaban a los cinco continentes. Al año siguiente, este símbolo, sobre un fondo blanco, se convirtió en la bandera olímpica. Los cinco aros son ahora uno de los símbolos más reconocidos del planeta. El origen de la llama olímpica se remonta a la antigua Grecia y, desde 1928, la llama ha ardido de forma continua en el estadio durante la celebración de los juegos. En la ceremonia de apertura, un atleta realiza el juramento olímpico en nombre de todos los participantes, y promete respetar las reglas y demostrar deportividad.

◀ *Esta antorcha de acero fue diseñada para los Juegos de 1936. Se utilizó para llevar por primera vez el fuego olímpico de Olimpia, Grecia, a Berlín, Alemania.*

### Los juegos paralímpicos

El deporte para las personas con discapacidades o necesidades especiales se desarrolló mucho durante el siglo XX. Tras la Segunda Guerra Mundial, un creciente movimiento a favor de un escenario internacional para atletas discapacitados llevó a la creación de unos juegos paralelos a los olímpicos. Las olimpiadas paralímpicas comprenden una gran variedad de pruebas, como atletismo, natación, baloncesto, esgrima, fútbol, halterofilia y judo, todas ellas divididas en distintas categorías de discapacidad. Los juegos han cosechado éxito tran éxito, y los atletas paralímpicos han cautivado al público con sus hazañas atléticas. En el año 2000, más de 3.800 atletas paralímpicos de 122 naciones compitieron en los Juegos de Sydney. Más de 1,1 millones de espectadores siguieron las pruebas en directo.

▲ *Los cinco aros del símbolo olímpico representan los continentes que participan en los juegos: África, Asia, América, Australasia y Europa. Este cartel de los Juegos de 1948 muestra los aros delante de un discóbolo de la antigua Grecia.*

◀ *El atleta paralímpico Stuart Braye espera el pistoletazo de salida durante la competición de 400 metros lisos de los juegos paralímpicos de 1992 en Barcelona. Braye, entrenador de discapacitados, obtuvo la medalla de bronce en la prueba con un tiempo de 60,92 segundos.*

## Cronología

**776 a.C.** Primeros juegos olímpicos, con una sola carrera.

**708 a.C.** Introducción del pentatlón (salto de longitud, disco, velocidad, jabalina y lucha).

**393 d.C.** El emperador romano Teodosio suprime las antiguas olimpiadas.

**Década de 1870** Excavación del escenario olímpico en Olimpia.

**1887** Pierre de Coubertin tiene la idea de revivir los juegos.

**1894** Fundación del COI en París.

**1896** Celebración de las primeras olimpiadas modernas en Atenas, Grecia.

**1900** Las mujeres participan en algunas pruebas olímpicas.

**1904** Primeras medallas de oro, plata y bronce.

**1908** Las olimpiadas admiten algunas pruebas de invierno.

**1912** Primeras pruebas femeninas de natación y saltos.

**1913** De Coubertin diseña el símbolo de los aros olímpicos.

**1916** Cancelación de los Juegos de Berlín por la I Guerra Mundial.

**1920** Aparición del lema y el juramento olímpicos.

**1924** Primeros juegos de invierno en Chamonix, Francia.

**1928** La llama olímpica se enciende por primera vez. Se introduce el atletismo femenino.

**1936** Primer relevo de la antorcha olímpica.

**1940** Cancelación de los Juegos de Tokio por la II Guerra Mundial.

**1944** No se celebran los juegos debido a la II Guerra Mundial.

**1960** Primeros Juegos Paralímpicos en Roma.

**1968** Comienzan los controles antidopaje en las olimpiadas.

**1976** Paralímpicos de invierno.

**1993** Inauguración del museo olímpico en Suiza.

**1994** Los Juegos de Invierno comienzan a celebrarse dos años después de los de verano.

# DEPORTES ANTIGUOS Y NUEVOS

Los deportes olímpicos no han sido siempre los mismos. Con los años han desaparecido unos y surgido otros. En las Olimpiadas de Atenas de 1896 participaron 245 atletas en nueve disciplinas, mientras que en los juegos de Atenas de 2004, más de 10.000 atletas competirán en 28 deportes y 301 pruebas distintas. Desde 1994, los Juegos Olímpicos se celebran cada dos años, alternando los de invierno y verano.

▲ *El salto de altura sin carrera estuvo presente en las olimpiadas de 1900 a 1912. Pero este no fue el deporte más extraño. Los Juegos de París de 1900, por ejemplo, incorporaron una prueba de tiro a la paloma y otra de 200 m obstáculos que incluía escalada y natación.*

**Deportes desaparecidos**

Se han añadido muchos deportes nuevos al programa olímpico, pero otros se han quedado en el camino. Las regatas con motor aparecieron en los Juegos de 1908, por ejemplo, mientras que la escalada de cuerda fue deporte olímpico de 1896 a 1932. Algunos deportes suprimidos, como el cricket (deporte olímpico en 1900), golf (1900 y 1904) y rugby (1900, 1904, 1920 y 1928) son muy populares en todo el mundo. Otros, como el lanzamiento de disco con dos manos y el levantamiento de peso con una mano, apenas se practican. Muchas pruebas se suprimieron debido a su falta de popularidad: el croquet dejó de ser olímpico después de que en 1900 tuviera un solo espectador.

▼ *El soka-tira fue olímpico en cinco ocasiones entre 1900 y 1920. En esta ocasión, Gran Bretaña derrota a EE.UU. en las Olimpiadas de Amberes de 1920.*

## Deportes de exhibición

Desde 1912, algunos deportes han aparecido en los juegos de verano como mera exhibición. Las olimpiadas les dan publicidad y más posibilidades de convertirse en deportes oficialmente olímpicos en juegos posteriores. Algunos son una demostración de los deportes autóctonos de la nación anfitriona. Tal es el caso del fútbol americano, que apareció en 1932 en las Olimpiadas de Los Ángeles, y el *korfball*, un deporte popular en Holanda y Bélgica, presente en 1920 y 1928. Más recientemente, los Juegos de Barcelona de 1992 acogieron exhibiciones de hockey sobre patines.

## Preceptos olímpicos

Para aspirar a ser olímpico, un deporte no debe incluir propulsión motorizada. Esto deja fuera a las carreras de motoras y de coches, entre otros. El deporte también debe someterse al código antidopaje, que combate el uso ilegal de drogas. El COI insiste en que para que un deporte pase a formar parte de los juegos, debe jugarse en 75 países en cuatro continentes, en el caso de pruebas masculinas, o en 40 países en tres continentes, para las pruebas femeninas. Pese a cumplir estos preceptos, algunos deportes populares como el squash, el kárate y el golf no están incuidos en las olimpiadas, mientras que otros menos populares, como el tiro o la lucha grecorromana, sí lo están. Algunas personas creen que las olimpiadas de verano son tan largas que deberían suprimirse pruebas en lugar de añadirse. Sin embargo, desde 1950 no se ha suprimido ningún deporte o disciplina de los juegos.

*▶ Los Juegos de Atlanta de 1996 sirvieron de debut a la popular bicicleta de montaña, que logró convertirse en disciplina olímpica en 1993. La prueba, de 40-50 km para hombres y 30-40 km para mujeres, atrajo a un gran número de espectadores tanto en los Juegos de Atlanta como en los de Sydney.*

*▼ Faissal Ebnoutalib, de Alemania, y Mohammad Alfararjeh, de Jordania, compiten en las Olimpiadas de 2000 en taekwondo, un arte marcial. Antes de lograr su categoría olímpica en 2000, el taekwondo apareció por primera vez como deporte de exhibición en los Juegos de Barcelona de 1992.*

*▲ El deporte de la cesta punta fue disciplina olímpica en una sola ocasión, en 1900. Desde entonces, el juego, que se disputa en un frontón con una cesta alargada y curva, ha sido deporte de exhibición en 1924, 1968 y en los Juegos de Barcelona de 1992 (en la fotografía).*

▲ *El cartel de las Olimpiadas de 1912 mostraba a atletas desnudos en referencia a la pureza de los antiguos juegos griegos. Algunos países lo prohibieron.*

# ESTOCOLMO 1912

Las primeras cuatro olimpiadas de la era moderna tuvieron cierta relevancia, pero se vieron ensombrecidas por una escasa organización y casos de malos jueces. El movimiento olímpico necesitaba unos juegos bien organizados y eso es lo que ofreció Suecia en 1912. Más de 2.500 atletas compitieron en 102 pruebas en unos juegos que presenciaron la aparición del cronómetro electrónico. El gran éxito de las Olimpiadas de Estocolmo permitió superar una interrupción de ocho años debida al estallido de la Primera Guerra Mundial.

▲ *La ceremonia inaugural se celebró en el estadio olímpico de Estocolmo. Construido sobre unos terrenos donados por el rey Gustavo V de Suecia, el estadio tenía un aforo de 22.000 espectadores. Por primera vez se utilizó un sistema de megafonía.*

## Juegos globales

Aunque la mayoría de las 28 naciones eran de Europa, los Juegos de 1912 fueron los primeros en que compitieron deportistas de los cinco continentes. Japón participó por primera vez en las olimpiadas, mientras que Australasia (un combinado de Autralia y Nueva Zelanda) apareció por última vez como tal y ganó dos oros, dos platas y tres bronces.

◀ *Hannes Kolehmainen cruza la llegada y gana los 5.000 metros lisos. El finlandés fue el atleta que más éxitos obtuvo en los juegos. Ganó también los 10.000 metros lisos y la carrera cross country individual.*

## Pruebas de resistencia

La carrera más larga celebrada en unas olimpiadas modernas tuvo lugar en 1912. La carrera de ciclismo por carretera, de más de 320 km, tuvo como vencedor a Rudolph Lewis, de Suráfrica, con un tiempo de 10 horas, 42 minutos y 39 segundos. El final de la competición de lucha grecorromana fue un duelo agotador. Tras más de nueve horas, el finlandés Ivar Böhling y el sueco Anders Ahlgren lucharon hasta llegar a un punto muerto sin que ninguno se alzara vencedor. Se declaró un empate y ambos hombres obtuvieron la plata, pero no el oro.

◀ *El pentatlón moderno fue deporte olímpico por primera vez en 1912. Los tres participantes suecos (en la fotografía) obtuvieron el oro, plata y bronce. En quinto lugar quedó George Patton, que más tarde se convertiría en un famoso general estadounidense en la Segunda Guerra Mundial.*

◀ *El atleta norteamericano Jim Thorpe supera el listón en el salto de altura. Thorpe se convirtió en la estrella de los Juegos de Estocolmo al ganar el pentatlón y el decatlón.*

## El atleta más grande del mundo

Jim Thorpe era un gran deportista que practicaba una gran variedad de deportes a alto nivel, entre ellos el fútbol americano y el lacrosse. En los Juegos de 1912 ganó medallas de oro en pentatlón y en el primer decatlón olímpico, batiendo los récords mundiales de ambas pruebas. Su actuación en decatlón fue tan buena que sus 8.412 puntos habrían sido suficientes para ganar una medalla de plata casi 40 años después, en los Juegos de Londres de 1948. Sin embargo, en 1913 se exigió a Thorpe la devolución de sus medallas de oro tras salir a la luz que había jugado al béisbol semiprofesional. Las medallas fueron devueltas a su familia en 1983, 30 años después de la muerte de Thorpe.

| MEDALLERO | O | P | B |
|---|---|---|---|
| EE.UU. | 25 | 19 | 19 |
| Suecia | 24 | 24 | 17 |
| Gran Bretaña | 10 | 15 | 16 |
| Finlandia | 9 | 8 | 9 |
| Francia | 7 | 4 | 3 |
| Alemania | 5 | 13 | 7 |
| Suráfrica | 4 | 2 | 0 |
| Noruega | 4 | 1 | 4 |
| Hungría | 3 | 2 | 3 |
| Canadá | 3 | 2 | 3 |

▲ *En 1912 se entregaron por última vez medallas de oro macizo. Hoy en día las medallas de oro son de plata chapada en oro.*

## La influencia sueca

Las mujeres fueron admitidas en las pruebas de natación y saltos por primera vez en Estocolmo, compitiendo en 100 metros estilos y en relevos libres 4 x 100 m. Pero todavía había solamente cinco pruebas femeninas, comparadas a las 87 masculinas. Hubo una gran conmoción cuando el boxeo quedó fuera de los Juegos Olímpicos por ser ilegal en Suecia. La lucha libre también se vio excluida. Los Juegos de 1912 fueron los últimos en los que se permitió a la nación anfitriona ejercer una influencia tan grande sobre el programa olímpico.

◀ *Una carrera de 100 metros estilos masculinos en la piscina descubierta construida para los Juegos de Estocolmo. La medalla de oro fue para el hawaiano Duke Kahanamoku, que también ganó el oro en las Olimpiadas de 1920 en Amberes, Bélgica.*

◀ *Ralph Rose, de EE.UU., a punto de lanzar el peso y ganar la medalla de oro. Rose también compitió en el inusual lanzamiento de peso con dos manos, logrando el oro con un lanzamiento de más de 27 metros.*

# EL LARGO CAMINO PARA SER SEDE OLÍMPICA

Ser la sede del mayor acontecimiento internacional no es nada fácil. Exige una gran planificación, inversión y compromiso. Pero el prestigio y la publicidad que aporta y la posibilidad de renovar una ciudad o región derivan en una competencia feroz. Todo comienza ocho años antes de la celebración de los juegos, cuando varias ciudades empiezan a trabajar en su candidatura para acoger el evento.

▲ *En 2001, Pekín, la capital de China, ganó la candidatura para los Juegos de 2008 frente a Osaka (Japón), París (Francia), Toronto (Canadá) y Estambul (Turquía).*

◀ *Jacques Rogge es el presidente del COI desde 2001. Rogge representó a Bélgica como regatista en los Juegos de 1968, 1972 y 1976.*

### Candidatas a ser la mejor

Cualquier ciudad o región puede presentar su candidatura a las olimpiadas, pero existe un límite de una por país. Una ciudad candidata tiene que obtener la aprobación nacional, ya que la celebración exige una inversión inmensa y un gran compromiso por parte de todo el país. En primer lugar, las ciudades forman comités y preparan presentaciones detalladas. Después, los miembros del COI visitan los escenarios para valorar la idoneidad de la ciudad como sede de los juegos. Muchas reuniones tienen lugar en secreto, ya que las ciudades rivales tratan de influir en la decisión del COI. En ocasiones, esto ha llevado a acusaciones de corrupción y el COI se vio obligado a endurecer sus normas tras descubrirse que algunos de sus miembros habían aceptado regalos ilegales a finales de la década de 1990. Durante el proceso de valoración, se descartan algunas candidaturas que no llegan a la lista final. La ciudad que obtiene la mayoría de los votos (más del 50%) es nombrada sede de los juegos. Si no hay mayoría, se elimina la candidatura con menos votos y se vuelve a votar. El resultado se revela mientras miles de personas esperan ansiosas. Para una nación, será una gran alegría; para los perdedores, una gran desilusión.

### Planificación y organización

Ser la sede de las olimpiadas es un gran reto. Los avances en las comunicaciones han llevado la emoción de los juegos a todos los rincones del mundo. A su vez, esto ha provocado un incremento en el número de personas que acuden a los juegos, como participantes y como espectadores. Una ciudad debe ser capaz de proporcionar alojamiento, transporte y otros muchos servicios vitales a los cientos de miles de visitantes adicionales que recibe. Se llevan a cabo grandes obras públicas para mejorar los nudos de transporte, y las delegaciones de todos los deportes olímpicos inspeccionan las instalaciones que ofrecerá la ciudad. Los preparativos para acoger los juegos son enormes y detallados, e incluyen el reclutamiento y preparación de miles de personas.

## Un gigante comercial

El primer escenario construido expresamente para unas olimpiadas fue el White City Stadium, erigido para los Juegos de Londres de 1908 por un coste superior a 55.000 euros. Las modernas instalaciones olímpicas pueden costar mil veces esa cifra. Se calcula que acoger los juegos de verano hoy puede suponer más de mil quinientos millones de dólares, sin incluir los gastos en nudos de transporte nuevos y otras mejoras metropolitanas. Muchas olimpiadas exigen la ayuda del gobierno del país. Se calcula que el gobierno habrá financiando el 15% del coste de los Juegos de Atenas 2004. Algunos críticos dicen que los juegos han adquirido tan envergadura que suponen un lujo que pueden permitirse pocos países. Los que están a favor de las olimpiadas defienden que, bien organizados, los juegos no tienen por qué resultar costosos. También pueden dejar alojamientos, transporte e instalaciones sociales y deportivas innovadoras que enriquecen la vida de los habitantes locales y los futuros visitantes.

▲ *La financiación necesaria para acoger las olimpiadas tiene distintas procedencias. Los patrocinadores y la publicidad (en la fotografía) aportan mucho dinero, al igual que la venta de entradas y artículos conmemorativos. Además, el COI vende los derechos audiovisuales para cubrir los juegos y dona el 60% de sus ingresos al comité organizador de la nación anfitriona.*

► *La villa olímpica de Sydney acogió a los atletas y miembros de los equipos durante los Juegos de 2000. Después, se convirtió en el barrio de Newington, ofreciendo apartamentos ecológicos con energía solar a cientos de personas.*

◄ *Para los Juegos de 2004, el gobierno griego ha invertido cientos de millones de dólares en ampliar su sistema de metro, construir un nuevo aeropuerto y unos 120 kilómetros de carretera, y plantar más de 250.000 árboles. Se han construido muchas instalaciones deportivas nuevas, mientras que otras se han renovado. Esta fotografía muestra dos canchas de tenis y el estadio olímpico (al fondo) en construcción en agosto de 2003, un año antes de la inauguración de los juegos.*

## Grandes ventajas

En épocas recientes, la competencia para ser sede de las olimpiadas de verano ha sido feroz. Al tratarse del mayor acontecimiento mundial, las olimpiadas ofrecen una oportunidad inmejorable de mostrar la ciudad y la nación al resto del mundo. Además de los miles de visitantes que acuden a los juegos como espectadores, otros cientos de miles que los han seguido por televisión deciden visitar esa ciudad o país en los años siguientes. Antes de los Juegos de 1992, por ejemplo, Barcelona ocupaba el puesto 16 entre los destinos turísticos más populares de Europa. El éxito de las olimpiadas derivó en un *boom* turístico que, en 1999, había convertido la ciudad en el tercer destino favorito del continente. El número de turistas que visitan Australia aumentó considerablemente después de los Juegos de Sydney, y se espera que ocurra lo mismo con las ciudades de Atenas y Pekín tras la celebración de sus juegos.

# SUEÑOS OLÍMPICOS

Todos los atletas que acuden a los juegos son olímpicos. Esto es un gran logro y, para muchos, el simple hecho de formar parte del equipo nacional es ya un gran premio. El deseo de lograr el éxito al más alto nivel está presente en muchos deportistas desde una temprana edad, y su inspiración puede proceder de haber visto los juegos o conocido a un deportista olímpico cuando eran niños. Pero entre el sueño y la realidad hay muchos años de sacrificio y trabajo duro.

▶ *La corredora de fondo británica Paula Radcliffe perdió por los pelos una medalla en 10.000 metros lisos en Sydney 2000, pero desde entonces ha utilizado esa decepción como motivación para ganar muchas carreras. Radcliffe entrena casi todo el año, corriendo cientos de kilómetros y empleando muchas horas en el gimnasio.*

### El entrenamiento

Los deportistas olímpicos tienen el don de desarrollar su deporte al más alto nivel. Los atletas deben ser fuertes tanto a nivel físico como mental, y gozar de atributos físicos como flexibilidad y potencia (especialmente importantes en pruebas como las carreras de velocidad o la halterofilia) o la capacidad de repetir un movimiento exacto una y otra vez con precisión milimétrica. Esto es vital en las pruebas de precisión como arco y tiro. Otros deportes exigen reacciones rápidas o resistencia extrema (la capacidad de rendir a gran nivel durante largos períodos sin agotarse). El talento sin más no es suficiente para triunfar, y por eso casi todos los atletas olímpicos entrenan mucho y de forma regular. Para muchos, el entrenamiento es una ocupación permanente, con programas especializados y específicos. Los entrenamientos pueden variar: desde mejorar el tono general y aumentar la fuerza en el gimnasio hasta potenciar la velocidad de las piernas con ejercicios intensivos.

▶ *Dos meses antes de las olimpiadas de Sydney, Michael Johnson se lesionó el ligamento izquierdo durante los 200 m lisos en las eliminatorias olímpicas de EE.UU.*

### Lograr la marca

Solamente unos cuantos de los atletas que sueñan con ir a las olimpiadas hacen realidad su sueño, ya que una serie de pruebas clasificatorias limitan el número de participantes. La selección para las pruebas atléticas individuales, por ejemplo, exige que los atletas hayan superado la marca olímpica en dicha prueba. Esto puede resultar muy difícil y lograrla tampoco garantiza un puesto en el equipo olímpico nacional. Las naciones pueden enviar entre uno y tres atletas a competir en la mayoría de las pruebas individuales, mientras que en la mayoría de los deportes de equipo sólo se permite un equipo por país. Muchos países realizan eliminatorias a fin de decidir quién irá a los juegos. Y a veces el resultado es sorprendente. Por ejemplo, en las clasificatorias de atletismo en pista de EE.UU. del año 2000, Maurice Greene y Michael Johnson (los hombres más rápidos del mundo en aquel momento en 100 y 100 metros lisos) se lesionaron corriendo los 200 metros. Por este motivo, no pudieron ser seleccionados para representar a EE.UU. en los 200 metros lisos de los Juegos de Sydney 2000.

## De amateur a profesional

Los juegos olímpicos fueron concebidos como una competición para atletas amateurs que no cobraban por realizar su deporte. Durante varios años, las olimpiadas fueron sólo para amateurs. Los deportistas profesionales o semiprofesionales (que cobran por jugar y competir) no eran admitidos y, cuando lo eran, se les retiraba las medallas. Con el paso del tiempo ha habido un cambio de actitud. Muchos de los participantes de Sydney 2000 eran profesionales, y determinados deportes profesionales como el tenis y el béisbol también han entrado en los juegos. Los mejores deportistas olímpicos tienen ahora la oportunidad de entrenar y jugar a su deporte a tiempo completo. También pueden tener acceso a las mejores instalaciones, los mejores entrenadores y equipos médicos. Sin embargo, muchos deportistas olímpicos siguen siendo aficionados que realizan enormes sacrificios para poder competir. Estos deportistas tienen que entrenar en su tiempo libre y para ir a los juegos han de costearse sus propios gastos u obtener el dinero de varias fuentes.

## Ganadores y perdedores

Por cada deportista olímpico que sube al podio a recibir una medalla de oro, hay cientos que tienen que enfrentarse a la decepción. Las actuaciones sorprendentes de atletas menos conocidos son una parte importante del gran atractivo de las olimpiadas. Lesiones, pérdidas de forma o simplemente no ser los mejores son las mayores pesadillas de los favoritos. Para todos los atletas, el simple hecho de competir es un gran triunfo, pero para aquellos de los que se espera la victoria, no ganar una medalla es una gran derrota. Perder es una experiencia dura, pero a la mayoría de los deportistas olímpicos les sirve para avivar el deseo de entrenar más y obtener mejores resultados en el futuro.

▲ *El mayor honor para un deportista olímpico es ser el abanderado de su equipo nacional en la ceremonia de apertura.*

▼ *El equipo nigeriano de relevos en 4 x 100 metros muestra su alegría al ganar el bronce en las Olimpiadas de Barcelona de 1992.*

# EN LA SOMBRA

Las olimpiadas pueden parecer un espectáculo de 10.000 participantes que deleitan a los espectadores de todo el mundo, pero sin los otros miles de personas presentes en los juegos, las olimpiadas no podrían celebrarse. En ellas trabaja gente de todo tipo, desde expertos en tecnología de la información y comunicaciones, encargados de que los resultados lleguen correctamente a los medios, a legiones de limpiadores que hacen desaparecer los millones de vasos desechables y otros residuos abandonados por los espectadores.

▲ *Era fácil identificar a los voluntarios olímpicos de los Juegos de Sydney gracias a su colorido uniforme. Más de 75.000 personas solicitaron los 47.000 puestos disponibles.*

◀ *Un médico atiende a Suzy Favor Hamilton, de EE.UU., que se cayó poco antes de cruzar la línea de llegada en la final de los 1.500 metros lisos femeninos en los Juegos de Sydney. Sufrió deshidratación durante la carrera, que ganó la argelina Nouria Merah-Benida.*

### Entrenadores y jugadores

Los equipos enviados por naciones poderosas, como EE.UU., Rusia, Alemania, China o Australia, pueden estar compuestos de cientos de jueces, entrenadores y especialistas médicos, además de técnicos y personal de apoyo. Por lo general, estas personas permanecen en la sombra, organizando a los participantes y asegurando que los deportistas y su equipamiento estén en perfectas condiciones para la competición. Muchos deportistas mantienen una relación estrecha con el entrenador, que tal vez les haya ayudado a lo largo de su carrera. Los entrenadores tratan de sacar lo mejor de sus hombres y mujeres desarrollando programas de entrenamiento que aseguren su rendimiento y aconsejándoles en todos los elementos de su técnica.

◀ *El entrenador del equipo femenino de waterpolo da instrucciones a sus jugadoras durante un descanso en la final de Sydney. Su equipo tuvo que conformarse con la medalla de plata tras ser derrotado 4-3 por Australia.*

## Los voluntarios

En Sydney hubo 47.000 y en Atenas habrá unos 60.000. Sin ellos, las olimpiadas serían un caos para los atletas, jueces y, sobre todo, para los visitantes y espectadores. Estas personas tan necesarias son voluntarios que entregan su tiempo libre para ayudar en la organización de los juegos. Los voluntarios son esenciales, no sólo para reducir el coste de los juegos, sino para dar a la comunidad local la oportunidad de involucrarse. Muchos miles de voluntarios trabajan en las instalaciones olímpicas y en la ciudad anfitriona, guiando y aconsejando a los atletas, funcionarios y turistas, y actuando como intérpretes, vigilantes y conductores. Con la llegada de tantas personas de todo el mundo, los voluntarios con conocimientos de otros idiomas son especialmente valorados. Los puestos del voluntariado se anuncian varios años antes de los juegos, y los elegidos reciben una amplia formación. Su entusiasmo y la cálida bienvenida que ofrecen a los visitantes extranjeros son piezas esenciales de la experiencia olímpica.

▼ *El cubano Anier Garcia está rodeado por cámaras de televisión y fotógrafos tras su victoria en la final masculina de 110 metros vallas en 2000. El interés de los medios de comunicación es notable. En los Juegos de Sydney, más de 15.000 periodistas filmaron e informaron de la acción mientras ocurría. Las secuencias fueron retransmitidas a 200 países: más que en ninguna de las olimpiadas anteriores.*

► *Cada prueba olímpica necesita de cierto número de jueces que aseguren que se cumplen las reglas. En la fotografía, el británico Linford Christie es informado de que ha sido descalificado en la final de 100 metros lisos de Atlanta 1996 tras dos salidas nulas.*

## El hotel más grande del mundo

Uno de los grandes proyectos que debe acometer la ciudad anfitriona es la construcción de una villa olímpica. En ella vive, come y comparte vivencias la mayoría de los participantes y miembros de los equipos durante los juegos. Alojar y alimentar a 16.000 personas de todos los continentes, religiones y estilos de vida es una operación realmente compleja. Las cantidades son asombrosas. Por ejemplo, en los Juegos de Sydney de 2000, se consumieron 350 toneladas de fruta y verduras, 82 toneladas de pescado, 100 toneladas de carne y tres millones de refrescos. Un equipo de unos 450 cocineros debe preparar estos y otros muchos ingredientes teniendo en cuenta la dieta y preferencia de los atletas, y debe hacerlo llegar a los habitantes de la villa en cuestión de 24 horas. La vida en la villa olímpica se hace extraña para algunos participantes, pero la mayoría habla positivamente de su estancia allí. Consideran que conocer a deportistas de otras pruebas y países es una experiencia realmente memorable.

► *En la villa olímpica hay todo tipo de instalaciones (desde un centro de aromaterapia hasta un salón de videojuegos) para que los deportistas se sientan cómodos y estén ocupados. Este es el salón de Internet de Sydney, en el que los olímpicos podían navegar en la red y utilizar el correo electrónico.*

▲ En 1988, el boxeador surcoreano Byun Jong-Il perdió dos puntos por dar un cabezazo. Se originó una pelea y Byun fue descalificado. Como protesta, se sentó en el ring y no se movió durante 67 minutos.

# PESADILLAS OLÍMPICAS

Pese a que su objetivo es promover la paz y la armonía, las olimpiadas han experimentado algunos momentos trágicos. Los juegos son una oportunidad única para que los mejores deportistas del mundo se reúnan, compitan y tal vez logren la fama y la gloria. En ocasiones, el deseo de triunfar o la decepción de la derrota ha sido tal que los participantes han hecho trampas, protestado o incluso reaccionado con violencia. Otros han arriesgado sus carreras y sus vidas usando drogas ilegales para mejorar sus marcas.

## Trampas y engaños

Los trucos, engaños e intentos de amañar resultados por parte de los participantes han sido una constante desde los primeros juegos de la era moderna. En 1904, por ejemplo, el primer hombre que acabó el maratón, el norteamericano Franz Lorz, reconoció haber recorrido en coche 17,5 de los 42 kilómetros tras sufrir un calambre. A veces las olimpiadas han estado mal organizadas o ha habido jueces parciales o errores de medida. En los Juegos de México de 1968, por ejemplo, más de una docena de jueces y árbitros de la prueba de boxeo fueron expulsados por incompetencia. Uno de los casos más escandalosos de engaño ocurrió en 1967, cuando el pentatleta soviético Boris Onischenko trucó su florete para que registrara un tocado cuando él apretaba un botón oculto en su vestimenta.

▲ En los Juegos de Montreal de 1976, un juez inspecciona el florete de Boris Onischenko después de que protestara un oponente, el británico, Jim Fox. Onischenko, que ya contaba con una plata anterior en la prueba, fue expulsado de los juegos.

## Malos perdedores

A ningún deportista olímpico le agrada perder. La mayoría se toma la derrota con deportividad, pero algunos protestan o se lo toman de forma personal. Esto a veces deriva en muestras de disgusto espontáneas, como cuando el esprínter británico Linford Christie tiró sus zapatillas a la papelera tras ser descalificado por dos salidas nulas en la final de los 100 metros lisos de Atlanta en 1996. En la final de hockey masculino de los Juegos de 1972, Pakistán perdió 1-0 frente a Alemania Occidental. Los miembros del equipo paquistaní arrojaron agua al presidente de la Federación Internacional de Hockey y pisotearon sus medallas de plata. Fueron expulsados de los juegos para siempre.

◄ La semifinal de waterpolo entre Hungría y la Unión Soviética acabó en un baño de sangre. La Unión Soviética había invadido Hungría semanas antes y el malestar se desató en la piscina durante el partido cuando los deportistas comenzaron a pelearse y, literalmente, tiñeron el agua de rojo. El juego se suspendió cuando Hungría ganaba 4-0. Hungría fue declarada vencedora y sus jugadores tuvieron que ser escoltados fuera de la zona de la piscina.

▲ *Knut Jensen (centro), un ciclista danés de 23 años, sufrió un ataque cardícaco en Roma en 1960 y murió una hora después de la carrera. La causa fue una sobredosis de anfetaminas, que obligaron a sus pulmones y corazón a ir más deprisa.*

## Las drogas en el deporte

El dopaje (la ingestión de sustancias prohibidas o restringidas para mejorar el rendimiento) es un gran problema en los deportes en general, y las olimpiadas no son una excepción. Existen muchos tipos de sustancias prohibidas, como los esteroides anabolizantes. Estos potencian el crecimiento muscular, permitiendo a los deportistas aumentar rápidamente el tamaño de sus músculos y su fuerza. Las drogas están prohibidas porque otorgan una "ventaja" injusta a los deportistas que las consumen y también porque constituyen un riesgo para la salud. Por ejemplo, si se toman durante mucho tiempo, los esteroides pueden dañar el hígado, el corazón y los pulmones, además de causar depresión y agresión incontrolada.

◀ *En las olimpiadas de 2000, tres búlgaros –Sevdalin Minchev (en la fotografía), Ivan Ivanov e Izabela Dragneva– dieron positivo por diuréticos y perdieron sus medallas. Los diuréticos hacen que el cuerpo elimine líquidos rápidamente, reduciendo el peso del atleta y enmascarando otras drogas.*

## Control antidopaje

El COI fue una de las primeras organizaciones deportivas que introdujo el control antidopaje. Apareció por primera vez de forma experimental en los Juegos de 1968 y se adoptó oficialmente cuatro años después. En los primeros juegos era fácil superar el control. Hoy en día los controles son más sofisticados, pero todavía están lejos de ser infalibles. Son habituales las apelaciones a los tribunales después de que un atleta haya dado positivo. Continuamente se diseñan nuevas drogas y esto dificulta los controles, pero el COI y otras organizaciones están en la lucha. En 1999 se creó la Agencia Mundial Anti-Dopaje (WADA) y los participantes se enfrentan ahora a sanciones de por vida por consumo repetido. Sin embargo, el juego de gato y ratón entre deportistas y autoridades continuará durante muchos años.

▲ *La mayor tragedia de la historia de las olimpiadas sucedió en los Juegos de Múnich en 1972. Once miembros del equipo israelí fueron secuestrados, y posteriormente asesinados, por el grupo terrorista palestino Septiembre Negro. Se suspendieron los Juegos de forma inmediata y, tras una ceremonia conmemorativa (en la fotografía), se decidió que continuarían como protesta contra el terrorismo.*

▲ *El cartel oficial de las Olimpiadas de 1936 muestra la Puerta de Brandenburgo, un monumento significativo de Berlín. Fue impreso en 19 idiomas.*

# BERLÍN 1936

Alemania fue nombrada sede de las Olimpiadas de 1936 en 1931, poco después de que Adolf Hitler y el Partido Nacional Socialista (Nazis) llegaran al poder. Hitler vio los juegos como una oportunidad para hacer pública su creencia en la superioridad racial del pueblo alemán. Había símbolos nazis por todas partes, la policía secreta vigilaba a los periodistas y los atletas judíos y negros fueron difamados en los medios de comunicación. No obstante, las instalaciones fueron excelentes y hubo actuaciones memorables.

► *La ceremonia de inauguración en el Estadio Olímpico de Berlín fue presidida por Adolf Hitler, el jefe de Estado de Alemania desde 1933. En los juegos participaron 466 atletas de 49 naciones que compitieron en 129 pruebas distintas. Se vendieron más de cuatro millones y medio de entradas para todos los eventos.*

| MEDALLERO | O | P | B |
|---|---|---|---|
| Alemania | 33 | 26 | 30 |
| EE.UU. | 24 | 20 | 12 |
| Hungría | 10 | 1 | 5 |
| Italia | 8 | 9 | 5 |
| Finlandia | 7 | 6 | 6 |
| Francia | 7 | 6 | 6 |
| Suecia | 6 | 5 | 9 |
| Japón | 6 | 4 | 8 |
| Países Bajos | 6 | 4 | 7 |
| Gran Bretaña | 4 | 7 | 3 |

◄ *El atleta griego Konstantin Kondylis hace historia al dar el primer relevo de la antorcha de los primeros Juegos Olímpicos de la era moderna. Unos 3.000 corredores llevaron la antorcha de Grecia a Berlín en un recorrido de 3.075 km por siete países participantes.*

### Juegos innovadores

Ensombrecidas por la política antisemita nazi, en ocasiones olvidamos que las Olimpiadas de Berlín fueron un éxito de organización. Destacaron por sus muchas innovaciones, como la llegada del fuego olímpico y sistemas de cronometraje más precisos. Fueron los primeros juegos retransmitidos por televisión: se mostraron en algunas pantallas de circuito cerrado de la ciudad, mientras que los documentales con los momentos más destacados volaban a otras ciudades europeas. El remo, el baloncesto y el balonmano hicieron su debut olímpico en Berlín, mientas que el polo hizo su última aparición. El programa gimnástico se amplió y dio la bienvenida a dos multimedallistas alemanes: Konrad Frey, que ganó tres oros, una plata y dos bronces, y Alfred Schwarzmann, que obtuvo tres medallas de oro y dos de bronce.

◀ *Jesse Owens recibe el testigo en la prueba de relevos de 4x100 m. Él formó parte del equipo norteamericano que ganó el oro y batió el récord mundial en un tiempo de 39,8 segundos.*

▶ *Owens conversa con Luz Long, el atleta alemán de quien se hizo amigo en los juegos y que más tarde moriría en la Segunda Guerra Mundial. Owens escribió: "Podrías fundir todas las medallas y copas que he ganado y no serían ni un chapado de la amistad de 24 quilates que siento por Luz Long."*

**Las olimpiadas de un hombre**

Pocos acontecimientos deportivos internacionales han estado tan claramente dominados como las Olimpiadas de 1936 por Jesse Owens. Hijo de un agricultor pobre, Owens había encendido el mundo del atletismo el año anterior batiendo cinco récords mundiales e igualando un sexto en una sola tarde. Pese a la gran competencia de algunas pruebas, Owens no decepcionó en Berlín. Se convirtió en el favorito de los espectadores alemanes y acabó con la idea de Hitler de que los juegos serían un escaparate para la "raza superior". Owens ganó medallas de oro en 100 m, 200 m y relevos 4 x100 m. Su prueba más dura sería el salto de longitud, donde corrió el riesgo de ser eliminado tras dos saltos nulos. Su principal rival, el atleta blanco alemán Luz Long, le ofreció consejos que le ayudaron no sólo a clasificarse para la final, sino también a ganar su cuarto oro por delante de Long, que logró la plata.

▲ *El baloncesto hizo su debut olímpico en 1936, cuando se jugaba al aire libre. En la fotografía vemos a Filipinas y México jugando un partido de clasificación. Al final, venció EE.UU.*

▶ *La saltadora norteamericana Marjorie Gestring ganó el oro en la competición de salto a la edad de 13 años y 9 meses. Continúa siendo la medallista de oro más joven de la historia de las olimpiadas de verano.*

**Récords de oro**

Los logros de Jesse Owens eclipsaron muchas otras actuaciones. En la piscina, Inge Sorensen, de Dinamarca, ganó una medalla de bronce en braza. A sus 12 años, se convirtió en la medallista olímpica más joven. La estrella nadadora de los juegos fue la holandesa de 17 años Hendrika 'Rie' Mastenbroek, que ganó tres oros y una plata. Hungría ocupó un sorprendente tercer puesto en el medallero, debido en parte a su gran participación en lucha y esgrima, donde, liderados por Kabos Endre, ganaron 24 de las 25 pruebas. El triunfante equipo de waterpolo de Hungría contaba con Oliver Halassy, que jugó a pesar de tener una pierna amputada por debajo de la rodilla.

# CARRERAS DE VELOCIDAD

▲ *Los atletas toman la salida en las eliminatorias de los 100 metros lisos masculinos de Atlanta. Para tener la oportunidad de convertirse en campeón olímpico, un corredor debe clasificarse entre los ocho que compiten en la final.*

He aquí los humanos más rápidos del planeta. Los 100 y 200 metros lisos son las pruebas más esperadas de las olimpiadas. Una serie de carreras clasificatorias deciden los ocho atletas que disputarán cada una de las finales. La tensión aumenta mientras los rivales estiran y se concentran, se sitúan en los tacos de salida y se preparan para reaccionar al oír la pistola. Años de entrenamiento culminan en apenas diez segundos de intensa emoción en los 100 metros y veinte segundos en los 200 metros.

▼ *Antes de tomar la salida de una carrera de velocidad, los corredores se sitúan en los tacos de salida y se concentran en la pista (1). Cuando oyen la señal, levantan las caderas (2) y se preparan para el pistoletazo de salida.*

▲ *Impulsándose en los tacos de salida (3), los corredores avanzan con zancadas cortas y potentes, acelerando (4) e incorporándose a una carrera completa. Un corredor alcanza su velocidad máxima a mitad de carrera. A partir de ahí, se trata de una lucha por evitar la fatiga y permanecer relajado a fin de mantener la postura, zancada y estilo necesarios.*

**País:** *Holanda*
**Olimpiadas:** *Berlín 1936, Londres 1948, Helsinki 1952*
**Pruebas:** *100 m, 200 m, 4 x 100 m relevos, 80 m vallas, salto de altura*
**Medallas:** *4 de oro*

### Fracciones de segundo

El cronometraje preciso es vital en muchas pruebas olímpicas, sobre todo en las de velocidad. La pistola de salida va conectada a un cronómetro electrónico que se activa con el disparo. Moverse o despegarse de los tacos cuenta como salida nula, y hay que volver a repetirla. El final de muchas carreras es tan ajustado que es necesario que los jueces consulten la *foto finish*. En la final de los 100 metros lisos femeninos de los juegos de 1992, la corredora americana Gail Devers perdió la plata por una centésima de segundo por detrás de la jamaicana Juliet Cuthbert.

▲ *En ocasiones la* foto finish *es la única manera de decidir el ganador de una carrera. Un corredor finaliza la carrera cuando atraviesa la línea de llegada con el pecho, pero no con los brazos, las piernas o la cabeza.*

### Historia de las pruebas de velocidad

El ganador de los 100 metros lisos de las primeras olimpiadas modernas fue el americano Thomas Burke, que corrió en 12 segundos. Con el paso del tiempo y la mejora de las técnicas, pistas, calzado y vestuario, el cronómetro se ha rebajado notablemente. En 1968, el americano James Hines fue el primer medallista de oro que rebajó la barrera de los 10 segundos, con un tiempo de 9,95 segundos en México. Las mujeres participaron por primera vez en velocidad y otras pruebas atléticas en 1928, cuando Fanny Blankers-Koen silenció a los críticos que decían que era demasiado mayor logrando cuatro medallas a los 30 años y convirtiéndose en la primera madre campeona olímpica.

▲ *El corredor griego Konstantinos Kenteris no puede ocultar la alegría de su triunfo en la final de los 200 metros lisos masculinos en Sydney. Kenteris completó su éxito con una medalla de oro en el Campeonato del Mundo de Atletismo de 2001 y al año siguiente se convirtió en campeón europeo de los 200 metros lisos.*

### Los 200 metros lisos

Los 200 metros lisos comienzan en la curva, con los tacos de salida escalonados a lo largo de la pista para que todos los atletas corran la misma distancia. Los corredores dan la curva tratando de mantenerse en su calle para no ser descalificados. La segunda mitad de la carrera tiene lugar en la recta y los atletas intentan mantener su forma y estilo. En los últimos 20 ó 30 metros, los corredores comienzan a decelerar mientras la fatiga de rendir al máximo pasa factura. El fruto de cientos de horas de esfuerzo y resistencia permite a los mejores reducir la deceleración y mantener un estilo fluido al cruzar la meta.

◀ *La corredora francesa de 200 metros lisos Marie-José Pérec da la curva a buen ritmo en Atlanta, donde ganó la medalla de oro en 1996. Empujados hacia el exterior de la calle al tomar la curva a gran velocidad, los corredores se inclinan hacia dentro para mantenerse en su calle.*

◀ *El atleta americano Maurice Greene se coloca el dorsal antes de correr los 100 metros y ganar la medalla de oro en las Olimpiadas de 2000.*

### Doblete de velocidad

La técnica y el ritmo extremo exigidos en los 100 y 200 metros lisos son parecidos, y algunos atletas participan en ambas carreras con la esperanza de alzarse con el gran premio de velocidad. En los juegos de Sydney 2000, la corredora americana Marion Jones consiguió lo que muy pocos atletas (incluso el americano Carl Lewis en 1984 y el soviético Valeriy Borzov en 1972) han logrado: ganar el oro en 100 y 200 metros lisos. Jones sumó un tercer oro en los relevos de 4 x 100 m, y otros dos bronces. Su medallero es el mayor obtenido por una mujer en cualquier deporte en unas solas olimpiadas.

# CARRERAS DE MEDIO FONDO

Las carreras de medio fondo, que consisten en dar una o más vueltas a la pista, son algunas de las pruebas más dramáticas de las olimpiadas. Es importante poseer fuerza, resistencia y velocidad, pero aún más valiosa es una buena técnica. Los atletas necesitan moverse deprisa para no perder oportunidades, pero reservando energía para el final, cuando el ritmo se acelera. La mayoría de los corredores de medio fondo son capaces de esprintar en los últimos 100 ó 200 metros de una carrera.

▲ *La prueba de 800 metros femeninos de Sydney es liderada por la mozambiqueña Maria Mutola, que ganaría la carrera. A pesar de que sólo tenía 27 años, eran ya sus cuartas olimpiadas.*

► *Michael Johnson fue el atleta dominante en los 200 y 400 metros lisos durante la década de 1990. Fue el primer hombre que ganó dos veces los 400 metros lisos y obtuvo tres oros más en los relevos de 4 x 400 metros (dos veces) y los 200 metros lisos.*

▲ *El desastre acecha durante la final de los 3.000 metros lisos femeninos en las Olimpiadas de Los Ángeles. Un choque accidental de piernas entre Zola Budd, descalza, que representaba a Gran Bretaña, y la norteamericana Mary Decker dejó a esta última lesionada y fuera de la carrera. Budd, una de las favoritas, se quedó en el séptimo lugar.*

### Cambio de longitud

Con el paso de los años, las carreras de medio fondo han experimentado cambios en su longitud. La milla fue reemplazada por los 1.500 metros como la prueba estrella del medio fondo y los 3.000 metros femeninos cayeron ante los 5.000 metros en 1996. Las pruebas de medio fondo solían estar dominadas por países de habla inglesa como Gran Bretaña, EE.UU. y Australia. En 1976, el cubano Alberto Juantorena se convirtió en el primer corredor de un país de habla no inglesa que ganó el oro olímpico en 400 u 800 metros. Desde entonces, los campeones del medio fondo olímpico proceden de todo el mundo.

▶ *El marroquí Said Aouita toma la salida en las Olimpiadas de Seúl en 1988. Aouita dominó las carreras de medio fondo en la década de 1980 compitiendo con éxito en los 800 y 1.500 metros y permaneciendo imbatido en los 5.000 metros durante una década.*

**Estrategias de carrera**

Los atletas de élite ven los 400 metros lisos –una vuelta a la pista– como un *sprint* continuo. Toman impulso en los tacos de salida escalonados en la curva de la pista y deben permanecer en sus calles durante toda la carrera. En los 800 metros, los corredores también comienzan de forma escalonada. Tras los primeros 100 metros pueden abandonar sus calles y acercarse hacia la interior (la distancia más corta). Muchas carreras de 800 metros, y todas las de fondo, no se corren a un ritmo frenético, sino que son pruebas cautelosas en las que los corredores buscan ocupar y mantener una buena posición antes de que comience el *sprint* de la última vuelta. Los corredores de los 800 metros, y sobre todo de 1.500 metros, tienen que estar muy atentos y permanecer alerta ante la posibilidad de que un corredor acelere de repente. También deben procurar no quedar encajonados en el interior para el *sprint* final.

**Carrera tras carrera**

Las pruebas de medio fondo comienzan con una serie de eliminatorias y semifinales que concluyen en la final. Estas rondas de carreras exigen mucho a los corredores, que deben esforzarse por clasificarse al tiempo que reservan fuerzas para la final. Algunos atletas dotados consiguen dos triunfos en las olimpiadas y compiten en 800 y 1.500 metros o corren los 1.500 metros y una prueba más larga, como los 5.000 metros. Correr los 400 y los 800 metros lisos es muy raro. Solamente Alberto Juantorena compitió en estas dos disciplinas en las mismas olimpiadas. Ganó ambas en los Juegos de Montreal y estableció un nuevo récord mundial en 800 metros.

**País:** *Cuba*
**Olimpiadas:** *Múnich 1972, Montreal 1976, Moscú 1980*
**Pruebas:** *400 m, 800 m*
**Medallas:** *dos de oro*

▶ *La rumana Gabriela Szabo ondea la bandera de su país y saluda al público tras lograr la victoria en los 5.000 metros femeninos en Sydney, donde obtuvo una medalla de bronce por detrás de Nouria Merah-Benida, de Argelia, y Violeta Szekely, de Rumanía.*

# CARRERAS DE FONDO

Extenuantes para los competidores y emocionantes para los espectadores, las carreras de fondo tienen una larga historia que se remonta a las antiguas olimpiadas. Las distancias que corren los atletas se han modificado con el paso del tiempo, pero normalmente varían desde las carreras de 5.000 y 10.000 metros hasta los 42,2 kilómetros del maratón. Las pruebas de fondo incluyen también la marcha, un deporte exigente y muy técnico, con carreras de 20 y 50 kilómetros para los hombres y de 20 kilómetros para las mujeres.

◀ *Las carreras y la marcha de fondo exigen fuerza y resistencia sobrehumanas. Aquí, el atleta eslovaco Peter Tichy se derrumba en brazos de un juez instantes antes de cruzar la línea de meta en la carrera de 50 kilómetros marcha en los Juegos de Atlanta 1996. Tichy compitió de nuevo en Sydney.*

▲ *Uno de los atletas más populares del mundo, Haile Gebrselassie, ponía a punto su excepcional resistencia y velocidad cuando era niño en Etiopía corriendo 10 kilómetros diarios para ir a la escuela. De adulto ganó el oro en los 10.000 metros en las Olimpiadas de Atlanta y Sydney.*

◀ *El mejor corredor de fondo de su tiempo, Emil Zatopek, de Checoslovaquia, estableció 20 récords mundiales en su carrera. En las Olimpiadas de 1952 en Helsinki, logró algo que ningún otro atleta ha conseguido jamás: ganar el oro en 5.000 metros, 10.000 metros y el maratón. Era su primera maratón.*

### Pruebas de fondo en pista

Los 5.000 y 10.000 metros masculinos y femeninos son las pruebas atléticas de más distancia que se celebran en pista. Al ir en grupo, parece que los atletas corren tranquilamente, pero su ritmo es sorprendentemente rápido e incesante. Los corredores de los 10.000 metros tardan poco más de un minuto en recorrer cada vuelta de la pista de 400 metros, 25 en total. Algunas carreras de 5.000 y 10.000 metros parecen tranquilas, pero en ocasiones se emplean tácticas fascinantes. Algunos atletas optan por ir en cabeza, mientras que otros prefieren quedarse en segunda línea y acelerar en las últimas vueltas o en los últimos 300 metros. A pesar de las largas distancias, las carreras a veces tienen un final tenso y muy emocionante.

## El maratón

El nombre de esta prueba extenuante tiene su origen en la antigüedad. En el 490 a.C., un soldado griego llamado Filípides (consulta la pág. 6) corrió desde Atenas hasta Maratón para llevar la noticia de la victoria de los atenienses sobre los persas. Para conmemorar esta hazaña, el primer maratón de la era olímpica moderna, celebrado en 1896, recorrió de nuevo los casi 40 kilómetros que separan ambas ciudades. En los Juegos de Londres de 1908, la distancia del maratón aumentó a algo más de 42 kilómetros. En la actualidad los corredores del maratón olímpico emplean menos de dos horas y cuarto en completar esta gran distancia, llevando sus cuerpos al límite del agotamiento. A lo largo de la carrera los corredores tratan de mantener un ritmo relativamente uniforme, pero la clave para entrar al estadio olímpico en cabeza está en saber cuándo reservar fuerzas y cuándo acelerar.

▶ *La atleta norteamericana Joan Benoit saluda al público tras su victoria en el primer maratón olímpico femenino, celebrado en los Juegos de 1984 en Los Ángeles. Aunque Benoit había ganado el prestigioso maratón de Boston en 1979 y 1983, la noruega Grete Waitz comenzó la carrera como favorita. Waitz obtuvo la medalla de plata, un minuto y 26 segundos por detrás de Benoit.*

◀ *El atleta debe cumplir dos reglas en la marcha. En primer lugar, debe mantener recta la pierna que adelanta, sin flexionar la rodilla, desde el momento en que el pie toca el suelo hasta que la pierna pasa bajo el centro del cuerpo. En segundo lugar, siempre debe mantener un pie en contacto con el suelo.*

◀ *Robert Korzeniowski celebra la victoria en 50 km marcha en los Juegos de 2000. El atleta polaco logró dos dobletes únicos en Sydney: ganó los 50 km en dos olimpiadas consecutivas y completó su palmarés con la victoria en 20 km marcha.*

## Marcha

Esta prueba exige gran resistencia y control corporal por parte de los atletas. Los campeones de marcha de ambos sexos pueden completar una carrera de 20 kilómetros en 15 ó 25 minutos más de lo que tardarían los mejores corredores del mundo en cubrir la misma distancia. Los atletas avanzan a una velocidad increíble, pero deben hacerlo respetando dos reglas (consulta el pie de foto superior). A lo largo de la carrera, los jueces observan los movimientos de los atletas. Si incumplen alguna de las dos reglas, reciben un aviso. En la marcha olímpica, tres avisos suponen la descalificación. Aunque los atletas pasan miles de horas practicando esta técnica, la presión de la competición puede hacer que cometan errores. En los Juegos de 2000, el mexicano Bernardo Segura cruzó la meta creyendo que había ganado la prueba de 20 km y descubrió que había sido descalificado en la última parte de la carrera.

# VALLAS Y RELEVOS

**País:** *EE.UU.*
**Olimpiadas:** *Montreal 1976, Los Ángeles 1984, Seúl 1988*
**Pruebas:** *400 metros vallas*
**Medallas:** *dos de oro, una de bronce*

Las pruebas de vallas y relevos exigen algo más que ritmo frenético y resistencia. Requieren una gran técnica en los atletas, que deben saltar las vallas o realizar el pase del testigo en cuestión de segundos. En todas las carreras de vallas, los corredores deben salvar los obstáculos sin saltar muy alto y volver a pisar la pista –donde se genera su velocidad– lo antes posible.

### Vallas

Los 100 metros vallas femeninos y los 110 metros vallas masculinos son algunas de las pruebas atléticas más técnicas. En ambas hay 10 vallas, que los corredores pueden derribar, aunque perdiendo cierta velocidad y arriesgándose a caer. Los 400 metros vallas también tienen 10 vallas espaciadas a lo largo del circuito, aunque algo más bajas que las vallas de 100 metros masculinos. La prueba agota la resistencia de los atletas, que tratan de mantener un ritmo de zancada regular (el número de zancadas que dan entre vallas) y una velocidad constante. Edwin Moses está considerado el mejor vallista de la era moderna: ganó dos medallas de oro en las olimpiadas y permaneció imbatido durante más de nueve años y 122 carreras.

◀ *El vallista toma impulso con la pierna posterior. La pierna delantera se lanza por encima de la valla, mientras que la otra pierna se eleva desde la rodilla con el pie girado hacia fuera para salvar el obstáculo. Una vez superada la valla, la pierna delantera toca la pista lo antes posible. La pierna posterior avanza hacia delante para dar la siguiente zancada.*

## Relevos

Las dos pruebas de relevos, la de 4 x 100 metros y la de 4 x 400 metros, gozan de gran popularidad entre el público. Ofrecen una serie de *sprints* con la emoción añadida del pase del testigo, cuando el receptor comienza a correr antes de recogerlo. En la carrera de 4 x 400 metros, la salida es escalonada y la primera vuelta se corre en las calles. Los relevistas esperan en su calle justo a la salida de la primera curva y, una vez pasado el testigo, se dirigen hacia la calle interior. En los siguientes tres pases, los ocho receptores luchan por conseguir una buena posición en el grupo. La vuelta final suele estar reservada al corredor más rápido del equipo de 400 metros lisos.

▲ *El británico Mark Hylton pasa el testigo a Du'aine Ladejo en una eliminatoria de relevos de 4 x 100 metros en los Juegos de Atlanta de 1996. Como los equipos de relevos son rotativos, ninguno de estos atletas formó parte del cuarteto que obtuvo la plata en la final por detrás de EE.UU.*

## En la zona

Las carreras de relevos, sobre todo la de 4 x 100 metros, con frecuencia se ganan y se pierden en la zona de entrega, un área de 20 metros de longitud señalado en la pista. El testigo debe estar únicamente en poder del receptor en el momento en que su mano abandona dicha zona. De no ser así, el equipo queda descalificado. El portador puede entregar el testigo hacia arriba o hacia abajo y debe procurar que el receptor pueda agarrarlo cómodamente. La caída del testigo no supone la descalificación oficial, pero en la práctica significa el final de la carrera, ya que se pierden unos segundos vitales.

◀ *Gail Devers, de EE.UU., compite en 100 metros vallas en Sydney. Tras superar una grave enfernedad, Devers logró ser tricampeona mundial de 100 metros vallas y ganar de dos oros olímpicos en 100 metros lisos. Un tirón muscular en la semifinal de vallas la obligó a abandonar los Juegos de Sydney, pero todavía está a tiempo de ganar una medalla olímpica en su prueba favorita.*

▼ *Los atletas superan la ría en la tercera eliminatoria de la carrera de obstáculos de los Juegos de 2000. De esta eliminatoria salieron los eventuales ganadores del oro, Reuben Kosgei, de Kenia (derecha), y el bronce, Ali Ezzine, de Marruecos (centro).*

## Carrera de obstáculos

Una de las pocas pruebas atléticas exclusivamente masculinas, los 3.000 metros obstáculos, combina el ritmo y la resistencia del medio fondo con la dificultad de saltar 28 vallas y siete rías. Estos obstáculos aportan gran emoción, ya que los atletas se tambalean y a veces se caen. Los corredores emplean la técnica de los 400 metros vallas para superar las barreras y muchos utilizan la parte superior de las rías como trampolín para salvar la mayor distancia posible de los 3,66 metros de agua. En épocas recientes la prueba ha estado dominada por Kenia, que ha obtenido el oro en todas las olimpiadas desde 1984.

# SALTO DE LONGITUD Y TRIPLE

Tanto el salto de longitud como el triple salto consisten en una carrera rápida y rítmica, seguida de una batida, o despegue, y una serie de movimientos en el aire antes de aterrizar. Los saltadores olímpicos de élite a veces compiten también en 100 metros lisos, ya que el ritmo y la aceleración extrema son parecidos. Los saltadores de triple salto también necesitan velocidad, unida a un gran control y a un ritmo pausado con el fin de dar tres saltos lo bastante largos para merecer una medalla olímpica.

▲ *Los saltadores de longitud corren hacia la tabla de batida antes de tomar impulso con el pie. Las piernas y los brazos van por delante del cuerpo, y en el aterrizaje proyectan los pies y piernas hacia delante para caer en el foso lo más lejos posible.*

### Carrera, vuelo y caída

Los saltadores de longitud olímpicos disponen de tres saltos clasificatorios. Los ocho mejores atletas disponen de otros tres saltos en la final. Antes de saltar, los competidores calculan un punto de salida al comienzo de la pista de 45 metros de longitud. Desde ahí, el saltador acelera hasta adoptar una posición erguida en el punto de velocidad máxima. Al despegar en la tabla de batida, el saltador trata de avanzar en el aire lo más posible antes de aterrizar. Los jueces miden los saltos tanto electrónicamente como en persona. La distancia se calcula desde el borde frontal de la tabla de batida hasta la huella más cercana dejada en la arena. Por este motivo, los saltadores procuran no sentarse al aterrizar ni dejar marcas en la arena por detrás de sus pies.

▲ *Carl Lewis recoge arena del foso tras ganar el salto de longitud en los Juegos de Atlanta de 1996. Lewis entró en el equipo de EE.UU. por los pelos y no logró clasificarse para la final hasta su último salto. Pero el campeón reservó su mejor talento para la final, donde batió el récord mundial de Mike Powell.*

### Distancias mejoradas

La mejora en la preparación de los atletas ha supuesto un aumento de la distancia que son capaces de saltar. La barrera de ocho metros –en otro tiempo considerada imposible de batir– es ahora superada por la mayoría de atletas masculinos. Los nueve mejores competidores de la final de salto de longitud masculino de los Juegos de Sydney, por ejemplo, saltaron más de ocho metros. Mike Powell, de EE.UU., tiene el récord mundial con un salto de 8,95 metros logrado en 1991. El actual récord mundial femenino fue establecido en 1988 cuando la soviética Galina Chistyakova saltó 7,52 metros. La alemana Heike Drechsler se convirtió en la campeona olímpica de salto de longitud de más edad cuando obtuvo su cuarto oro consecutivo en las Olimpiadas de 1996 con un salto de 8,50 metros.

► *La saltadora de longitud nigeriana Chioma Ajunwa saluda desde lo alto del podio en las Olimpiadas de 1996. Su triunfo fue una sorpresa, ya que hasta entonces sólo había participado en tres competiciones. Su salto de 7,12 m superó en 10 cm al de la italiana Fiona May.*

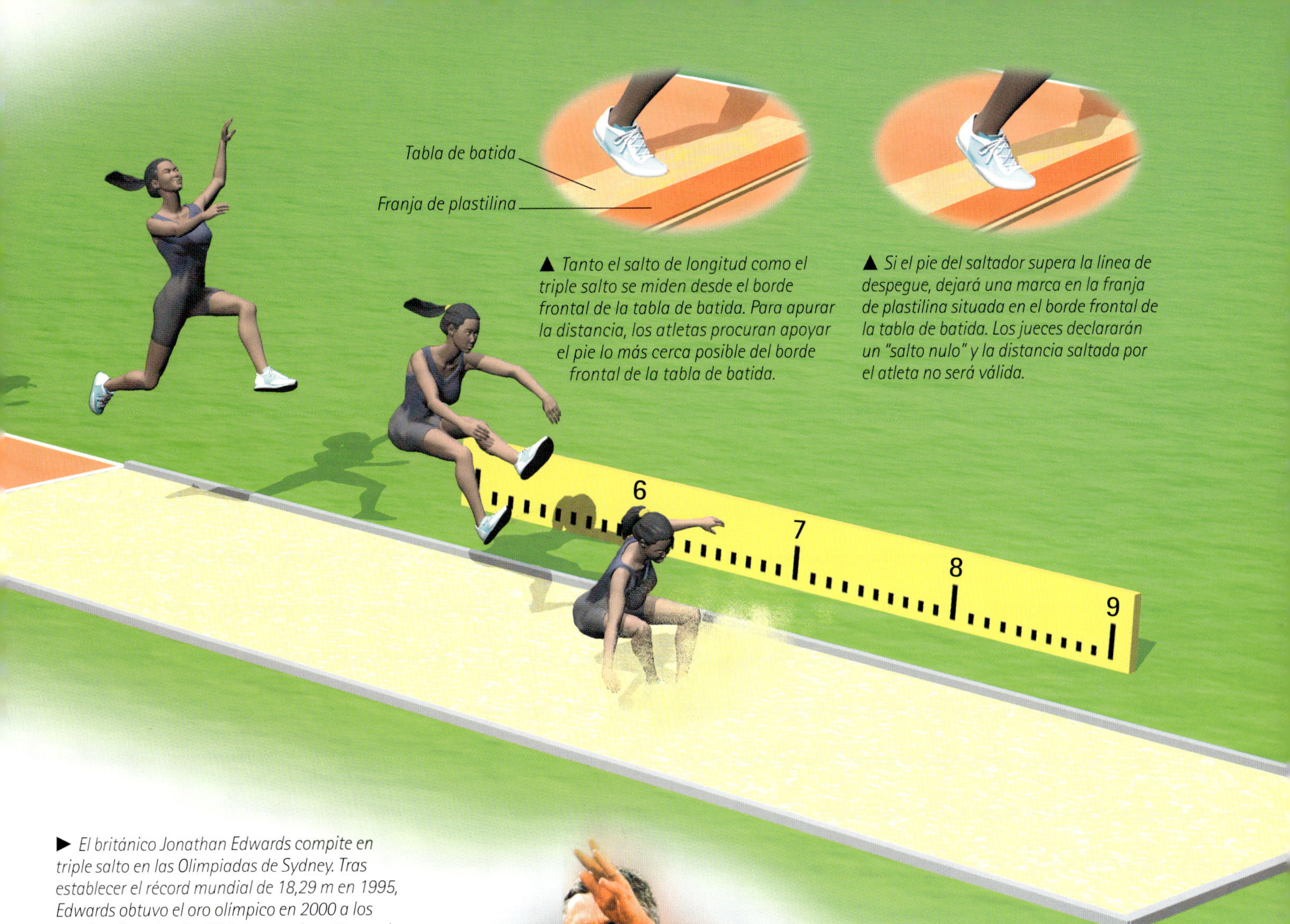


▲ *Tanto el salto de longitud como el triple salto se miden desde el borde frontal de la tabla de batida. Para apurar la distancia, los atletas procuran apoyar el pie lo más cerca posible del borde frontal de la tabla de batida.*

▲ *Si el pie del saltador supera la línea de despegue, dejará una marca en la franja de plastilina situada en el borde frontal de la tabla de batida. Los jueces declararán un "salto nulo" y la distancia saltada por el atleta no será válida.*

► *El británico Jonathan Edwards compite en triple salto en las Olimpiadas de Sydney. Tras establecer el récord mundial de 18,29 m en 1995, Edwards obtuvo el oro olímpico en 2000 a los 34 años. Su salto de 17,71 m superó en 24 cm al del medallista de plata, el cubano Yoel García.*

**Triple salto**

Aunque el triple salto femenino no hizo su debut olímpico hasta el 2000, la competición masculina ha estado presente en todos los juegos modernos. De hecho, fue la primera prueba de las Olimpiadas de 1896, lo que convirtió a su vencedor, James Connolly, en el primer medallista de oro de la era moderna. La prueba exige una gran técnica y disciplina. Los atletas deben aprovechar al máximo la velocidad de la carrera con una serie de movimientos ejecutados de manera continua. Connolly ganó los Juegos de 1896 con un salto de 13,71 centímetros. En la actualidad, los saltadores de triple salto suelen superan los 17 metros, mientras que el récord mundial femenino, establecido por la atleta ucraniana Inessa Kravets, está en 15,50 metros.

**Anatomía del triple salto**

El saltador debe adquirir bastante velocidad en la carrera antes de despegar en la primera fase del salto. La rodilla de la pierna delantera se lanza hacia arriba, pero sobre todo hacia delante, mientras que la otra pierna queda por detrás. Al acabar esta primera fase, el saltador extiende la pierna delantera para aterrizar con toda la planta del pie. A continuación, ejecuta una especie de salto "a la pata coja" para impulsarse de nuevo y dar una zancada lo más larga posible. La pierna delantera se mantiene flexionada de manera que el muslo va en paralelo al suelo. Cuando el pie toca el suelo, comienza la fase del salto. El atleta despega, proyecta ambos brazos hacia delante y eleva los pies por delante del cuerpo antes de realizar un aterrizaje similar al del salto de longitud.

# SALTO DE ALTURA Y PÉRTIGA

Dos de las pruebas atléticas más espectaculares, el salto de altura y el salto con pértiga, han formado parte de la competición olímpica masculina desde hace mucho tiempo, mientras que el salto de altura femenino apareció en los juegos en 1928 y la pértiga femenina debutó en 2000. Para triunfar en estas disciplinas se precisa fuerza, velocidad, agilidad y coordinación. Los atletas deben cronometrar perfectamente su carrera y luego concentrar toda su energía y técnica en el salto y el paso del listón.

▲ *La saltadora de altura rusa Yelena Yelesina supera el listón en las Olimpiadas de 2000 en Sydney. La veterana atleta, que fue campeona europea de salto de altura en 1989, superó 2,01 metros para hacerse con el oro a los 30 años.*

**El salto de altura**

La pista de salto de altura consta de un pasillo de arena y un listón apoyado en dos soportes encajados en los saltómetros situados aproximadamente a cuatro metros de distancia (consulta el diagrama). La altura del listón va aumentando, primero en tramos de cinco centímetros y después en unidades más pequeñas. En cada altura, los saltadores disponen de 90 segundos para realizar cada uno de los tres intentos por superar el listón. Los participantes pueden tocar el listón y hacer que se tambalee, pero no deben derribarlo. Los atletas que lo derriban tres veces seguidas, quedan eliminados. El ganador es el atleta que realiza el salto a mayor altura, y si dos o más saltadores logran la misma altura, el saltador que menos veces ha derribado el listón.

▲ *El cuerpo del saltador rota mientras supera el listón con la cabeza por delante. El saltador arquea la espalda para superar el centro del listón.*

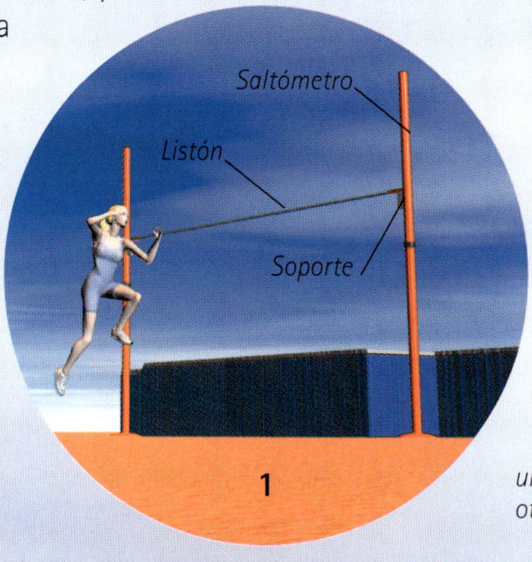


◀ *Tras una carrera ligera en curva, el saltador apoya un pie en el suelo. Impulsa los brazos y la rodilla de la otra pierna hacia arriba mientras da un gran salto.*

**País:** *Rumanía*
**Olimpiadas:** *Melbourne 1956, Roma 1960, Tokio 1964*
**Prueba:** *Salto de altura*
**Medallas:** *dos de oro*

**Campeones de salto de altura**

El salto de altura ha dado muchos campeones y campeonas famosos. Una de las mejores fue la doble medallista de oro olímpica Iolanda Balas, que batió el récord mundial femenino en 14 ocasiones y se mantuvo imbatida en más de 140 competiciones consecutivas entre 1957 y 1967. La saltadora de Alemania Occidental Ulrike Meyfarth, ganadora de dos competiciones olímpicas de salto de altura con 12 años de diferencia (1972 y 1984), fue la primera saltadora que superó dos metros en una competición olímpica. En los Juegos de 1968 de México, el norteamericano Dick Fosbury revolucionó el salto de altura con una nueva técnica que se denominó el salto Fosbury (consulta la página 40). Todos los saltadores de élite de la actualidad emplean este método.

▼ *El saltador levanta las caderas por efecto del impulso generado en el salto. El atleta mira por encima del hombro hacia el extremo de la colchoneta y trata de mantenerse relajado.*

▲ *Cuando las caderas del saltador han superado el listón, levanta un poco las piernas. El saltador aterriza de espaldas en la colchoneta situada en el foso de caída.*

## El salto con pértiga

El salto con pértiga es una prueba atlética en la que los participantes utilizan un palo largo y flexible para saltar alturas de más de 5,50 metros (hombres) y 4,50 metros (mujeres). Un pertiguista campeón necesita las habilidades de un esprínter, un gimnasta y un acróbata. El ejercicio comienza con el pertiguista corriendo por la pista para adquirir velocidad mientras sujeta la pértiga en paralelo al suelo. Se precisa una coordinación milimétrica para picar la pértiga, de unos cinco metros de longitud, en el cajetín de 20 centímetros situado entre los dos saltómetros. La pértiga se dobla bajo el peso del cuerpo del atleta en el impulso y, gracias a una buena postura, se desdobla e impulsa al saltador hacia el listón, que debe ser superado sin derribarlo. El ucraniano Sergei Bubka es el mejor pertiguista de la era moderna: en 1988 se convirtió en el primer hombre que superó los seis metros en competición.

▼ *El atleta surafricano Okkert Brits demuestra lo mucho que se dobla la pértiga durante la fase de picado e impulso del salto con pértiga. Brits, que agarra la pértiga por el extremo, está a punto de impulsarse hacia arriba e invertir el cuerpo hasta quedar boca abajo.*

◀ *La pertiguista danesa Marie Bagger compite en la final femenina de los Juegos de Sydney. Mientras la pértiga se desdobla, Bagger permanece en vertical boca abajo, con las piernas extendidas. Después, rota hasta quedar de cara al listón, se impulsa sobre la pértiga y eleva los brazos para pasar el listón.*

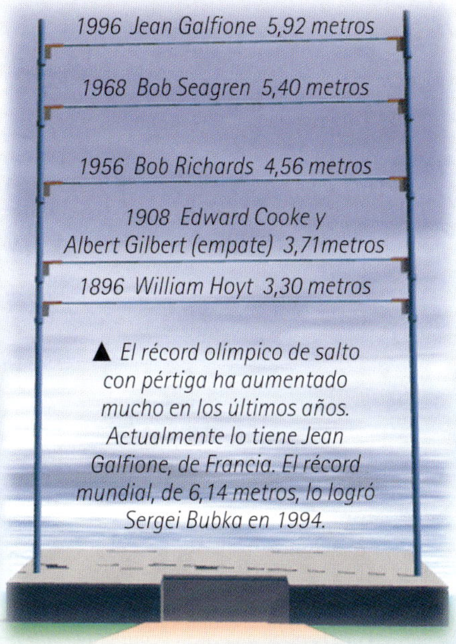


▲ *El récord olímpico de salto con pértiga ha aumentado mucho en los últimos años. Actualmente lo tiene Jean Galfione, de Francia. El récord mundial, de 6,14 metros, lo logró Sergei Bubka en 1994.*

# MARTILLO Y PESO

El lanzamiento de martillo y peso, dos de las pruebas atléticas más duras, exigen una inmensa fuerza. Los lanzadores de martillo y peso pasan mucho tiempo en el gimnasio desarrollando los músculos y el físico adecuados. Sin embargo, ambas pruebas requieren disciplina técnica y gran concentración para lograr el movimiento corporal y el ritmo necesarios para alcanzar distancias olímpicas.

◄ *El lanzador finlandés Olli-Pekka Karjalainen mantiene el ritmo mientras gira en el círculo y se detiene para completar el lanzamiento.*

**El lanzamiento de martillo**

El lanzamiento de martillo masculino apareció por primera vez en las Olimpiadas de 1900, pero tendría que pasar un siglo antes de que la prueba femenina hiciera su debut en Sydney. El martillo es una bola metálica que va unida a una empuñadura por medio de un cable de 1,2 metros. El martillo masculino pesa 7,26 kg, y el femenino, 4 kg. Se lanza desde un círculo de 2,1 metros de diámetro cuyo fondo y laterales están protegidos por una valla denominada jaula.

◄ *Polonia logró un doblete en martillo masculino y femenino en Sydney con el oro de Kamila Skolimowska (izquierda) y Szymon Ziolkowski. Skolimowska estableció un nuevo récord olímpico con un lanzamiento de 71,16 m.*

◄ *Agarrando la empuñadura con ambas manos, el lanzador comienza a girar el martillo por encima de su cabeza en la parte posterior del círculo (1). El lanzador rota sobre sí mismo tres o cuatro veces mientras continúa girando el martillo (2). Lanza el martillo de manera que vuela hacia delante y hacia arriba en un ángulo ideal de unos 45º, alcanzando una velocidad de hasta 110 km/h (3).*

## Mismo peso, distancias distintas

Tanto en el lanzamiento de peso como en el de martillo, los atletas disponen de tres lanzamientos preliminares, en los que los ocho mejores logran otros tres intentos. El martillo pesa igual que el peso, pero al estar unido a un cable puede ser lanzado a mayor distancia. El récord mundial de lanzamiento de peso masculino está en 23,12 m y fue logrado por el americano Randy Barnes en 1990. El récord mundial de lanzamiento de martillo masculino de 86,74 m, conseguido en 1986 por el soviético Yuri Sedykh, es uno de los hitos atléticos que se han mantenido durante más tiempo. Es importante soltar el martillo en el punto exacto. Hasta 1958, el arco de lanzamiento era un ángulo de 90°. La reducción del ángulo hasta 40° en 1970 obligó a una mayor precisión en el lanzamiento.

▶ *El finlandés Arsi Harju se alza con el triunfo tras lanzar su peso a 21,29 m en la segunda ronda de la competición masculina de las Olimpiadas de Sydney y obtener la medalla de oro. Fue la primera medalla de Finlandia en los juegos del 2000.*

▶ *La norteamericana Connie Price-Smith calcula el lanzamiento y corrige su postura antes de tomar impulso y lanzar el peso. Price-Smith compitió en cuatro olimpiadas consecutivas entre 1988 y 2000.*

## El lanzamiento de peso

Desde un círculo de 2,1 m de diámetro y con un tablón de frenado de 10 cm ante sí, el atleta debe lanzar el peso con un solo brazo de forma que caiga dentro de la superficie del arco de lanzamiento de 40°. El peso suele ser una bola metálica maciza de cobre o bronce que pesa 7,26 kg para los hombres y 4 kg para las mujeres. El peso se sujeta en la base de los dedos y se apoya en el cuello mientras se toma impulso antes de lanzarlo extendiendo el brazo.

## Generar velocidad y potencia

Los lanzadores de peso emplean dos técnicas para generar velocidad y potencia en el círculo. El método de rotación, también llamado técnica Baryshnikov, consiste en dar un giro parecido al de los lanzadores de disco (consulta las págs. 36-37), apoyándose en la pierna contraria al brazo con el que se lanza. El lanzamiento lineal se llama técnica O'Brien en honor al doble medallista de oro americano Parry O'Brien. Cuando este comenzó a utilizar esta técnica en 1952, se convirtió en el primer hombre que alcanzó la barrera de los 18 m y, más tarde, el primero en superar los 19 m. Al empezar de espaldas al arco y luego dar un giro de 180°, mejoró 16 veces el récord mundial.

▲ *En las olimpiadas de Sydney, la bielorrusa Yanina Karolchik se reservó el mejor lanzamiento de su vida para la última ronda. Karolchik lanzó a 20,56 m y ganó el oro por delante de Larisa Peleshenko y Astrid Kumbernuss.*

# DISCO Y JABALINA

▲ *El norteamericano Al Oerter consiguió cuatro medallas de oro consecutivas en disco. Su última victoria, en la fotografía, fue en los Juegos de 1968 en México.*

De estas dos pruebas de las antiguas olimpiadas, el disco ha aparecido en todas las olimpiadas modernas, y la jabalina, en todas desde 1908. Las dos exigen potencia, velocidad y coordinación, pero son también deportes muy técnicos en los que el ángulo de lanzamiento es decisivo. Los competidores disponen de tres intentos para clasificarse, y los ocho que han lanzado más lejos disponen de otros tres intentos en la final.

## Moviéndose en círculos

La competición de disco tiene lugar en un círculo de lanzamiento de 2,5 m de diámetro protegido por una jaula. Al igual que en el lanzamiento de peso, los lanzadores deben entrar y salir del círculo desde atrás y el disco debe tocar el suelo completamente dentro del arco de 40°. Los lanzadores de disco comienzan balanceando el disco hacia atrás y hacia delante antes de dar giro y medio para situarse al otro lado del círculo. Con cada giro, el disco adquiere más velocidad: cuanto mayor sea la velocidad de lanzamiento, mayor distancia recorrerá el disco.

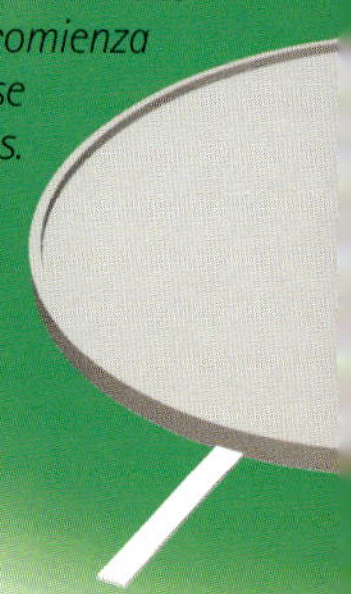

► *El atleta apoya en el suelo la pierna contraria al brazo con que lanza para tener un punto fijo sobre el que moverse. El brazo lanzador comienza a arquearse hacia atrás.*

◄ *La atleta alemana Ilke Wyludda ganó la prueba de disco femenina con un lanzamiento de 69,66 m. Compartió podio con la rusa Natalya Sadova, que obtuvo la plata, y la bielorrusa Ellina Zvereva, que más tarde ganaría el oro en los Juegos de 2000.*

◄ *El lanzador gira, atravesando el círculo con las piernas flexionadas y el tronco y la cabeza erguidos. Un lanzador diestro gira sobre el pie derecho y apoya el izquierdo cerca de la parte delantera del círculo.*

▼ *El atleta toma impulso moviendo varias veces hacia delante y hacia atrás el brazo con el que sujeta el disco.*

## El ángulo de ataque

El disco pesa dos kilos en la competición masculina y un kilo en la femenina. El disco genera empuje mientras vuela por el aire, siempre y cuando se lance con el ángulo correcto: entre 34° y 37°. Coordinar la postura correcta de cuerpo, brazo y mano para lograr este ángulo al tiempo que se genera impulso es realmente complicado y exige que el atleta perfeccione la técnica con cientos de lanzamientos en los entrenamientos. La marca de clasificación en las Olimpiadas de 2004 está fijada en 64,60 para hombres y 63,40 para mujeres.

▶ *Con los hombros hacia delante, el atleta lanza el disco desde la parte delantera de su mano, presionando en el borde con los dedos para que gire en el ángulo correcto.*

## La técnica del lanzamiento de jabalina

Los lanzadores de jabalina comienzan al final de un recorrido de unos 30 metros. Efectúan entre 10 y 12 zancadas para adquirir velocidad, sujetando la jabalina en paralelo al suelo justo por encima del hombro. El siguiente paso es transmitir la mayor velocidad posible a la jabalina: para ello, echan el brazo de la jabalina hacia atrás y se detienen súbitamente. La jabalina sale despedida con un movimiento potente y controlado. Lanzada correctamente –en dirección ascendente con un ángulo de 40°–, la jabalina adquiere una velocidad de 100 km/h.

◀ *El atleta de la República Checa Jan Zelezny dominó la competición de jabalina durante la década de 1990. Hijo de padres lanzadores de jabalina, Zelezny ganó la plata en 1998 y tres oros consecutivos en 1992, 1996 y 2000.*

## La jabalina

Los antiguos olímpicos utilizaban una tira de cuero para lanzar una jabalina de rama de olivo a gran distancia. Los lanzadores modernos emplean velocidad, potencia y una coordinación perfecta en las pruebas de lanzamiento más espectaculares. La jabalina debe lanzarse por encima del hombro, y los jueces señalan el punto donde toca el suelo. Aunque no es necesario que quede clavada, debe aterrizar de punta. Las técnicas de jabalina mejoraron en el siglo XX hasta el punto de que en 1984 el alemán oriental Uwe Hohnl la lanzó a una distancia de 104,8 metros. En 1986 se modificó el centro de gravedad y la empuñadura de la jabalina. Aun así, los hombres pueden superar los 85-90 metros en condiciones óptimas. Jan Zelezny ganó los Juegos del 2000 con un lanzamiento de 90,17 metros.

*La jabalina mide entre 2,6 y 2,7 m de longitud y pesa 600 gramos.*

▼ *Los lanzadores de jabalina adquieren velocidad en la carrera. Luego apoyan los dos pies en el suelo y lanzan la jabalina con un movimiento rápido de cuerpo y brazo. Tras soltarla, la pierna derecha del lanzador se adelanta, se apoya en el suelo y actúa como freno para impedir que el atleta supere el tablón de frenado.*

# MULTIPRUEBAS

▲ *El norteamericano Bob Mathias resultó imbatido en todos los decatlones en que participó, entre ellos dos competiciones olímpicas. En los Juegos de 1952, obtuvo 912 puntos: la mayor puntuación en la historia del decatlón olímpico.*

Cuatro pruebas atléticas de las olimpiadas de verano exigen destreza en más de una disciplina. Estos deportes multipruebas están considerados por muchos participantes y espectadores los mayores desafíos de los juegos. Cada multiprueba requiere que los atletas dominen diversas técnicas y empleen toda su resistencia y fuerza mental.

### Heptatlón

Desde 1964 hasta 1980, las mujeres compitieron en pentatlón olímpico, que constaba de cinco pruebas: salto de longitud, lanzamiento de peso, salto de altura, 80 metros vallas y 200 metros lisos. En 1984 fue sustituido por el heptatlón, de siete pruebas, que se celebra a lo largo de dos días consecutivos. Los tiempos de los atletas en las pruebas de pista y su mejor lanzamiento o salto se transforman en puntos. Gana el atleta que obtiene más puntos. El heptatlón es para muchos el último desafío del atletismo femenino, y al menos así lo fue para la leyenda estadounidense Jackie Joyner-Kersee. Una serie de actuaciones sorprendentes durante la década de 1980 y principios de los años 90 culminó en dos medallas de oro olímpicas. Sus 7.291 puntos de los Juegos de Seúl, en 1988, continúan siendo un récord mundial y olímpico.

**País:** *EE.UU.*
**Olimpiadas:** *Los Ángeles 1984, Seúl 1988, Barcelona 1992, Atlanta 1996*
**Pruebas:** *heptatlón, salto de longitud*
**Medallas:** *tres de oro, una de plata, dos de bronce*

◀ *El decatleta británico Daley Thompson se convirtió en el segundo deportista olímpico que ganó medallas de oro consecutivas en decatlón en Moscú 1980 y en Los Ángeles 1984.*

### Decatlón

El decatlón masculino es una de las pruebas más populares del programa olímpico de atletismo. La emoción aumenta a medida que los atletas compiten por la medalla de oro durante dos días en 10 disciplinas. Al igual que en el heptatlón, los logros se transforman en puntos. Los atletas ejecutan cinco pruebas cada día y la competición alcanza el clímax con la prueba final, los 1.500 metros lisos. Tanto el decatlón como el heptatlón resultan extenuantes para el cuerpo y la mente del atleta. Un día típico puede durar hasta 10 horas y los competidores deben permanecer concentrados en todo momento. Deben dejar de lado las lesiones fastidiosas o los malos resultados en pruebas anteriores si pretenden recuperarse y ganar una medalla.

► *La triatleta suiza Brigitte McMahon compite en las tres disciplinas del triatlón femenino en los Juegos de 2000: natación en el puerto de Sydney, ciclismo y, por último, la carrera por las calles de la ciudad. En una final emocionante, McMahon dejó atrás a la triatleta local Michellie Jones en los últimos 100 metros y ganó el oro con un tiempo de dos horas y 40 segundos.*

▼ *La heptatleta británica Denise Lewis supera el listón del salto de altura en el heptatlón de las Olimpiadas de Sydney. Lewis logró completar los dos días de pruebas a pesar de sufrir varias lesiones y obtuvo el oro por delante de la rusa Yelena Prokhorova.*

## Triatlón

El triatlón es uno de los deportes olímpicos más nuevos: la primera competición de triatlón tuvo lugar en 1974. La multiprueba hizo su debut olímpico en Sydney y comprende varios deportes en los que hombres y mujeres compiten a la vez. A nivel olímpico, el triatlón comienza con 1,5 kilómetros a nado, seguidos de 40 kilómetros en bicicleta y una agotadora carrera de 10 kilómetros. El cronómetro no se detiene de principio a fin y resulta esencial perder el menor tiempo posible en la transición de una a otra disciplina. Los atletas se entrenan en natación, ciclismo y carrera, ya que cualquier mejora en su técnica, multiplicada por las grandes distancias que deben recorrer, puede marcar la diferencia en los puestos finales de esta prueba.

◄ *Stephanie Cook, de Gran Bretaña, compite en la disciplina de hípica del pentatlón femenino moderno, que hizo su debut olímpico en el año 2000. Cook se convirtió en la primera medallista de oro de esta multiprueba.*

## Pentatlón moderno

Introducido en los Juegos de 1912, el pentatlón moderno combina cinco disciplinas distintas. El tiro, la natación y la hípica son pruebas cronometradas. En la prueba de esgrima, los atletas se enfrentan en duelo uno a uno. Los resultados de estas cuatro pruebas se transforman en puntos que deciden el orden de salida en la prueba final, los 3.000 metros *cross-country*. Sale primero el atleta que ha logrado más puntos y luego le siguen los demás atletas por orden de puntos obtenidos. Una vez en marcha, la prueba de *cross-country* es una carrera abierta en la que resultará campeón olímpico el primer pentatleta que cruce la línea de llegada.

**Heptatlón:** 100 m vallas, salto de altura, peso, 200 m lisos, salto de longitud, jabalina, 800 m lisos

**Decatlón:** 100 m lisos, salto de longitud, peso, salto de altura, 400 m lisos, 110 m vallas, disco, pértiga, jabalina, 1.500 m lisos

**Triatlón:** natación, ciclismo, carrera

**Pentatlón moderno:** Tiro, esgrima, natación, hípica, *cross-country*

▲ *Uno de los carteles oficiales mostraba un motivo inspirado en los aztecas, señores de un gran imperio en el valle de México en los siglos XV y principios del XVI.*

# MÉXICO 1968

Cuando México fue declarada sede olímpica para los Juegos de 1968 surgió una preocupación. A una altura de 2.200 metros, el aire contiene un 30% menos de oxígeno que a nivel del mar. Los competidores de pruebas de resistencia sufrieron y los tiempos fueron lentos. En cambio, prosperaron las pruebas de distancias cortas y otras disciplinas de potencia, y se establecieron 34 récords mundiales y 38 olímpicos.

◀ *La vallista mexicana Enriqueta Basilio de Sotelo porta la antorcha olímpica en la ceremonia de apertura de los Juegos de 1968. Fue la primera mujer que encendió la llama olímpica.*

## Tiempos difíciles

Las Olimpiadas de México tuvieron lugar durante una época de gran malestar en diversas partes del mundo. Se prohibió la participación de Suráfrica por motivo de su política de *apartheid*, las tensiones raciales crecían en EE.UU. y los tanques soviéticos habían invadido Checoslovaquia meses antes de la ceremonia de apertura. La gimnasta checa Vera Caslavska, crítica respecto a la invasión soviética, se había mantenido oculta antes de los Juegos, pero emergió triunfante para dominar la gimnasia femenina ganando dos oros y dos platas.

▶ *El atleta norteamericano Dick Fosbury deleitó al público en México con un innovador estilo en la prueba de salto de altura. El llamado "salto Fosbury" le valió la medalla de oro olímpica.*

▶ *Los esprinters Tommie Smith y John Carlos ganaron el oro y el bronce en los 200 metros lisos. En el podio alzaron sus puños con un guante negro como protesta contra el racismo en EE.UU. Ambos hombres fueron expulsados de la villa olímpica. El medallista de plata australiano Peter Nelson portaba una insignia en solidaridad.*

## Mucho de que hablar

Los atletas norteamericanos dieron que hablar en los Juegos de México. Dick Fosbury ganó el salto de longitud con una técnica nueva y Wyomia Tyus se convirtió en la primera mujer que obtenía medallas de oro consecutivas en 100 metros lisos. El programa atlético masculino estuvo dominado por Europa del Este y la Unión Soviética, pero fue el norteamericano Al Oerter quien acaparó todos los titulares con una cuarta medalla de oro en disco (pág. 36). Tommie Smith batió el récord mundial al ganar los 200 metros lisos, pero es más recordado por su saludo de "poder negro" junto a su compañero de equipo, John Carlos.

▶ *Bob Beamon accedió a la final de salto de longitud con su último salto de las eliminatorias. Pero su primer salto en la final, una sorprendente marca de 8,90 metros, batió el entonces récord mundial y lo superó en 55 centímetros. El récord de Beamon se mantuvo durante 23 años y nunca se ha superado en las Olimpiadas.*

▲ *El equipo ciclista de persecución por equipos de Alemania Occidental batió el récord mundial durante la eliminatoria, ganó la final, pero sería descalificado cuando los rivales de Alemania del Este informaron de ciertos asuntos ilegales. Los alemanes occidentales finalmente recibieron la medalla de plata una vez acabados los juegos.*

## Márgenes ganadores

El norteamericano Bob Beamon ganó el salto de longitud con 71 centímetros, pero este no fue el único gran margen ganador en México. Los atletas africanos destacaron en las carreras de fondo y medio fondo. Los corredores keniatas ganaron los 1.500 metros lisos, los 3.000 metros obstáculos y los 10.000 metros lisos. El segundo puesto de los 10.000 metros lisos fue para el etíope Mamo Wolde, que también ganó el maratón en dos horas y 20 minutos, más de tres minutos por delante del medallista de plata, el japonés Kenji Kimihara. En los 50 kilómetros marcha, el alemán oriental Christoph Höhne venció con un margen de 10 minutos.

▶ *En la final de los 400 metros vallas, David Hemery obtuvo el oro y estableció el récord mundial en 48,12 segundos. Fue la única medalla de oro de Gran Bretaña en los Juegos de 1968.*

▶ *Vera Caslavska ejecuta un ejercicio en la barra de equilibrio. Caslavska ganó su primera medalla olímpica, una plata, en 1960. Los tres oros y la plata de los Juegos de 1964 y las seis medallas obtenidas en México la convierten en una de las atletas con más medallas de la historia de las olimpiadas.*

| MEDALLERO | O | P | B |
|---|---|---|---|
| EE.UU. | 45 | 28 | 34 |
| Unión Soviética | 29 | 32 | 30 |
| Japón | 11 | 7 | 7 |
| Hungría | 10 | 10 | 12 |
| Alem. Este | 9 | 9 | 7 |
| Francia | 7 | 3 | 5 |
| Checoslovaquia | 7 | 2 | 4 |
| Alem. Oeste | 5 | 11 | 10 |
| Australia | 5 | 7 | 5 |
| Gran Bretaña | 5 | 5 | 3 |

## Juegos innovadores

México ofreció un gran número de innovaciones técnicas, como el uso del cronómetro electrónico en muchas pruebas. Las mujeres tuvieron que someterse a pruebas médicas para determinar su sexo y también se introdujeron pruebas toxicológicas. La preocupación por el aumento de las drogas en los deportes olímpicos y la muerte del ciclista Knut Jenseen en las Olimpiadas de Roma de 1960 (pág. 19) empujó al COI a formar una comisión médica y a publicar listas de sustancias prohibidas. El pentatleta sueco Hans-Gunnar Lijenwall fue el pimer deportista olímpico descalificado por consumo de drogas, tras dar positivo en un control de alcohol.

▲ *Aleksandr Popov es el nadador con más triunfos de Rusia. Dominó las pruebas de estilos durante la década de 1990, ganando cuatro medallas olímpicas de oro y cinco de plata.*

# NATACIÓN

En 1896, tres marineros se zambulleron en las gélidas aguas de la bahía de Zea, en la costa griega, para nadar aproximadamente 100 metros hasta la orilla. Desde estos humildes comienzos, la natación olímpica ha prosperado hasta convertirse en una de las grandes atracciones de los juegos. Las pruebas celebradas en el pabellón acuático ofrecen siempre un llenazo, ya que los espectadores adoran el glamour y la emoción que genera la natación olímpica.

**En la piscina**

Las primeras pruebas de natación olímpica tenían lugar en ríos y lagos, además de en el mar. Los Juegos de 1908 contaron con una gigantesca piscina de 100 metros, pero las piscinas olímpicas modernas tienen una longtiud estipulada de 50 metros y una anchura suficiente para ocho calles separadas por corcheras. Las carreras recorren varias distancias: desde los rapidísimos 50 metros hasta los 800 metros femeninos y 1.500 masculinos. Las carreras de 50 y 100 metros son pruebas de velocidad y exigen un ritmo frenético de principio a fin. En las carreras de larga distancia, el nadador debe elegir una estrategia: nadar toda la carrera al mismo ritmo o reservar energía para nadar una segunda mitad más rápida.

► *La nadadora holandesa Inge de Bruijn saluda al público tras finalizar una eliminatoria para los 100 metros mariposa femeninos en Sydney, una de las tres pruebas que ganó.*

▲ *El australiano Scott Miller demuestra una excelente técnica de salida durante una eliminatoria para los 200 metros mariposa en los Juegos de 1996.*

**Estilos diferentes**

La competición olímpica contempla cuatro estilos de natación: braza, espalda, mariposa y libre. Técnicamente, el estilo libre significa cualquier estilo que elija el nadador, pero en la práctica significa crol, el más rápido. El crol, la mariposa y la braza comienzan con una salida de cabeza desde la plataforma de salida, tras la cual los nadadores tienen que ascender 15 metros bajo el agua antes de salir a flote. En cualquier prueba de natación, una salida nula implica la descalificación del nadador. En la braza, la cabeza del nadador debe abrir la superficie del agua en cada brazada. Al finalizar un largo, los nadadores de espalda y crol pueden tocar la pared con cualquier parte del cuerpo, y la mayoría da una voltereta en el agua y se impulsa con los pies. Los nadadores de braza y mariposa deben tocar la pared de la piscina con ambas manos antes de virar para realizar el próximo largo.

## Relevos y pruebas de estilos

En las carreras de relevos, los equipos constan de cuatro nadadores que nadan a crol 100 metros en el caso de los relevos de 400 metros o 200 metros en el caso de los 800 metros. Los nadadores no deben abandonar la plataforma de salida más de 0,03 segundos antes de que su compañero toque la banda magnética de la pared; de lo contrario, quedan descalificados. Las pruebas de estilos combinan los cuatro estilos. En los 200 metros estilos individual, los nadadores nadan 50 metros con cada estilo: mariposa, espalda, braza y crol. El orden es el mismo para los 400 metros estilos individual, aunque aquí las postas son de 100 metros. En los relevos de estilos cada nadador ejecuta un estilo en este orden: espalda, braza, mariposa y crol.

*▲ La leyenda de la natación Mark Spitz avanza en el agua rumbo al triunfo en los 200 metros mariposa masculinos en las Olimpiadas de 1972. Esta victoria fue una de las siete logradas por el norteamericano en los juegos: el mayor medallero individual de oro en cualquier deporte en una sola olimpiada.*

## Grandes campeones

La natación ofrece una gran variedad de pruebas y los campeones con frecuencia acaban las olimpiadas con más de una medalla. Aunque cada estilo requiere una técnica completamente distinta, muchos grandes nadadores se han especializado en varios (normalmente mariposa y crol) para ganar el oro olímpico en distintas pruebas. El australiano Ian Thorpe y el holandés Inge de Bruijn lograron esta hazaña en los Juegos de Sydney. Otros grandes campeones han demostrado una longevidad sorprendente para ganar medallas en tres o más olimpiadas. La australiana Dawn Fraser fue la primera mujer que defendió un título olímpico de natación cuando ganó los 100 metros libres en los Juegos de 1960 en Roma. En 1964 ganaría la misma prueba por tercera vez.

**Nacionalidad:** *Australia*
**Olimpiadas:** *Melbourne 1956, Roma 1960, Tokio 1964*
**Pruebas:** *100 m y 400 m estilos, 4 x 100 m relevos de estilo libre, 4 x 100 m relevos de estilos*
**Medallas:** *cuatro de oro, cuatro de plata*

*▲ El australiano Ian Thorpe se impulsa en la pared de la piscina en la salida de una carrera de 100 m espalda.*

*▼ El australiano Kieren Perkins toma aire mientras recorre los 1.500 metros libres en los Juegos de Atlanta. Perkins fue un as en esta prueba, logrando el oro en 1992 y 1996, y la plata en 2000.*

# SALTOS, WATERPOLO Y NATACIÓN SINCRONIZADA

▼ *Una saltadora se eleva en el aire durante los entrenamientos para la competición femenina de salto de plataforma de las Olimpiadas de Atlanta.*

La natación no es el único deporte que entretiene a los espectadores en el pabellón acuático. Los saltos y la natación sincronizada requieren flexibilidad y precisión milimétrica. En ambas pruebas, los jueces valoran la calidad técnica y artística. En cambio, el waterpolo es un deporte de equipo que se juega en la piscina.

### Saltos: trampolín y plataforma

El salto fue uno de los primeros deportes que ofreció pruebas para hombres y mujeres. El salto masculino hizo su debut en 1904, mientras que el femenino se introdujo ocho años después. Las competiciones de salto olímpico tienen lugar a dos alturas: el salto de trampolín se realiza a tres metros por encima del agua y el salto de plataforma a 10 metros por encima de la superficie. Los saltadores compiten en una fase preliminar en la que los 18 mejores pasan a la semifinal. Los doce mejores semifinalistas pasan a la final. En cada fase, los participantes realizan cierto número de saltos que deben elegir de entre las decenas de saltos posibles. Las pruebas sincronizadas (en las que dos saltadores saltan a la vez) hicieron su debut en Sydney.

► *Este es un salto interior con medio mortal en posición encogida (con las rodillas pegadas al pecho). Tiene un grado de dificultad de 1,9, una puntuación media en el coeficiente de dificultad de la prueba de salto de trampolín.*

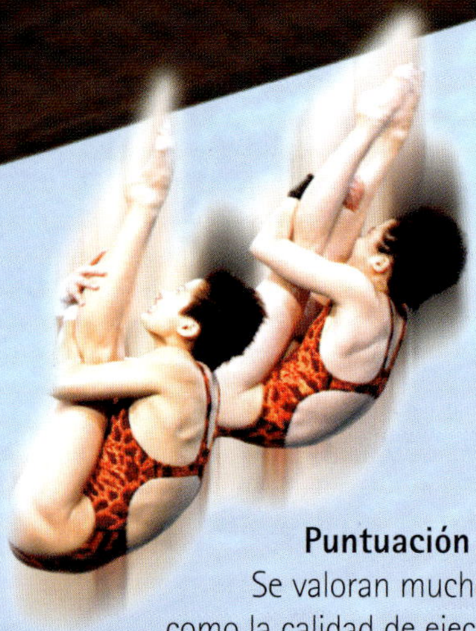

◄ *Las chinas Na Li y Xue Sang se sujetan el cuerpo en simetría casi perfecta durante un salto sincronizado en los Juegos de Sydney. La pareja ganó la prueba de salto de plataforma con un amplio margen de 30 puntos y también obtuvo el oro en trampolín.*

### Puntuación

Se valoran muchos elementos de los saltos, como la calidad de ejecución de los movimientos en el aire y la limpieza de la entrada en el agua. Siete jueces puntúan las pruebas individuales. Se eliminan la puntuación máxima y mínima, y se suman las otras cinco. Cada salto tiene un coeficiente de dificultad que se expresa con un número. La puntuación de un saltador se multiplica por el coeficiente de dificultad y luego por 0,6 para obtener el resultado final. Esta fórmula recompensa a los saltadores que se arriesgan con saltos desafiantes, pero también da la oportunidad de lograr una puntuación competitiva a los que ejecutan saltos más sencillos de forma casi perfecta.

## Waterpolo

El waterpolo, disciplina olímpica desde 1900, es el deporte de equipo más duradero de la era moderna, aunque su versión femenina no se introdujo hasta los Juegos de 2000. Se juega entre dos equipos de siete jugadores que tratan de encajar un balón en la portería (de 3 m de ancho por 90 cm de alto) del equipo contrario. Los jugadores pueden utilizar cualquier parte del cuerpo para empujar el balón por la superficie del agua o pasarlo a los compañeros, pero está prohibido golpear el balón o arrastrarlo bajo el agua. El portero es el único que puede agarrarlo con las dos manos. Cuando un equipo posee el balón, dispone de 35 segundos para marcar gol; de no ser así, el balón pasa al equipo contrario. Hay faltas ordinarias y graves. Tres faltas graves suponen la expulsión de un jugador. A lo largo del partido, los jugadores están en constante movimiento, ya sea nadando para adoptar una posición de ataque o defensa, o removiendo el agua para mantenerse a flote. Cuando van a lanzar, los jugadores se impulsan hacia arriba y sacan el cuerpo del agua. Esto ayuda a generar un tiro potente.

▲ *El húngaro Tamas Marcz marca al ruso Alexander Erychov durante la final de waterpolo de 2000. Hungría ganó 13-6 y obtuvo su séptima medalla de oro en la prueba.*

► *El portero italiano Francesco Attolico para un balón en Sydney. Los guardametas son los únicos jugadores que pueden tocar el fondo de la piscina en waterpolo.*

▲ *El equipo francés de natación sincronizada, en acción durante su rutina libre en las Olimpiadas de Sydney. Pese a lograr una buena puntuación, se vieron desplazadas al bronce por Canadá.*

► *El equipo francés ejecuta una hermosa figura libre durante un entrenamiento en Sydney.*

## Natación sincronizada

La natación sincronizada, que tuvo su origen en Canadá y EE.UU., hizo su debut olímpico en Los Ángeles en 1984. En este deporte, parejas o equipos de ocho nadadoras realizan, al ritmo de la música, rutinas compuestas de muchas figuras distintas tanto bajo el agua como en la superficie. Las participantes deben realizar una rutina técnica y una rutina libre, ambas en un tiempo limitado. En la rutina técnica, las nadadoras ejecutan una serie de figuras específicas en un orden establecido, mientras que en la rutina libre las nadadoras crean su propia coreografía con figuras espectaculares. Las nadadoras pueden permanecer bajo el agua hasta 60 segundos por secuencia y deben coordinar sus acciones perfectamente con sus compañeras. Las rutinas son valoradas por 10 jueces, divididos en dos grupos. Un grupo valora la calidad técnica y el otro la calidad artística. Las nadadoras logran que sus rutinas parezcan fáciles, pero en realidad precisan de mucha fuerza, resistencia y trabajo duro.

# REMO, VELA Y CANOA/KAYAC

Tres disciplinas náuticas atraen a numeroso público que contempla asombrado el gran nivel de resistencia, fuerza y calidad técnica de los deportistas. El remo y la vela hicieron su debut en los Juegos de París de 1900, mientras que el piragüismo apareció por primera vez como deporte de exhibición en las Olimpiadas de Amberes de 1920, antes de convertirse oficialmente en deporte olímpico en los Juegos de Berlín de 1936.

▲ *Competición femenina de K4 de 500 metros de los Juegos de Sydney. La denominación K4 hace referencia al número de palistas que ocupan el kayac. También hay competiciones olímpicas de K1 y K2 para uno y dos palistas.*

▲ *El equipo de cuatro sin timonel de Gran Bretaña compite en una eliminatoria de los Juegos de 2000, rumbo hacia su histórico quinto oro olímpico para Steve Redgrave (tercero desde el frente) y tercer oro para Matthew Pinsent (delante).*

**El remo**
El remo olímpico, uno de los deportes de resistencia más duros, tiene lugar en un recorrido de 2.000 metros. Los remeros se esfuerzan hasta el límite, en la fase final de las carreras, pese a estar casi agotados, y alcanzan velocidades sorprendentes de hasta 10 metros por segundo (36 km/h). En las pruebas de equipo para dos, cuatro u ocho personas, los remeros deben sincronizar sus movimientos y aunar su ritmo para avanzar deprisa y sin dar tirones.

▼ *Las mujeres del equipo femenino de ocho con timonel de Rumania, a punto de conseguir el oro el Sydney y repetir la hazaña de 1996.*

***Scull* y remo en punta**
El remo es uno de los deportes que más participantes atrae a las olimpiadas. En los Juegos de Atenas de 2004, más de 500 remeros competirán en una docena de pruebas distintas. Existen dos categorías: las pruebas de *scull*, en las que cada participante maneja dos remos, y las de remo en punta, en las que agarran un solo remo con las dos manos. Algunas pruebas llevan timonel. Esto significa que una persona, el timonel, se sienta en la popa del barco para marcar el ritmo y virar el timón. Las embarcaciones más grandes son las de ocho con timonel, considerada la prueba de remo por excelencia. Todas las pruebas incluyen una serie de eliminatorias que deciden las seis embarcaciones que acceden a la final.

## Piragüismo

Las canoas y los kayacs son embarcaciones similares, pero se manejan con distintas técnicas de remo. Los canoístas navegan arrodillados y utilizan un remo con una sola pala, mientras que los palistas de kayac navegan sentados y usan un remo de dos palas, una en cada extremo. Se celebran pruebas de velocidad para canoas y kayacs en recorridos de aguas tranquilas de diferentes distancias. Las mujeres recorren 500 metros en velocidad y los hombres 500 y 1.000 metros. También hay carreras de eslalon en aguas bravas, donde los piragüistas avanzan por aguas rápidas y turbulentas. El objetivo es atravesar, en el menor tiempo posible, una serie de 20 a 50 puertas dispuestas en un recorrido diseñado para la prueba.

◄ *El windsurf ha formado parte del programa olímpico desde 1984. En la fotografía, windsurfistas de Suecia y Nueva Zelanda se disputan la supremacía en la prueba Mistral de Sydney 2000.*

▲ *El piragüista italiano Pierpaolo Ferrazzi introduce su pala en las aguas bravas del recorrido de eslalon kayac de Sydney. Ferrazzi, que obtuvo el oro en el debut olímpico de esta prueba en 1992, ganó el bronce en 2000 por detrás del alemán Thomas Schmidt y el británico Paul Ratcliffe.*

## La vela

Las olimpiadas incluyen una serie de pruebas de vela, cada una para un tipo de embarcación distinta. En los Juegos de Sydney hubo nueve tipos de embarcación, entre las que destacan las de un regatista, como la Finn y la Europa, además de las de 49ers para dos personas y las Solings para tres. Algunas pruebas están restringidas a hombres o a mujeres, mientras que otras, como la clase Tornado, están abiertas a ambos sexos. En casi todas las pruebas, los regatistas participan en una serie de carreras (11 en la mayoría de las clases, 16 en la prueba de 49er) en las que todas las embarcaciones compiten juntas. La puntuación depende de los puestos de llegada: uno para el primer lugar, dos para el segundo, etcétera. Gana el velero que acumula menos puntos en la serie de carreras.

◄ *El británico Ben Ainslie compite en la clase Laser individual de los Juegos de 2000. Ainslie ganó la competición, celebrada en el puerto de Sydney, mejorando su medalla de plata de las Olimpiadas de Atlanta de 1996.*

**País:** *Unión Soviética*
**Olimpiadas:** *Melbourne 1956, Roma 1960, Tokio 1964*
**Pruebas:** *remo scull individual*
**Medallas:** *tres de oro*

# SEÚL 1988

Las Olimpiadas de Seúl, los segundos juegos de verano celebrados en Asia, estuvieron marcadas por el regreso de muchas naciones que habían boicoteado los Juegos de 1980 o 1984. Las únicas ausencias fueron Corea del Norte, Cuba y Etiopía. Los juegos son recordados por el gran nivel de seguridad sin precedentes y por la descalificación por consumo de drogas más sonada de la era moderna. Sin embargo, fueron también un escaparate para la cultura de Corea del Sur y contaron con actuaciones memorables.

▲ *El cartel oficial de los Juegos de 1988 mostraba a un corredor portando la antorcha olímpica como símbolo de los ideales olímpicos de armonía y progreso.*

◀ *Ben Johnson saluda al público tras ganar los 100 metros lisos y batir el récord mundial con un tiempo de 9,79 segundos. Días después de su victoria se le retiraría la medalla.*

◀▲ *En 1936, el atleta coreano Sohn Kee-chung fue obligado a participar en el maratón olímpico con un nombre japonés porque su país estaba entonces bajo ocupación japonesa. Ganó la medalla de oro. Más de 50 años después, a la edad de 76 años, Sohn entró al estadio olímpico portando la antorcha para inaugurar los Juegos de Seúl, un momento de gran emoción.*

**El escándalo Ben Johnson**

Lo que ocurrió en la final de los 100 metros lisos en Seúl conmocionó a los espectadores de todo el mundo. El esprínter canadiense Ben Johnson barrió a sus competidores, incluidos Carl Lewis y Lindford Christie, logrando un récord mundial que le valió el oro. Pero la gloria de Johnson duró bien poco, ya que dio positivo en un control antidroga por un esteroide prohibido, el estanozolol. Pese a las protestas, Johnson se vio desprovisto del oro y el récord mundial, y recibió una sanción de dos años de la Federación Internacional de Atletismo. Esta se convertiría en una sanción de por vida tras volver a dar positivo en 1993. La descalificación de Johnson fue el caso de consumo de drogas más sonado de los diez ocurridos en las Olimpiadas de Seúl.

## Nuevas llegadas

El tenis hizo su primera aparición olímpica en 1924. El sorprendente ganador del torneo masculino fue el checoslovaco Milosav Mercir, quien venció a Tim Mayotte y al favorito Stefan Edberg en su camino a la medalla de oro. El tenis de mesa se estrenó en los juegos y demostró gozar de gran popularidad. Corea del Sur ganó en dobles femeninos y obtuvo el oro y la plata en individual masculino, mientras que China ganó el individual femenino y los dobles masculinos. También hicieron su debut la carrera ciclista de velocidad y el arco en equipo, y el taekwondo apareció como deporte de exhibición.

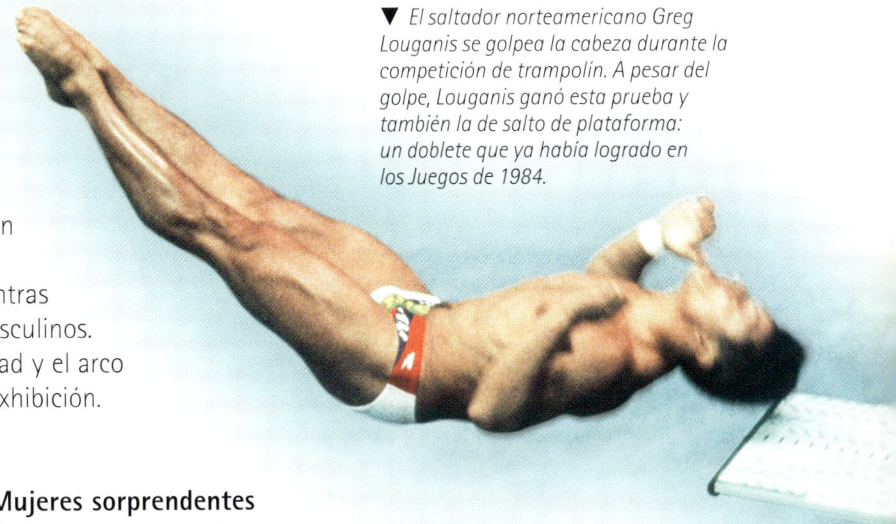

▼ *El saltador norteamericano Greg Louganis se golpea la cabeza durante la competición de trampolín. A pesar del golpe, Louganis ganó esta prueba y también la de salto de plataforma: un doblete que ya había logrado en los Juegos de 1984.*

◀ *En la final femenina de la primera competición de tenis en 64 años, la alemana occidental Stefi Graff obtuvo el oro tras derrotar 6-3, 6-3 a la argentina Gabriela Sabatini.*

## Mujeres sorprendentes

Hubo muchas actuaciones femeninas memorables en las Olimpiadas de Seúl. La esgrimista sueca Kerstin Palm pasó a ser la primera mujer que compitió en siete olimpiadas, mientras que la medalla de plata en ciclismo de la alemana oriental Christa Luding-Rothenburger la convirtió en la única atleta que ha ganado medallas en las olimpiadas de invierno y verano del mismo año: siete meses antes, en los Juegos de Calgary, había ganado el oro y la plata en patinaje de velocidad. En atletismo destacó la lanzadora de peso soviética Natalya Lisovskaya. Sus seis lanzamientos superaron a los del resto de las participantes.

▼ *Jackie Joyner-Kersee, de EE.UU., a punto de conseguir la medalla de oro en salto de longitud. Joyner-Kersee ganó también el heptatlón, mientras que su cuñada, Florence Griffith-Joyner, obtuvo tres oros y una plata en pista.*

## En el agua

En 1984, el nadador norteamericano Matt Biondi había ganado un oro olímpico como parte del equipo de relevos de 4 x 100 metros estilos. Cuatro años después, Biondi regresó a la competición olímpica en una forma inmejorable y ganó cinco medallas de oro, una de plata y una de bronce. Su derrota en la final de 200 metros estilos fue una sorpresa. El surfista y nadador australiano Duncan Armstrong, en el puesto 46 del *ranking* mundial, logró su mejor tiempo y obtuvo el oro.

| MEDALLERO | O | P | B |
|---|---|---|---|
| Unión Soviética | 55 | 31 | 46 |
| Alem. Este | 37 | 35 | 30 |
| EE.UU. | 36 | 31 | 27 |
| Corea del Sur | 12 | 10 | 11 |
| Alem. Oeste | 11 | 14 | 15 |
| Hungría | 11 | 6 | 6 |
| Bulgaria | 10 | 12 | 13 |
| Rumanía | 7 | 11 | 6 |
| Francia | 6 | 4 | 6 |
| Italia | 6 | 4 | 4 |

▼ *El norteamericano Matt Biondi celebra su victoria en 50 metros estilos por delante de su compatriota y poseedor del entonces récord mundial, Thomas Jagger.*

# ARCO, TIRO OLÍMPICO Y ESGRIMA

El tiro con arco, el tiro olímpico y la esgrima, tres deportes con orígenes en las guerras y combates de la antigüedad, exigen nervios de acero y una precisión milimétrica. Los arqueros y tiradores repiten la mima acción una y otra vez, sabiendo que un desliz de unos milímetros podría significar el fin de sus esperanzas olímpicas. Los campeones de esgrima precisan de precisión y rapidez de reacción, además de la capacidad para adivinar los movimientos del contrario en un combate de ataque y contraataque.

*◄ En las Olimpiadas de 1996, la arquera holandesa Ljudmila Arzhannikova apunta y se prepara para disparar. Los arqueros llevan un dedal y un peto que les protegen de posibles quemaduras causadas por la fricción de la flecha al salir disparada del arco a velocidades de más de 240 km/h.*

*▲ La diana del tiro con arco tiene diez círculos. Cuanto más cerca del centro se clava una flecha, más puntos logra. Dar en el centro supone 10 puntos.*

**El tiro con arco**

Antes de 1920, el tiro con arco había sido deporte olímpico en contadas ocasiones, pero después de esa fecha no volvió a aparecer en los juegos hasta 1972. Los participantes disparan mangas que constan de determinado número de flechas, que deben dispararse dentro de un tiempo limitado. En la eliminatoria celebrada antes de la competición olímpica, los arqueros disparan 12 mangas de seis flechas cada una (un total de 72 flechas) para elegir a los 64 mejores. Estos arqueros tienen que competir en una nueva serie de eliminatorias. Cuando sólo quedan cuatro, dos semifinales y una final deciden los ganadores. En las olimpiadas se celebran pruebas individuales masculinas y femeninas. En 1968 se introdujo una prueba de equipo para tres arqueros.

## Tiro olímpico

Los Juegos de 1900 ofrecieron tiro a vuelo, pero en las olimpiadas modernas, los participantes apuntan a dianas artificiales. En las pruebas de escopeta, los tiradores tienen que seguir y disparar a "palomas de cerámica" (platos de cerámica que se lanzan al aire con un artilugio llamado *trap* a velocidades de unos 100 km/h) a distintas alturas. Hay pruebas de *trap*, doble *trap* y *skeet*, en las que se lanzan dos platos, uno a cada lado del jugador. Los tiradores de rifle y pistola apuntan a dianas de papel fijas o en movimiento. Los tiradores de rifle disparan desde tres posiciones diferentes: de pie, de rodillas y tumbados boca abajo. el nivel de puntería exhibido en las olimpiadas es asombroso. Por ejemplo, en los Juegos de 1996, el australiano Michael Diamond compitió en la modalidad de trap masculino y consiguió 149 de 150 dianas, y 25 de 25 en la final.

▶ *El tirador italiano y medalla de oro en 1996 Roberto di Donna se prepara para disparar durante la final de la competición de pistola de aire comprimido desde 10 metros de los Juegos de 2000.*

## Esgrima

Este deporte dinámico es uno de los únicos cuatro que han aparecido en todas y cada una de las olimpiadas modernas. El objetivo del combate, en el que los esgrimistas llevan vestimenta y caretas protectoras, es tocar el cuerpo del rival con la punta del arma. Hay pruebas individuales y de equipo con tres tipos de armas: florete, sable y espada. Las reglas son distintas para cada arma. En el caso del florete, la zona de tocado está limitada al torso; la zona de marcaje del sable es el torso, los brazos y la cabeza; y la de la espada comprende todo el cuerpo, incluida la cabeza. En los combates cortos pero extremadamente tensos, los esgrimistas atacan avanzando y defendiéndose esquivando las estocadas del contrario. El deporte exige experiencia y sangre fría, y los campeones de esgrima suelen permanecer en la competición durante muchos años. El húngaro Aladar Gerevich, por ejemplo, ganó la prueba de sable individual en seis juegos consecutivos entre 1932 y 1960.

▲ *La esgrimista rusa Olga Charkova (izquierda) y la norteamericana Iris Zimmerman (derecha) compiten en la prueba individual femenina de florete en Sydney 2000. La pista es rectangular y mide 14 metros de largo por 1,5 metros de ancho. Las armas están dotadas de sensores que registran electrónicamente cada tocado.*

▲ *La esgrima en silla de ruedas es popular en los Paralímpicos. La polaca Jadwiga Polasik (derecha) se enfrenta a la húngara Palfi en su rumbo al oro de 2000. Polonia ganó tres de las cuatro medallas de esgrima femenina de los juegos.*

# HALTEROFILIA, LUCHA Y BOXEO

Los amantes de la fuerza bruta acuden a las pruebas olímpicas de halterofilia, lucha y boxeo para presenciar hazañas épicas de fuerza realizadas por los competidores. Estos atletas se entrenan duro para lograr físicos imponentes, pero cada prueba exige tácticas inteligentes y una gran calidad técnica. Los tres deportes tienen competiciones con diversas divisones de peso.

▲ *Naim Suleymanoglu, la leyenda de la halterofilia turca y ganador de tres medallas de oro olímpicas, se prepara para levantar las pesas en los Juegos de 1996. En 1988, el combinado total de sus dos alzados fue de 342,5 kilogramos, y él pesaba menos de 62 kilogramos (el límite para los pesos pluma).*

### Halterofilia

Una gran emoción envuelve las competiciones olímpicas de halterofilia, en las que los deportistas deben levantar y controlar unas pesas, o halteras, que pueden ser varias veces más pesadas que ellos. Los participantes anuncian su peso de inicio y disponen de tres oportunidades para levantar cada peso. Hay dos tipos de movimientos en los juegos: el de dos tiempos con cargada y envión (consulta el diagrama) y la arrancada, donde el alzado debe completarse en un solo movimiento. En la prueba combinada, los levantadores realizan los dos movimientos y su mejor alzado en cada categoría se suma para obtener el peso total combinado. La halterofilia femenina debutó en los Juegos de 2000; las atletas chinas ganaron el oro en cuatro de las siete divisiones.

▲ *La cargada y el envión componen un movimiento en dos tiempos. El levantador tira de la barra hacia su pecho empleando los músculos de muslos y espalda, y luego se agacha para controlar la barra. En el envión, el atleta se impulsa extendiendo las piernas y el cuerpo. El atleta debe mantener los pies, piernas y brazos extendidos para que el alzado sea válido.*

▼ *El ruso Aleksandr Karelin (de rojo) está considerado el mejor luchador de lucha grecorromana en categoría superpesada de la historia. Aquí, pelea con Siamak Ghaffari, de EE.UU., en 1996. Ganó su tercer oro en juegos consecutivos.*

### Lucha

Existen dos modalidades olímpicas de este deporte: la libre olímpica y la grecorromana. En ambas, los combates constan de dos asaltos de tres minutos y tienen lugar en el interior de un círculo amarillo de siete metros de diámetro. Los luchadores tratan de derribar al contrario haciendo que toque el tapiz con los hombros, lo que se denomina un "tocado". Se puntúa por agarres, o presas, y tocados, y los luchadores ganan cuando logran una ventaja de 10 puntos o anotando más puntos que su rival al final del combate. En la lucha grecorromana no se puede emplear las piernas en los agarres, que sólo pueden hacerse por encima de la cintura. La lucha libre permite apresar por encima y debajo de la cintura, y emplear las piernas para apresar o levantar.

## Boxeo

El boxeo olímpico está abierto a competidores amateur que se han clasificado en torneos regionales celebrados en cada continente. Los combates se dividen en cuatro asaltos de dos minutos. Los púgiles obtienen puntos cuando golpean a su rival en los lados o la parte frontal del cuerpo por encima de la cintura, o en la cabeza, con los nudillos del guante. No puntúan los golpes dados con otras partes del guante, en los brazos o con poca fuerza. Un boxeador cuyas manos o cuerpo tocan el suelo está fuera de combate y recibe una cuenta de ocho segundos. El árbitro decidirá si puede continuar. Un boxeador que no se ha puesto en pie después de 10 segundos es declarado fuera de combate, o noqueado, y pierde el combate. La seguridad es muy importante en el boxeo olímpico, y las amonestaciones por "golpes bajos" y otras tácticas de juego sucio pueden llevar a la descalificación del púgil. Desde 1984, es obligatorio el uso de casco protector y los púgiles deben tener entre 17 y 34 años. Siempre hay médicos a un lado del cuadrilátero y tienen la potestad de detener el combate por motivos médicos.

◀ *Un joven Cassius Clay ocupa orgulloso el podio tras recibir la medalla de oro en la prueba de semipesados en las Olimpiadas de Roma de 1960. Clay se haría boxeador profesional y, poco después, en 1964 cambió su nombre por el de Muhammad Ali. Otros medallistas olímpicos que lograron el éxito profesional son el británico Lennox Lewis y los norteamericanos George Foreman y Joe Frazier.*

▲ *El húngaro Laszlo Papp fue el boxeador que ganó tres oros olímpicos en la categoría de peso medio y medio ligero (1948-56). Más tarde fue el preparador del equipo de boxeo de Hungría durante 21 años.*

▶ *En los Juegos de 2000 Ricardo Williams Junior (de rojo) lanza su puño izquierdo mientras se inclina hacia la derecha para esquivar un golpe de Olusegun Ajose. Williams ganó la medalla de plata en la división de peso welter ligero.*

# JUDO Y TAEKWONDO

Las dos artes marciales olímpicas aparecieron en los juegos como deportes de exhibición (el judo en los juegos de Tokio de 1964 y el taekwondo en los de Seúl de 1988). Hoy en día tienen estatus olímpico. Los deportistas de judo y taekwondo precisan equilibrio, aplomo y reacciones rápidas y contundentes. También necesitan agilidad mental y una gran fuerza para responder a los movimientos del rival en un fascinante combate cuerpo a cuerpo.

▲ *El francés David Douillet derrota al japonés Shinichi Shinohara y obtiene la medalla de oro de judo en pesos pesados de las Olmpiadas de Sydney. Douillet ganó también el oro en 1996 y el bronce en 1992.*

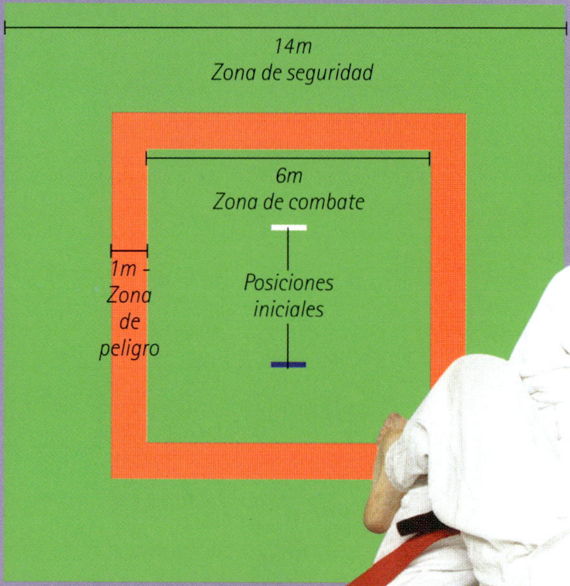


◄ *Los combates de judo tienen lugar sobre tatamis. La acción se desarrolla en la zona de combate , rodeada por una franja roja llamada "zona de peligro". La zona de seguridad protege a los que caen fuera.*

► *La belga Nicole Flagothier es derribada por la británica Nicola Fairbrother en los Juegos de 1992. Fairbrother obtuvo la plata en la categoría de peso ligero.*

**Judo**

La palabra japonesa judo significa "camino suave". Desarrollado a finales del siglo XIX, es una forma de combate y autodefensa sin armas en la que los dos competidores, llamados judocas, utilizan la fuerza del ataque de su adversario para desequilibrarlo. Bajo la atenta mirada de un árbitro, los judocas suman puntos ejecutando derribos y agarres, e inmovilizando al adversario contra el suelo. Japón es la nación dominante, pero la creciente popularidad de este deporte ha derivado en medallistas olímpicos de muchas naciones como Corea del Sur, Rusia, Georgia, Francia, Países Bajos y Cuba.

▲ *Apresada desde atrás, la judoca de blanco realiza un derribo con la cadera llamado* harai goshi*: uno de los más comunes.*

▲ *Agarrando a su rival por la cintura, la judoca atacante lanza hacia atrás la pierna derecha para barrer a su adversaria con la cadera.*

▲ *Utilizando los brazos para completar el derribo, la judoca de blanco tira a su rival, que aterriza con la espalda.*

### *Ippon* y *waza-ari*

Un combate de judo termina inmediatamente si un judoca logra puntuar un *ippon*. Éste se obtiene ejecutando un derribo. El rival debe caer de espaldas y el derribo debe realizarse con un nivel casi perfecto de fuerza, control y velocidad. También se puede obtener un *ippon* inmovilizando al adversario contra el tatami durante 25 segundos, o si este indica que se rinde golpeando el tatami dos veces mientras está inmovilizado. El *waza-ari* vale medio *ippon* y se obtiene inmovilizando al contrario durante 20 segundos o si un derribo satisface el criterio de la mayoría de los jueces. Dos *waza-ari* logrados por el mismo judoca significan la victoria. Si un combate no acaba de este modo, gana el judoca que suma más puntos tras cumplir cuatro minutos (en judo femenino) o cinco (en masculino).

▲ *El británico Darren Kail combate con el ucraniano Sergiy Sydorenko en la competición de 66 kg de judo para ciegos de los Paralímpicos de 2000. Las reglas son casi idénticas a las del judo convencional, pero los judocas comienzan a un brazo de distancia.*

### Taekwondo

A pesar de tener su origen en la tradición de las artes marciales centenarias, el taekwondo se formalizó como deporte en la segunda mitad del siglo XX. Se convirtió en deporte olímpico en 2000, ofreciendo una fascinante fusión de elegancia y agilidad por una parte, y potencia y energía por otra. La fuerza de las patadas y golpes realizados por los dos adversarios es tal que los participantes deben llevar protecciones que incluyen casco, peto protector y protectores de espinillas, ingles y antebrazos.

▼ *El australiano Paul Lyons realiza una espectacular patada con los dos pies durante los Juegos de Sydney. Lyons compitió en la categoría más ligera del taekwondo masculino. La competición femenina también está dividida en cuatro categorías por pesos. Hombres y mujeres visten el dobok, un uniforme que consiste en una chaqueta y unos pantalones blancos.*

### Puntos y penalizaciones

El taekwondo es un deporte rápido en el que los participantes han de ejecutar una serie de golpes (principalmente patadas) mientras esquivan o evitan los ataques del adversario y mantienen el equilibrio. El objetivo es derribar al rival o sumar más puntos a lo largo del combate. Tres jueces otorgan puntos, mientras que un árbitro controla el combate que tiene lugar en un tatami cuadrado de 12 metros. Cada combate se compone de tres asaltos de tres minutos cada uno. Se obtienen puntos por encajar un golpe tácticamente correcto en una de las zonas autorizadas: la cabeza, el abdomen y los lados del cuerpo. Las faltas restan puntos. Estas se dividen en faltas *kyong-go* (medio punto o aviso), por ofensas como fingir una lesión o sujetar al oponente, y faltas *gam-jeom* (un punto entero), por ofensas como derribar al oponente. Si un participante acumula una tercera falta, pierde inmediatamente.

# GIMNASIA

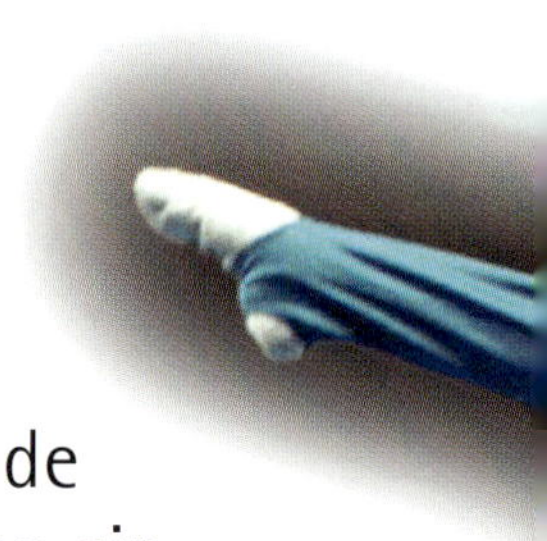

La gimnasia, en todas sus formas, ha sido un deporte sobrecogedor y muy popular en todas las olimpiadas de la era moderna. Unos juegos de verano sin la elegancia, fuerza y magnífica agilidad de sus gimnastas son simplemente impensables. La gimnasia se divide en artística y rítmica (que hizo su debut en los Juegos de Los Ángeles de 1984) y trampolín, la prueba olímpica más nueva.

◄ *La gimnasta rítmica bielorrusa Yulia Raskina ejecuta un ejercicio con la cinta. Raskina obtuvo 39,548 de 40 puntos y ganó la plata en la prueba individual, por detrás de la rusa Yulia Barsukova, que obtuvo 39,632 puntos.*

► *El trampolín hizo su debut olímpico en Sydney. En la fotografía, la rusa Irina Karavaeva realiza un vuelo durante la final femenina, en la que compiten las ocho mejores gimnastas de la eliminatoria. Karavaeva ganaría la medalla de oro. Su compatriota Alexander Moskalenko ganó el oro en la prueba masculina.*

LEYENDA OLÍMPICA

Olga Korbut (nacida en 1955)

**País:** *Unión Soviética*
**Olimpiadas:** *Múnich 1972, Montreal 1976*
**Prueba:** *Gimnasia artística*
**Medallas:** *cuatro de oro, dos de plata*

### Gimnasia rítmica y trampolín

La gimnasia rítmica, que es exclusivamente femenina, tiene pruebas individuales y por equipos. Las participantes ejecutan rutinas en una pista cuadrada de 13 metros con cinco aparatos distintos: cuerda, pelota, mazas, cinta y aro. Las rutinas tienen música y coreografía, deben durar entre 75 y 90 minutos, y utilizar toda la pista mientras el aparato está en movimiento constante. Tres grupos de jueces evalúan los méritos técnicos, ejecución y méritos artísticos. La competición de trampolín comienza con una eliminatoria de dos rutinas: una obligatoria y otra original. Se puntúa por estilo y ejecución de los movimientos en ambas rutinas. Los mejores gimnastas pasan a la final, donde ejecutan una sola rutina original. Las rutinas no tienen límite de tiempo, pero los participantes deben realizar tres acrobacias, incluido aterrizar hacia delante y hacia atrás, y dar un salto mortal con tirabuzón. Los gimnastas tratan de hacer movimientos espectaculares en sus rutinas, como el *triff* (un triple salto mortal con tirabuzón) y el Randolph (un salto mortal hacia delante con dos tirabuzones y medio).

## Gimnasia artística

En el deporte olímpico de la gimnasia artística, o deportiva, los gimnastas realizan ejercicios en diversos aparatos. Obtienen medalla los mejores gimnastas individuales de cada aparato: barra de equilibrio, caballo de salto, barras asimétricas y suelo en la competición femenina, y barra fija, barras paralelas, anillas, caballo con arcos, caballo de salto y suelo en la masculina. También hay pruebas por equipos y medallas individuales para los mejores, cuyas marcas se toman de los ejercicios en todos los aparatos. Dos jueces valoran el grado de dificultad de cada ejercicio, mientras que otros seis califican la ejecución, siendo 10 la puntuación máxima. Cada error resta puntos. Por ejemplo, caerse de un aparato supone 0,5 puntos, mientras que un pequeño error de colocación puede significar 0,1 puntos. Se descartan las puntuaciones más alta y más baja, y se hace una media con las otras cuatro para obtener la puntuación final.

◀ *El ucraniano Oleksandr Beresh realiza un movimiento en las barras paralelas durante la prueba masculina por equipos de Sydney. Su equipo ganó la plata por detrás de China. Al final de la rutina, el gimnasta desmonta y aterriza junto al aparato.*

▼ *La rumana Nadia Comaneci, fotografiada en la barra de equilibrio, sorprendió a los espectadores en los Juegos de Montreal 1976 con sus ejecuciones perfectas en varios aparatos. Se convirtió en la primera gimnasta que obtenía un 10 unánime de los jueces en las olimpiadas.*

▶ *En la competición de caballo de salto masculino, los gimnastas, como el norteamericano Blaine Wilson (en la fotografía), se acercan al caballo a gran velocidad. Impulsándose en un trampolín, apoyan las dos manos en el potro y realizan giros acrobáticos en el aire.*

## Elegancia bajo presión

La gimnasia ha sido una parte importante de las olimpiadas durante más de un siglo, pero en la década de 1970 el deporte recibió un gran empuje en su popularidad gracias a dos gimnastas en concreto. La soviética Olga Korbut realizó actuaciones de gran estilo y originalidad, mientras que los ejercicios perfectos de la rumana Nadia Comaneci fueron simplemente sobrecogedores. La elegancia y el aplomo que muestran las gimnastas a veces enmascara la gran fuerza necesaria para mantener una postura en las anillas o en los ejercicios de suelo. Pero los gimnastas necesitan muchísimo más que fuerza: flexibilidad increíble, precisión milimétrica, vena artística y ejercicios originales, entre otras cosas. En todas las pruebas con aparatos, es muy importante aterrizar en perfecto equilibrio y sin dar ningún pasito.

◀ *La rusa Elena Zamolodtchikova realiza su ejercicio de suelo en los Juegos de Sydney. En la prueba femenina, el ejercicio de suelo tiene música. Las gimnastas deben interpretar la música con gracia, además de ejecutar una serie de movimientos como volteretas, giros y saltos mortales.*

# BARCELONA 1992

▲ *El logotipo oficial de las Olimpiadas de Barcelona era un colorido símbolo que representaba un atleta saltando una valla formada por los aros olímpicos.*

Barcelona tuvo que esperar antes de ser nombrada sede olímpica. La ciudad española esperaba acoger los Juegos de 1924, pero una decisión de última hora trasladó el evento a París. En 1992, Barcelona demostró ser una excelente anfitriona para las primeras olimpiadas en 20 años que no sufrieron boicot alguno. Los juegos son recordados por una serie de competiciones emocionantes, geniales ceremonias de apertura y clausura, poca controversia y muchos éxitos deportivos.

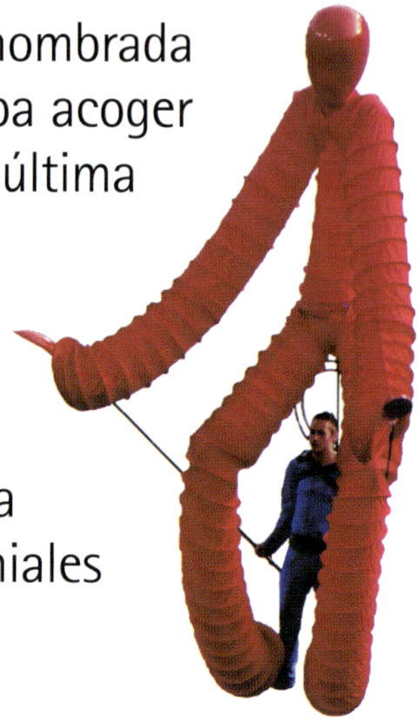

▲ *La ceremonia de inauguración tuvo una audiencia global de casi dos mil millones de personas.*

### Éxito paralímpico

Las Olimpiadas de Seúl de 1984 fueron las primeras en las que los paralímpicos tuvieron acceso a las instalaciones olímpicas y compitieron en los mismos lugares que los deprotistas olímpicos. El éxito de las Olimpiadas Paralímpicas de Seúl continuó en Barcelona gracias a la ayuda de más de 8.000 voluntarios. Participaron más de 3.000 atletas de 83 nacionalidades que lograron 279 récords mundiales. Sus hazañas fueron seguidas en vivo por millón y medio de personas, lo que cimentó el futuro de los Juegos Paralímpicos.

◀ *La atleta paralímpica Tanni Gray triunfó en Barcelona, ganando medallas de oro en cuatro pruebas: 100 m, 200 m, 400 m y 800 m lisos.*

### Bienvenidas todas las naciones

Un récord de 9.367 participantes de 169 naciones hizo de los Juegos de Barcelona los más grandes hasta entonces. El final del sistema de segregación racial en Suráfrica propició el regreso de ese país al movimiento olímpico tras una ausencia de 32 años. La Unión Soviética estaba en pleno proceso de disolución en distintas repúblicas independientes, y sus atletas participaron bajo la denominación de Comunidad de Estados Independientes. Namibia, Croacia y Eslovenia hicieron su debut olímpico, mientras la Alemania unificada competía por primera vez desde 1936, obteniendo 33 medallas de oro. En hockey masculino, Andreas Keller se convirtió en la tercera generación de su familia que representaba a Alemania y ganaba una medalla olímpica en dicho deporte.

◀ *El equipo de baloncesto de EE.UU., que reunía a las superestrellas de la liga profesional NBA, fue apodado* Dream Team. *Hasta llegar a la final, el equipo encestó más de 100 puntos en cada partido. En la fotografía, Michael Jordan (9) recupera un rebote rodeado de sus compañeros de equipo (de izquierda a derecha) Larry Bird, Magic Johnson y Scottie Pippen.*

► *Vitaly Scherbo ejecuta una cruz perfecta en su ejercicio de anillas. Scherbo, del Equipo Unificado, ganó esta prueba y otras cinco competiciones gimnásticas, ocupando el primer puesto del medallero individual de los Juegos de Barcelona.*

| MEDALLERO | O | P | B |
|---|---|---|---|
| E. Unificado | 45 | 38 | 29 |
| EE.UU. | 37 | 34 | 37 |
| Alemania | 33 | 21 | 28 |
| China | 16 | 22 | 16 |
| Cuba | 14 | 6 | 11 |
| España | 13 | 7 | 2 |
| Corea del Sur | 12 | 5 | 12 |
| Hungría | 11 | 12 | 7 |
| Francia | 8 | 5 | 16 |
| Australia | 7 | 9 | 11 |

## Sueños, pero pocas pesadillas

El miedo al terrorismo hizo que el gobierno español gastara unos 400 millones de dólares en seguridad. No hubo incidentes, pero sí mucha emoción en las pruebas.

El británico Linford Christie se convirtió en el ganador de más edad de los 100 metros lisos masculinos, mientras que el favorito Sergei Bubka fracasó en el salto de pértiga.

El bádminton hizo su debut olímpico, y Corea del Sur e Indonesia se disputaron el oro.

El judo femenino y el béisbol masculino también hicieron su presentación. Un cambio en el reglamento del baloncesto permitió el acceso de jugadores profesionales, y el *Dream Team* norteamericano dominó los juegos, ganando partidos con una ventaja de 43,3 puntos y derrotando incluso a la medalla de plata, Croacia, por un margen de 32 puntos.

► *Una de las escenas más memorables de Barcelona la protagonizó el corredor británico de 400 metros lisos Derek Redmond, que sufrió una lesión de ligamentos en la semifinal. Acabó la carrera ayudado por su padre, cojeando y con un dolor tremendo.*

▲ *El equipo alemán de hockey femenino defiende un saque de esquina en Barcelona. El equipo llegó a la final, donde fue derrotado por España. El equipo alemán masculino llegó más allá, obteniendo el oro tras derrotar a Australia en la final.*

## En el agua

La vela y el remo fueron un éxito en Barcelona. El príncipe Felipe, hijo del rey de España Juan Carlos I, compitió en una prueba de vela individual, pero no ganó ninguna medalla. La final de remo ocho con timonel presenció el triunfo de Canadá sobre Rumanía con un margen de apenas 30 centímetros. En la misma prueba, Carlos Font, el timonel de la embarcación española se convirtió en el participante más joven desde 1896. Tenía sólo 11 años.

► *En los 10.000 m, la etíope Derartu Tulu (izquierda) fue la primera mujer negra africana que ganó un oro olímpico. Elana Meyer (derecha), de Suráfrica, fue plata.*

# CICLISMO

El ciclismo, en sus muchas formas, ha formado parte de las olimpiadas desde los primeros juegos de 1896. Algunas pruebas, como la carrera de 2.000 metros tándem, se han quedado por el camino, mientras que se han incorporado carreras nuevas como el *keirin*. A comienzos de la década de 1990, se permitió la participación de ciclistas profesionales (que compiten en el Tour de Francia o la Vuelta a España), lo cual añadió glamour al ya popular espectáculo olímpico.

▲ *La prueba de ciclismo en carretera de Sydney comienza con una salida masiva. Las bicicletas de carretera se parecen más a una bici normal que a las máquinas aerodinámicas de ciclismo en pista.*

◀ *El francés Miguel Martínez salva un descenso del recorrido de bicicleta de montaña de los Juegos de Sydney, donde obutvo el oro en cross-country masculino. Este deporte exige equilibrio y resistencia.*

**Ciclismo de montaña**

El ciclismo se divide en pruebas de montaña, en carretera o en pista. La montaña, que es la última incorporación a los juegos, exige fuerza y habilidad para sortear el abrupto terreno del recorrido de *cross-country*. La carrera, de unas dos horas y cuarto de duración, consiste en dar determinado número de vueltas a un recorrido con colinas escarpadas, barrancos y descensos difíciles. En total, supone entre 40 y 50 kilómetros para los hombres y entre 30 y 40 kilómetros para las mujeres. El terreno es tan difícil que, en ciertos lugares, algunos ciclistas desmontan y cargan con la bici. Otros se arriesgan a seguir montados con la esperanza de ganar tiempo. Los choques y los pinchazos son habituales, y los ciclistas llevan cajitas de herramientas por si acaso.

▶ *Gran Bretaña adelanta a Rusia para ganar los cuartos de final de la prueba de persecución por equipos en el velódromo de Sydney. Las bicicletas, que no tienen frenos, están fabricadas con materiales ligeros, como el titanio y la fibra de carbono.*

## Ciclismo en carretera

Existen dos pruebas olímpicas en carretera que recorren distancias diferentes: la contrarreloj individual (unos 50 km para los hombres y 30 km para las mujeres) y la carrera por carretera (unos 220 km para los hombres y 110 km para las mujeres). La contrarreloj es una carrera contra el cronómetro en la que los ciclistas salen escalonados con 90 segundos de diferencia y luchan por completar el recorrido en el tiempo más rápido para ganar el oro. En la carrera por carretera, el campeón es un individuo, pero el trabajo en equipo es muy importante. Los ciclistas de una nación cuidan de su mejor hombre dejándole rodar tras ellos para que se mantenga fresco para el *sprint*. Jeannnie Longo-Ciprelli compitió en cinco olimpiadas toda una hazaña. A los 41 años consiguió el bronce en Sydney.

◀ *La ciclista holandesa Leontien Zijlaard compite en la persecución individual en 2000, prueba que finalmente ganó. Las ruedas de su bici no tienen radios. La ciclista se agarra al manillar e inclina el cuerpo hacia delante para lograr una postura lo más aerodinámica posible.*

## En el velódromo

La mayoría de las pruebas ciclistas tienen lugar en la pista en pendiente del velódromo. Las carreras en pista se dividen en pruebas de velocidad (entre 500 m y 2.000 m) y de resistencia (hasta 60 km). En la persecución individual, dos ciclistas comienzan en puntos opuestos de la pista. El objetivo es completar un recorrido de 4.000 m (masculino) o 3.000 m (femenino) en menos tiempo que el rival. La persecución por equipos es similar, pero exige la cooperación de los ciclistas. El cronómetro de cada equipo se detiene cuando el tercer ciclista atraviesa la meta, resultando ganador el tiempo más bajo. La prueba también puede ganarse si un equipo alcanza y adelanta al contrario. La contrarreloj de 1.000 metros es un *sprint* recto en el que los ciclistas aceleran al máximo desde la salida. Una de las pruebas más emocionantes es el *keirin*, en la que un vehículo motorizado (el *derny*) marca el ritmo de los ciclistas durante los primeros 1.400 de los 2.000 m de la carrera. Encontes, los ciclistas inician un *sprint* espectacular hasta la meta.

**País:** *Francia*
**Olimpiadas:** *Los Ángeles 1984, Seúl 1988, Barcelona 1992, Atlanta 1996, Sydney 2000*
**Pruebas:** *contrarreloj, en carretera*
**Medallas:** *una de oro, dos de plata, una de bronce*

# EQUITACIÓN

Hace más de 2.600 años, la carrera de cuadrigas era una de las pruebas más espectaculares y peligrosas de las antiguas olimpiadas. El moderno programa ecuestre de salto, doma y circuito se introdujo en los Juegos de 1912. Desde entonces se ha mantenido tal cual, incluso pese a la crisis de 1956, cuando las leyes de cuarentena australianas no permitieron la entrada de caballos extranjeros en el país y las pruebas ecuestres tuvieron que celebrarse en Estocolmo, Suecia.

**País:** *Alemania Occidental*
**Olimpiadas:** *Melbourne 1956, Roma 1960, Tokio 1964, México 1968, Múnich 1972, Montreal 1976*
**Prueba:** *salto (individual y por equipos)*
**Medallas:** *cinco de oro, una de plata, una de bronce*

◀ *La equitación es uno de los pocos deportes olímpicos en los que hombres y mujeres compiten en los mismos equipos o entre sí. Aquí, la norteamericana Margie Goldstein monta un caballo llamado Perrin y salta una barrera durante una prueba clasificatoria de salto individual en los Juegos de Sydney.*

**Saltos**

En el concurso de salto olímpico, los jinetes y los caballos deben compenetrarse extremadamente bien para completar un recorrido que tiene entre 15 y 20 obstáculos. Estos incluyen fosos de agua, barreras y combinación de obstáculos, compuestos de dos o tres barreras situadas a poca distancia. El objetivo es completar el recorrido sin recibir penalizaciones, llamadas faltas. Se comete falta cuando el caballo derriba parte de un obstáculo, rehúsa saltar un obstáculo al primer intento, mete una pata en el agua de un foso o salta en el orden incorrecto. Si hay un empate por el primer puesto, entonces se modifica el recorrido y desempatan en una carrera contrarreloj. Gana el que cometa menos faltas. En caso de nuevo empate, gana el más rápido.

## Doma

La doma, en ocasiones descrita como ballet para caballos, tiene su origen en un método de adiestramiento militar de caballos. El jinete y el caballo deben trabajar en perfecta armonía para realizar una serie de movimientos complicados, como la figura del ocho, a tres velocidades distintas: paso, trote y galope. Cinco jueces califican la actuación de cada jinete y caballo, puntuando cada movimiento que realizan. Debe parecer que el jinete está sentado perfectamente erguido en todo momento y el caballo debe responder a las instrucciones del jinete con movimientos sutiles. Los jinetes no pueden hablar ni hacer ningún sonido a los caballos, y no se permiten látigos. Cuatro jinetes compiten en la prueba por equipos, en la que se suman las puntuaciones de los tres mejores para hallar el total del equipo. La ronda final de la prueba individual es de estilo libre y en ella el jinete realiza su rutina al ritmo de la música.

▲ *La doma exige sombrero de copa, frac oscuro y pantalones de montar blancos. En la fotografía, la australiana Kristy Oatley-Nist compite en doma individual en los Juegos de Sydney.*

◀ *Los tres medallistas de la competición de circuito individual de Sydney 2000 celebran su victoria. David O'Connor aparece en medio con el oro, rodeado de Andrew Hoy con la plata (izquierda) y Mark Todd con el bronce.*

▼ *La amazona británica Leslie Law guía a su caballo por el agua durante la competición de circuito por equipos de Sydney. Law era miembro del cuarteto británico que ganó la plata en esta prueba.*

## Circuito

El circuito ecuestre dura tres días. Tanto en las competiciones por equipos como en la individual, caballos y jinetes realizan una prueba de doma y completan un recorrido de salto de obstáculos. Entre estas dos pruebas tiene lugar la más dura: la disciplina de fondo. Celebrada a lo largo de un recorrido de 25 kilómetros, la prueba de fondo consta de distintas fases que incluyen una carrera de obstáculos, en la que deben saltar tres barreras tres veces cada una, y una carrera de *cross-country*, en la que caballo y jinete deben superar desniveles, dunas y fosos de agua naturales. Además, hay un recorrido de salto de obstáculos (normalmente más bajos que los del concurso de saltos) al final de este día agotador. Los jinetes tratan de completar las diversas secciones del circuito dentro del tiempo estipulado y sin cometer faltas causadas por derribos, caídas u otras penalizaciones.

▶ *La australiana Gillian Rolton se cae de su caballo, Peppermint Grove, durante la competición de circuito por equipos de los Juegos de Atlanta de 1996. Pese a fracturarse la clavícula y dos costillas, Rolton volvió a montar y completó el circuito. El equipo australiano aseguró la medalla de oro.*

# BALÓN Y PELOTA 1

Algunos de los deportes de equipo más populares del mundo se cuentan entre los deportes de balón y pelota. El béisbol y el *softball* constan de un equipo de nueve jugadores: un *pitcher*, o lanzador, que arroja la pelota y un *catcher*, o receptor, que la atrapa si falla el bateador rival, y otros siete jugadores de campo. El hockey y el baloncesto permiten tantas sustituciones como se desee durante el partido, siempre que no se exceda el número máximo de jugadores.

▲ *La emoción del béisbol deriva de los intentos de los corredores de tocar una base antes de que la pelota le llegue al jugador que la guarda. Aquí, el norteamericano Ernie Young llega antes que la pelota y no es eliminado.*

◀ *Ernie Young se prepara para lanzar durante la semifinal de 2000 entre EE.UU. y Corea del Sur. El bateador debe protegerse la cabeza con un casco, ya que la pelota viaja a velocidades de hasta 160 km/h.*

### Béisbol

El béisbol apareció como deporte de exhibición en siete ocasiones antes de hacer su debut olímpico oficial para hombres en 1992. Los equipos se turnan para atacar (batear y correr) y defender (parar y atrapar), y cada uno dispone de nueve entradas para lograr más carreras que los rivales. Se consigue una carrera cuando un bateador avanza por las tres bases y regresa a la base donde comenzó, la base meta. Un jugador es eliminado si no lanza uno de tres golpes legales al campo de juego o si batea la pelota y los contrarios la atrapan sin que toque el suelo. Cuando un jugador batea la pelota, debe correr a la base siguiente y llegar allí antes de que la pelota le llegue al rival que guarda la base meta. Los equipos se intercambian cuando se eliminan tres jugadores. Cuba, que obtuvo el oro en 1992 y 1995, y EE.UU., que triunfó en Sydney, son grandes rivales en béisbol.

▶ *Las receptoras de* softball *llevan guantes para atrapar la pelota en el aire. Luego se la pasan a la otra mano para lanzársela a otra compañera situada en una base.*

### *Softball*

El *softball* es un deporte olímpico exclusivamente femenino. Llegó a los juegos en 1996, cuatro años después de su primo, el béisbol, con el que comparte muchas similitudes. También es un deporte de lanzar y atrapar, pero la distancia entre lanzadora y bateadora es menor que en el béisbol. Con una distancia de 18,3 m entre las cuatro bases, el *softball* es más rápido que el béisbol, cuya distancia entre bases es de 27,43 m. La pelota es más grande y más blanda que en béisbol, y se lanza por debajo del hombro. Hasta ahora EE.UU. ha ganado las dos competiciones olímpicas, derrotando a Japón 2-1 en una tensa final en Sydney.

▶ *Las lanzadoras de* softball *mueven enérgicamente el brazo para generar impulso. Cuando el deporte debutó en los Juegos de Atlanta, el lanzamiento más rápido del torneo alcanzó los 118 km/h.*

## Hockey sobre hierba

El hockey es un juego de campo que es olímpico desde 1908 para los hombres y desde 1988 para las mujeres. Los equipos constan de 11 jugadores que golpean la pelota con un palo, llamado *stick*, con dos caras, una plana y otra redondeada. Los jugadores sólo pueden golpear la pelota con la cara plana y tampoco pueden tocarla con ninguna parte del cuerpo. Los porteros son la excepción. Van provistos de almohadillas protectoras y pueden emplear el cuerpo para realizar paradas, siempre que lo hagan desde el interior del círculo de tiro. Los tiros a puerta también deben lanzarse desde dentro de este círculo de unos 15 metros de diámetro. El juego consta de dos tiempos de 35 minutos y una prórroga si el partido acaba en empate. Dos árbitros controlan el juego, cubriendo cada uno la mitad del campo, que en las olimpiadas es de hierba artificial. India y Pakistán han dominado este deporte desde siempre, pero últimamente se enfrentan a la dura competencia de Alemania, Países Bajos, Australia y Gran Bretaña.

◀ *Los jugadores de hockey sobre hierba empujan, pasan y desvían la pelota con sus* sticks *en un juego vertiginoso que exige gran forma física y trabajo en equipo. Aquí, Kuhan Shanmuganathan, de Malaisia, (de naranja) evita el regate del argentino Edgardo Palios en los Juegos de 1996.*

▼ *Este jugador de baloncesto emplea su gran agilidad para saltar sobre la cancha y encestar una canasta (situada a una altura de 3,05 metros), que vale dos puntos.*

## Baloncesto

El baloncesto, presente en las olimpiadas desde 1936, es un deporte con equipos de cinco jugadores que se juega en una cancha de 28 metros de largo por 15 metros de ancho. Cada partido consta de dos tiempos de veinte minutos, en los que el cronómetro se pone en marcha sólo cuando el balón está en juego. Los jugadores mueven el balón con diversos pases o lo botan a la vez que corren. No pueden correr mientras lo agarran con las dos manos y no pueden volver a botarlo después de haberlo parado. Los equipos logran dos puntos por un tiro desde cerca de la canasta y tres puntos por un tiro desde fuera de la línea de tres puntos. Si se comete falta sobre un atacante, su equipo recibe tres tiros libres, que valen un punto cada uno. El baloncesto es un juego rápido en el que el balón siempre está en movimiento. Cuando un jugador atrapa el balón, dispone de cinco segundos para pasarlo y su equipo sólo tiene 30 segundos para encestar, o la posesión pasa al equipo rival. EE.UU. ha ganado 16 oros olímpicos.

▲ *El baloncesto en silla de ruedas goza de gran popularidad en los Paralímpicos. Aquí, la británica Kristina Small lanza contra Australia en los Juegos de 2000.*

# BALÓN Y PELOTA 2

Fútbol, voleibol y balonmano son deportes de equipo rápidos que atraen al gran público. El fútbol fue el primero en llegar a los juegos en 1960, mientras que el voleibol debutó en Tokio en 1964. El balonmano era un deporte de aire libre con equipos de 11 jugadores en 1936, pero regresó a las olimpiadas en 1972 como un juego de interior con equipos de siete. El volley playa hizo su debut olímpico en 1996.

▲ *Los futbolistas pueden emplear cualquier parte del cuerpo, excepto las manos y los brazos, para impulsar el balón. Aquí, un futbolista lo controla con el pecho.*

◄ *El equipo noruego de fútbol femenino posa con sus medallas en 2000. La final contra EE.UU. acabó en empate (2-2) y el juego continuó en la prórroga. Noruega marcó un tercer gol y se hizo con el oro.*

▼ *El equipo masculino de Camerún celebra la victoria tras ganar el oro en los Juegos de Sydney venciendo a España en la tanda de penaltis.*

**Fútbol**

Este es el deporte de balón que se juega en equipo más popular del mundo. Lo practican y siguen tanto hombres como mujeres. Los equipos constan de once jugadores, que tratan de marcar más goles que los rivales en dos tiempos de 45 minutos cada uno. El fútbol es también un acontecimiento esperado en las olimpiadas: en 1956, por ejemplo, en la ciudad australiana de Melbourne, un partido de primera ronda entre Suecia y Brasil congregó a 93.000 personas. Cuando la competición olímpica llega a los cuartos de final, se juega una prórroga en los partidos que acaban en empate. Si los equipos siguen empatados al finalizar la prórroga, el juego concluye con una tensa y emocionante tanda de penaltis.

▼ *El portero es el único jugador de fútbol que puede tocar el balón con las manos cuando está en juego, y siempre que lo haga dentro del área de penalti, también llamada área grande.*

**De amateur a profesional**

Hasta la creación de la Copa del Mundo en la década de 1930, las olimpiadas fueron el escenario del campeonato de fútbol internacional más grande del mundo. Tradicionalmente, solo se permitía participar en los juegos a los jugadores amateur, pero desde la década de 1980 se ha permitido el acceso de jugadores profesionales (con algunas restricciones de edad). Sydney 2000 vio a profesionales tan conocidos como el brasileño Ronaldinho, el camerunés Lauren y el japonés Hidetoshi Nakata tomar parte en un torneo que produjo una media de más de tres goles por partido. En la década de 1990, la competición femenina irrumpió en los juegos, obteniendo EE.UU. la primera medalla de oro en 1996. Diez equipos femeninos y 16 masculinos competirán por el oro en los Juegos de Atenas de 2004.

## Voleibol

Tanto el voleibol como el volley playa se juegan en un campo rectangular de 9x18 metros con una red elevada a una altura de 2,43 metros para los hombres y 2,24 metros para las mujeres. En el voleibol, dos equipos de seis jugadores golpean por turnos el balón con la mano para pasarlo al campo contrario por encima de la red en no más de tres toques. Los jugadores pueden emplear cualquier parte del cuerpo para golpear el balón, pero no pueden volver a tocarlo antes de que lo haya hecho otro jugador. El volley playa se juega sobre un terreno de juego cubierto de arena nivelada. Las reglas son casi las mismas y el balón tiene el mismo tamaño (aunque inflado a más presión para que sea más pesado y resulte más estable frente al viento). Solo hay dos jugadores por equipo, lo que les obliga a cubrir una gran superficie y compenetrarse bien. Los jugadores se aprovechan de la debilidad del rival.

▼ *La australiana Kerri Pottharst se lanza para tocar el balón en la final de volley playa femenino de Sydney. Pottharst y su compañera Natalie Cook derrotaron a las favoritas brasileñas en la final y sumaron este oro al bronce que habían obtenido cuatro años antes.*

► *El holandés Reinder Nummerdor bloquea un tiro del español Rafael Pascual durante la competición de voleibol masculina de Sydney. El equipo holandés ganó el partido por tres sets a uno (25-18, 25-17, 24-26, 25-21).*

## Balonmano

El balomano es un deporte rápido en el que casi toda la acción se centra en torno a las porterías. Este deporte es especialmente popular en el este de Europa. El balomnano olímpico es un juego con equipos de siete jugadores que se practica en un terreno de juego rectangular de 40 x 20 metros. Los jugadores pasan, lanzan y atrapan un balón pequeño, con el objetivo de encajarlo en la portería contraria. Un semicírculo situado a seis metros de la portería delimita el área de meta, que solo puede ser ocupada por el portero. El portero es también el único jugador que puede utilizar los pies y las piernas por debajo de la rodilla para detener el balón. Cuando un jugador atrapa el balón, dispone de tres pasos y tres segundos de posesión antes de pasarlo. También pueden botarlo como un balón de baloncesto y rodarlo por el suelo. El reglamento permite realizar todos los cambios y sustituciones que se deseen.

◄ *Dinamarca: las campeonas de balonmano femenino posan para una foto tras ganar el oro de nuevo en 2000. Las danesas remontaron una desventaja de seis puntos y vencieron a Hungría 31-27 en la final, en la que Anette Hoffman Moberg marcó 11 goles.*

◄ *La brasileña Viviani Emerick se eleva en el aire para tirar a puerta durante los Juegos de Sydney. El balón de balonmano tiene un perímetro de 54 a 56 centímetros en la competición femenina y de 58 a 60 centímetros en la masculina.*

▲ *Gran Bretaña se enfrenta a China en los dobles de bádminton de las Olimpiadas de 2000. China logró un éxito sorprendente en Sydney: sus tres parejas femeninas consiguieron medallas y el equipo de bádminton recogió ocho de las 15 medallas posibles.*

# DEPORTES DE RAQUETA

El tenis es uno de los deportes de raqueta más populares y practicados del mundo. Su regreso a la competición olímpica en 1988 deleitó a millones de seguidores. El tenis de mesa y el bádminton también son relativamente nuevos en los juegos (debutaron en 1988 y 1992), pero los dos cuentan con legiones de aficionados, sobre todo en Europa y Asia.

**Bádminton**

El bádminton, que en sus orígenes era un juego de persecución practicado entre los ricos a finales del siglo XIX, es hoy el juego de raqueta más rápido del mundo. Los jugadores deben estar en gran forma y ser excelentes atletas. Se puede jugar en individuales o por parejas y consiste en golpear con una raqueta ligera un volante de plumas o sintético por encima de la red hacia el otro lado de la pista. Se conceden puntos cuando el jugador que da el servicio obliga a su rival a cometer un fallo (estrellar el volante contra la red o enviarlo fuera de la pista, por ejemplo) o si consigue que el volante toque el suelo de la pista del lado del adversario. Los partidos se componen de tres juegos y los jugadores han de ser muy ágiles y reaccionar deprisa para atacar y defender, ya que el volante viaja a velocidades de hasta 260 km/h.

► *Durante un partido de dobles de bádminton, el surcoreano Yoo Yong-Sung salta para dar un* smash. *Él y su compañero, Lee Dong-Soo, ganaron una medalla de plata en esta competición en los Juegos de 2000.*

► *En este partido de tenis de mesa de Sydney 2000, el jugador atacante emplea su cuerpo para realizar un espectacular* smash. *Aunque golpea la pelota con gran fuerza, debe calcular la dirección con precisión milimétrica para que la pelota caiga en la mitad de la mesa del rival. La mesa de juego es un rectángulo de 3,45 m de largo por 1,92 m de ancho.*

**Tenis de mesa**

Millones de personas han disfrutado con un partidillo de ping pong ocasional, pero eso tiene poco que ver con el tenis de mesa de las olimpiadas. Los recientes cambios en las reglas de puntuación y servicio han propiciado un juego de ataque en el que los participantes son capaces de golpear la pelota a velocidades de hasta 160 km/h. Las finales olímpicas de tenis de mesa se componen de siete juegos. Para ganar un juego, un jugador debe conseguir 11 tantos o, si ambos jugadores empatan a 10, adelantarse en dos puntos. El tenis de mesa no sólo es un deporte espectacular, es también un juego de precisión, velocidad y tácticas. Los campeones pueden golpear la pelota con una gran variedad de golpes, dándole efecto para que cambie de trayectoria al botar. Los golpes con efecto hacen que la pelota se desvíe bruscamente en el aire, mientras que los *top-spins* hacen que la pelota se eleve, bote y acelere en la otra mitad de la mesa.

◀ *El jugador de tenis de mesa que recibe debe reaccionar deprisa para responder al potente ataque de su adversario. Los golpes defensivos a veces dan a la pelota un efecto hacia atrás que hace que pierda velocidad después de botar.*

▶ *El ruso Yevgeny Kafelnikov lanza un servicio durante la competición de individuales masculina de los Juegos de Sydney. El servicio es un arma potente en el tenis masculino. El jugador que saca, o sirve, trata de enviar la pelota al jugador al resto a gran velocidad o con efecto para que resulte imposible devolverla. Se denomina* ace *a un saque que el restador no puede tocar con su raqueta.*

**Tenis**

El tenis regresó a la competición olímpica en Seúl 1988, tras una ausencia de 64 años, ahora con la presencia de tenistas profesionales. El tenis olímpico, al igual que el bádminton y otros grandes torneos, es una competición eliminatoria con pruebas individuales y por equipos para hombres y mujeres. En ambos casos los partidos se componen de tres sets, a excepción de la final masculina, que cuenta con cinco sets. Los tenistas que pierden en las semifinales se disputan el tercer puesto y la medalla de bronce. Los tenistas de élite deben ser capaces de prever los golpes del rival, recorrer la pista deprisa y tener un servicio fuerte y preciso que no se vea afectado por la presión. Algunos tenistas prefieren mantenerse en la línea de fondo de la pista, dando golpes largos y grandes carreras. Otros optan por subir a la red y atacar con voleas y espectaculares golpes de *smash*.

▶ *La tenista norteamericana Venus Williams mantiene la vista en la pelota mientras se prepara para golpearla con las dos manos. Williams obtuvo dos oros en los Juegos de Sydney, derrotando a la rusa Yelena Dementyeva en individuales y ganando los dobles junto a su hermana Serena.*

# SYDNEY 2000

El 15 de septiembre de 2000, el mayor espectáculo del mundo llegó a Australia por segunda vez. Las Olimpiadas de 1956 en Melbourne habían sido un acontecimiento feliz pero relativamente discreto. Las Olimpiadas de Sydney elevaron los juegos a un nivel completamente distinto. 16 días después, tras decenas de escenas memorables y actuaciones increíbles, José Antonio Samaranch, presidente del COI, declaró los Juegos de Sydney los mejores de todos los tiempos. Pocos discreparon.

▲ *Logotipo oficial de las Olimpiadas de verano de 2000, los Juegos más grandes de todos los tiempos, con 10.651 atletas de 199 naciones compitiendo en 300 pruebas. Se utilizaron 36 escenarios, incluido el gigantesco Sydney Stadium en Homebush Bay.*

▼ *Cathy Freeman cautivó a sus compatriotas y al mundo entero con una victoria en 400 metros lisos bajo extrema presión. Freeman, símbolo del pueblo aborigen australiano, fue la portadora de la antorcha olímpica en la inauguración.*

## Gran apoyo popular

El éxito de Sydney se debió en gran parte al público australiano, que acudió en masa a los estadios y casi agotó los cinco millones de entradas a la venta. Los atletas australianos respondieron con su mejor actuación olímpica, obteniendo 58 medallas. Los australianos mostraron su apoyo, apasionado pero justo, hacia todos los participantes. En el salto de longitud masculino, por ejemplo, el público aplaudió con entusiasmo al cubano Iván Pedroso, incluso después de haber arrebatado el oro al australiano Jai Taurima.

▲ *Steve Redgrave celebra el quinto oro olímpico de su carrera, obtenido como parte del equipo británico de remo en modalidad cuatro sin timonel.*

◀ *Ian Thorpe, apodado el Thorpedo, a punto de ganar el oro y establecer un nuevo récord mundial en 400 m estilos. Thorpe obtuvo un total de tres oros y dos platas en el modernísimo Aquatic Centre de Sydney.*

### Actuaciones sobresalientes

Un sinfín de grandes historias salpicaron las Olimpiadas de Sydney. Se esperaba que la leyenda del ciclismo Lance Armstrong venciera en la prueba de 50 km contrarreloj, pero perdió frente al ruso Vyacheslav Ekimov. Otro ruso, Alexandr Karelin, perdió su récord en lucha grecorromana, imbatido durante 13 años, frente al americano Rulon Gardner. Dos deportistas alemanas, la saltadora de longitud Heike Drechsler y la piragüista Birgit Fischer, obtuvieron el oro en su madurez, venciendo a oponentes mucho más jóvenes. En el caso de Fischer había 20 años de diferencia entre sus dos medallas en remo. Las estrellas de natación fueron Ian Thorpe, de Australia, e Inge de Brujin, de los Países Bajos, quienes ganaron tres oros y una plata.

| MEDALLERO | O | P | B |
|---|---|---|---|
| EE.UU. | 39 | 25 | 33 |
| Rusia | 32 | 28 | 28 |
| China | 28 | 16 | 15 |
| Australia | 16 | 25 | 17 |
| Alemania | 14 | 17 | 26 |
| Francia | 13 | 14 | 11 |
| Italia | 13 | 8 | 13 |
| Países Bajos | 12 | 9 | 4 |
| Cuba | 11 | 11 | 7 |
| Gran Bretaña | 11 | 10 | 7 |

◀ *La espectacular ceremonia de clausura, celebrada en el Sydney Stadium en Homebush Bay, atrajo a 110.000 espectadores entusiastas.*

▶ *Annet Davis, de EE.UU., y Sarah Stratton, de Australia, disputan un punto en la competición de volley playa femenina, celebrada en la famosísima playa Bondi de Sydney.*

### Medallas memorables

El remero británico Steve Redgrave consiguió su quinto oro en cinco olimpiadas, una hazaña jamás lograda antes en un deporte de resistencia. Colombia celebró la primera medalla de oro de su historia cuando María Isabel Urrutia, de 35 años, obtuvo un oro en halterofilia –la primera vez que la halterofilia femenina aparecía en los Juegos–. También hicieron su debut olímpico la natación sincronizada, el salto de pértiga femenino, el triatlón y el taekwondo. El campeón de Corea del Sur Kim Kyong-Hun obtuvo el oro en este último deporte. Grecia y China también lograron medallas en esta disciplina.

# GRANDES RIVALIDADES

La historia de las olimpiadas, como la de todos los grandes eventos deportivos, está salpicada de historias de grandes rivalidades entre atletas excelentemente dotados o entre equipos y naciones. De cuando en cuando, la intensidad de la competición acaba en discordia, pero en su mayoría estas rivalidades se controlan y sirven para motivar a los deportistas olímpicos a cotas más altas.

▲ *El atleta británico Daley Thompson (izquierda) y el alemán occidental Jürgen Hingsen (derecha) alcanzaban cotas cada vez más altas del decatlón mientras rivalizaban por el triunfo. Thompson ganó el oro en 1980 y 1984.*

▼ *La rivalidad entre los corredores de fondo Haile Gebrselassie (izquierda) y Paul Tergat (derecha) ha dado algunas de las carreras más emocionantes y finales más trepidantes de la historia del deporte. Gebrselassie ha logrado siempre el oro olímpico, relegando por décimas a su rival a la segunda posición en dos ocasiones.*

**Duelo de decatletas**

A finales del la década de 1970 y 1980, el decatlón estuvo dominado por el británico Daley Thompson y un trío de Alemania Occidental (Guido Kratschmer, Siggy Wentz y Jürgen Hingsen). La rivalidad entre Thompson y Hingsen era tan feroz que batieron récords mundiales en decatlones de todo el mundo. Tras ganar el oro en los Juegos de 1980, Thompson se enfrentaba a una dura prueba en las Olimpiadas de Los Ángeles, sobre todo cuando Hingsen batió el récord mundial de Thompson. Los dos hombres mejoraron inmediatamente sus marcas y batieron récords olímpicos durante la competición, antes de que finalmente ganara Thompson. La lista de méritos de Thompson aumentó con un nuevo récord mundial. "Algún día le ganaré. Claro, que entonces igual tendré 80 años", bromeó Hingsen a posteriori. La rivalidad continuó en unas terceras olimpiadas en 1988, pero una lesión de Thompson y la descalificación de Hingsen de los 100 metros lisos por salidas nulas les apartaron de las glorias anteriores.

## Rivales sonrientes

Etiopía contra Kenia, Haile Gebrselassie contra Paul Tergat. Una de las grandes rivalidades atléticas del mundo tuvo lugar en las carreras de fondo de 5.000 m lisos, *cross-country* y maratón. Dos de sus grandes encuentros fueron en las olimpiadas, ambos en 10.000 m lisos. En los Juegos de 1996, Gebrselassie derrotó a Tergat por apenas unos metros. Tergat batió el récord de Gebrselassie en 1997 y también le ganó en algunas otras pruebas. Pero Gebrselassie era el favorito y la pareja renovó su intensa pero amistosa rivalidad en Sydney 2000. En una dramática carrera, Tergat logró adelantarse en la última zancada. Tras más de 27 minutos de carrera, únicamente nueve centésimas de segundo separaron el primer puesto de Gebrselassie del segundo de Tergat. Su rivalidad ha dado algunas de las llegadas a meta en carreras de fondo más emocionantes de la historia olímpica.

▲ *Los baloncestistas norteamericanos celebran la victoria al término de la final de 1972. En realidad, el partido no había acabado y sus rivales soviéticos se alzaron con la victoria en los últimos segundos. EE.UU. no recogió las medallas, que continúan en poder del COI.*

## Rivalidades por equipos

Las grandes rivalidades no se limitan a dos atletas individuales. Existe una rivalidad larga e intensa, por ejemplo, entre los boxeadores de Cuba y EE.UU., los jugadores de hockey de India y Pakistán, y los equipos de levantamiento de peso de Grecia, Turquía y Bulgaria. Una de las rivalidades más vivas tiene lugar en la piscina entre las naciones punteras en natación, EE.UU. y Australia. Comenzó en la década de 1920, cuando el nadador norteamericano Johnny Weissmuller dominaba muchas pruebas, y ha llevado a estas dos naciones a ocupar el primer y segundo lugar en el medallero de la natación en nueve ocasiones.

## Demasiado lejos

En ocasiones la rivalidad se transforma en hostilidad o en negativa a aceptar la derrota. En 1996, tras una épica semifinal de voleibol femenino en la que Cuba derrotó a Brasil, las jugadoras comenzaron a empujarse unas a otras. No se descalificó a ningún equipo y Cuba conservó el oro. En plena guerra fría, la rivalidad deportiva entre EE.UU. y la Unión Soviética se disparó, alcanzando el culmen en la final de baloncesto de 1972, cuando, a falta de unos segundos y con EE.UU. un punto por delante en el marcador, surgió la controversia acerca de si el equipo soviético había pedido tiempo muerto. El juego se reinició varias veces y, justo cuando la bocina señalaba el final del partido, los soviéticos encestaron. Los norteamericanos no aceptaron el resultado ni tampoco las medallas de plata.

# CONTRA TODO PRONÓSTICO

Ganar una medalla olímpica es el final de un largo y, en ocasiones, doloroso viaje para muchos participantes. Todos los deportistas olímpicos deben controlar sus dudas y temores, llevar sus cuerpos al límite y superar a sus rivales para obtener un codiciado lugar en el podio. Enfermedades, lesiones y otras circunstancias han obligado a algunos participantes a ir aún más allá para lograr su premio.

▲ *Un año antes de los Juegos de Sydney, una motocicleta dejó al tirador francés Franck Dumoulin en una silla de ruedas. No solo logró competir en Sydney, sino que su impresionante actuación le valió el oro en tiro de pistola desde 10 metros.*

► *Wilma Rudolph ganó tres medallas de oro en los Juegos de 1960, que sumó al bronce en relevos 4 x 100 metros obtenido a los 16 años en 1956. Su elegancia y asombrosa velocidad le valieron el apodo de la Gacela Negra.*

### Una lucha cuesta arriba

Muchos deportistas han tenido que superar problemas de su infancia para convertirse en campeones olímpicos. La esgrimista húngara Ildiko Ujlaki-Rejto nació sorda y necesitaba que sus entrenadores le escribieran mensajes. A pesar de ello, llegó a ser una esgrimista de primera clase que compitió en cinco olimpiadas (1960-76) y ganó siete medallas. La corredora norteamericana Wilma Rudolph cogió neumonía y escarlatina a los cuatro años. Quedó paralítica y los médicos le dijeron que nunca volvería a caminar. Rudolph no solo aprendió a caminar, sino también a correr... a velocidades de vértigo. Fue la primera mujer que corrió los 200 m lisos en menos de 23 segundos, y en 1960 se convirtió en la leyenda de los Juegos de Roma al ganar tres oros en 100 y 200 m lisos, y en relevos 4 x 100 m.

▼ *La danesa Lis Hartel contrajo la polio cuando tenía 20 años y quedó paralizada por debajo de las rodillas. En los Juegos de 1952 y 1956 (pese a que tenían que montarla y desmontarla del caballo), Hartel ganó la plata en la prueba de doma ecuestre.*

### Regresos espectaculares

Algunos deportistas han tenido el coraje de regresar tras sufrir accidentes o enfermedades graves. El caso del húngaro Oliver Halassy es extraordinario. Perdió la pierna izquierda a la altura de la rodilla en un accidente de tranvía, y a pesar de ello, compitió en la exigente prueba de waterpolo y formó parte del victorioso equipo húngaro de las Olimpiadas de 1936. La leyenda del ciclismo norteamericano Lance Armstrong reveló en 1996 que padecía un cáncer de testículos potencialmente mortal. Tras varias operaciones y tratamientos de radiaciones, Armstrong consiguió no sólo sobrevivir a la enfermedad, sino también ganar dos de los más codiciados premios de ciclismo, el Tour de Francia, y un bronce en los Juegos de Sydney.

### Kip Keino

Kipchoge 'Kip' Keino era un corredor relativamente desconocido cuando hizo realidad su sueño de llegar a los Juegos de México de 1968. Posteriormente sería recordado y admirado por unas olimpiadas extraordinarias. El policía keniata tenía cálculos biliares y, mientras lideraba el grupo en su primera prueba, los 10.000 metros lisos, se desmayó de dolor y salió tambaleándose de la pista a falta de sólo dos vueltas. Se puso en pie para acabar la carrera, aunque más tarde sería descalificado. Cuatro días después, participó en los 5.000 metros lisos y ganó la medalla de plata. Todavía con grandes dolores, el día de la final de 1.500 metros lisos, cogió un autobús de la villa olímpica al estadio. El autobús encontró un atasco, así que Keino se bajó y corrió dos kilómetros hasta el estadio. Llegó instantes antes del comienzo de la carrera, en la que marcó un ritmo rápido para tratar de neutralizar al supuesto favorito, Jim Ryun de EE.UU. Sorprendentemente, Keino ganó el oro con una ventaja de 20 metros respecto a Ryun.

◀ *Jim Abbott era el lanzador estrella del equipo norteamericano de béisbol que triunfó en los Juegos de 1988. Abbot nació sin mano derecha. Cuando lanzaba, se ponía un guante en la mano derecha, que luego pasaba deprisa a la izquierda para recoger cualquier pelota que le llegara. Posteriormente, Abbott se dedicó al béisbol profesional.*

◀ *Kip Keino en las Olimpiadas de Múnich de 1972, donde ganó el oro en 3.000 metros obstáculos pese a su escasa experiencia y a participar en la carrera como un desafío.*

### Por el bien del equipo

Cada deportista olímpico trata de hacer lo mejor por su equipo. Algunos llevan esto hasta el límite, luchando contra el dolor cuando muchos se retirarían. En los Juegos de 1936, el jinete alemán Konrad von Wangenheim se cayó del caballo y se fracturó la clavícula. Continuó montando y, pese a sufrir una segunda caída al día siguiente, ayudó a su equipo a ganar la medalla de oro. Un drama similar ocurrió durante los Juegos de 1976. El japonés Shun Fujimoto estaba en medio de su ejercicio de suelo cuando se rompió la rótula. Aunque parezca increíble, siguió compitiendo por su equipo. Obtuvo 9,5 en el caballo con arcos antes de acometer las anillas, donde realizó una salida con triple salto mortal. El aterrizaje ejerció una tremenda presión en la rodilla herida, pero el gimnasta mantuvo la postura para los jueces antes de desmayarse de dolor. El 9,7 que obtuvo Fujimoto no solo fue su mejor puntuación en ese aparato, sino también una baza vital que llevó al equipo japonés a la gloria del oro, aventajando a la Unión Soviética únicamente por 0,4 puntos.

▼ *El gimnasta japonés Shun Fujimoto se rompió una rótula mientras competía, pero optó por ignorar el terrible dolor para mantener las esperanzas del oro de su equipo. Continuó, ocultando su dolor, sin decírselo a nadie y sin tomar calmantes, para lograr el oro.*

# DATOS Y CIFRAS OLÍMPICAS

**Mayor medallero**
Larissa Latynina, Unión Soviética, 1956–64: 18 medallas (9 oro), gimnasia
Nikolay Andrianov, Unión Soviética, 1972–80: 15 medallas (7 oro), gimnasia

**Mayor medallero (no gimnasia)**
Edoardo Mangiarotti, Italia, 1936–60: 13 medallas (6 oro), esgrima
Paavo Nurmi, Finlandia, 1920–28: 12 medallas (9 oro), atletismo
Mark Spitz, EE.UU., 1968–72: 11 medallas (9 oro), natación
Matt Biondi, EE.UU., 1984–92: 11 medallas (8 oro), natación
Birgit Fischer, Alemania, 1980–2000: 10 medallas (7 oro), piragüismo

**Mayor medallero en unas olimpiadas**
Aleksandr Dityatin, Unión Soviética, 1980: 8 medallas (3 oro), gimnasia
Mark Spitz, EE.UU., 1972: 7 medallas (7 oro), natación
Willis Lee, EE.UU., 1920: 7 medallas (5 oro), tiro
Matt Biondi, EE.UU., 1988: 7 medallas (5 oro), natación
Mariya Gorokhovskaya, Unión Soviética, 1952: 7 medallas (2 oro), gimnasia

**Medallista de más edad**
Oscar Swahn, Suecia, 1920:
72 años y 280 días, medalla de plata en tiro

**Participante femenina de más edad**
Lorna Johnstone, Gran Bretaña, 1972:
70 años, puesto 12 en la prueba de doma

**Participante de más edad Sydney 2000**
Bruce Meredith, Islas Vírgenes EE.UU.:
63 años, tiro

**Participantes más jóvenes**
Dimitrios Loundras, Grecia, 1896: 10 años, gimnasia
Carlos Front, España, 1992: 11 años, remo ocho con timonel
Luigina Giavotti, Italia, 1928: 11 años, gimnasia

**Juegos de la era moderna**

| Año | Sede olímpica | Participantes | Naciones | Pruebas |
|---|---|---|---|---|
| 1896 | Atenas, Grecia | 241 | 14 | 43 |
| 1900 | París, Francia | 1.225 | 24 | 95 |
| 1904 | Saint Louis, EE.UU. | 689 | 13 | 91 |
| 1908 | Londres, RU | 2.035 | 22 | 110 |
| 1912 | Estocolmo, Suecia | 2.547 | 28 | 102 |
| 1920 | Amberes, Bélgica | 2.669 | 29 | 154 |
| 1924 | París, Francia | 3.092 | 44 | 126 |
| 1928 | Amsterdam, Países Bajos | 3.014 | 46 | 109 |
| 1932 | Los Ángeles, EE.UU. | 1.408 | 37 | 117 |
| 1936 | Berlín, Alemania | 4.066 | 49 | 129 |
| 1948 | Londres, RU | 4.099 | 59 | 136 |
| 1952 | Helsinki, Finlandia | 4.925 | 69 | 149 |
| 1956 | Melbourne, Australia | 3.184 | 67 | 145 |
| 1960 | Roma, Italia | 5.348 | 83 | 150 |
| 1964 | Tokio, Japón | 5.140 | 93 | 163 |
| 1968 | México, México | 5.530 | 112 | 172 |
| 1972 | Múnich, Alem. Occidental | 7.123 | 121 | 195 |
| 1976 | Montreal, Canadá | 6.028 | 92 | 198 |
| 1980 | Moscú, Unión Soviética | 5.217 | 80 | 203 |
| 1984 | Los Ángeles, EE.UU. | 6.797 | 140 | 221 |
| 1988 | Seúl, Corea del Sur | 8.465 | 159 | 237 |
| 1992 | Barcelona, España | 9.367 | 169 | 257 |
| 1996 | Atlanta, EE.UU. | 10.318 | 197 | 271 |
| 2000 | Sydney, Australia | 10.651 | 199 | 300 |
| 2004 | Atenas, Grecia | 10.500 (aprox.) | 201 | 301 |
| 2008 | Pekín, China | – | – | – |

*Fuente: Página web del Comité Olímpico Internacional (www.olympic.org)*

# INCREÍBLE PERO CIERTO

En 1900, la norteamericana Margaret Abbot participó en lo que ella creía que era una competición local de golf. Cuando ganó, se convirtió en la primera campeona olímpica de esa disciplina.

El regatista Hank Lammens fue descalificado de los Juegos de 1992 por olvidarse el chaleco salvavidas.

El australiano Henry Pearce llevaba tanta ventaja en la prueba de remo individual de 1928 que se detuvo para dejar paso a unos patos. Después, siguió remando y ganó el oro.

El boxeador surafricano Thomas Hamilton-Brown perdió un combate muy disputado en los Juegos de 1936 y se consoló con una comilona. Cuando los jueces descubrieron que en realidad había ganado, pesaba demasiado para participar en el siguiente combate.

El corredor cubano Félix Carbajal llegó al maratón de 1904 con zapatos y pantalones largos, tras hacer autoestop durante horas. Durante la carrera, Carbajal sintió hambre y comió una manzana verde de un árbol. Un dolor de estómago le obligó a retirarse.

En la prueba de disco de 1932, el francés Jules Noël bebió champán entre los lanzamientos. Perdió la medalla de bronce por 10 cm.

El atleta norteamericano George Eyser ganó las pruebas gimnásticas de cuerda, barras paralelas y caballo con arcos en las Olimpiadas de 1904 a pesar de tener una pierna ortopédica.

Los jueces de los Juegos de 1932 perdieron la cuenta de las vueltas de los 3.000 metros obstáculos y obligaron a los atletas a correr 400 metros más.

Dos de los veleros participantes en la vela de 1990 fueron descalificados por usar motores secretos.

En 1896 se celebró una carrera de natación de 100 metros estilos para marineros de la marina griega.

Ni Giovanni Pettenella ni Pierre Trentin querían dar la primera pedalada en la semifinal de 1.000 metros de ciclismo en 1964. Permanecieron inmóviles durante 21 minutos y 57 segundos. Al final, Petenella ganó la carrera y la consiguiente medalla de oro.

El recorrido ciclista de los Juegos de 1920 incluía un paso a nivel. Algunos ciclistas sufrieron más de cuatro minutos de retraso por culpa de un tren.

Cuando el canadiense George Lyon ganó la competición de golf en 1904, subió a recibir el trofeo caminando sobre las manos.

El combinado danés y sueco de soka-tira de los Juegos de 1900 contaba con un hombre menos, así que le pidieron al periodista danés Edgar Aaybe que se les uniera. Ganaron el oro.

---

# MOMENTOS MEMORABLES

Las olimpiadas de verano han generado cientos de momentos memorables de triunfo, desastre, coraje, amistad y espíritu deportivo. Muchos aparecen en el texto de este libro. He aquí otros cinco.

**Deportividad cronometrada**
El finlandés Paavo Nurmi ya había ganado ocho medallas de oro en fondo y medio fondo cuando se preparaba para tomar la salida de la semifinal de 3.000 metros obstáculos en los Juegos de 1928. Nurmi, famoso por correr con un cronómetro en la mano, se cayó y perdió el reloj en la ría. El atleta francés Lucien Duquesne se detuvo a ayudarle a recuperar el cronómetro. Nurmi correspondió corriendo al lado de Duquesne y ofreciéndole el primer lugar en la línea de llegada, pero el francés declinó el honor.

**La atleta definitiva**
Mildred 'Babe' Didrikson era una increíble deportista "todoterreno" que destacó en béisbol, baloncesto y, tras su carrera olímpica, en golf, al que jugó a nivel profesional. A los 21 años, Didrikson se clasificó para ocho pruebas olímpicas de los Juegos de 1932, pero sólo se la permitió competir en tres. Ganó la jabalina con un récord olímpico y luego los 80 metros vallas en un tiempo récord mundial de 11,7 segundos. En el salto de altura, Didrikson y su compañera norteamericana Jean Shirley alcanzaron la misma altura, pero Didrikson fue relegada a la medalla de plata por su inusual técnica de salto. Didrikson está considerada una de las atletas más grandes de todos los tiempos.

**La maravilla descalza**
El corredor de fondo etíope Abebe Bikila llegó al maratón de 1960 siendo un desconocido. Tampoco tenía experiencia, ya que hasta entonces sólo había corrido dos maratones. Bikila triunfó y ganó la medalla de oro, batiendo el récord mundial con un tiempo de una hora, 15 minutos y 16 segundos. Logró esto corriendo descalzo, aun cuando parte del recorrido era a través de calles adoquinadas. Bikila dejó boquiabiertos a los espectadores de las siguientes olimpiadas al ganar de nuevo el maratón, esta vez apenas seis semanas después de una operación de apéndice.

**Cinco de cinco**
En 1996, el británico Steve Redgrave estableció un récord olímpico en remo al convertirse en la primera persona que ganaba la medalla de oro en ese deporte en cuatro olimpiadas consecutivas. Redgrave entrenó sin descanso para Sydney 2000, pese a padecer colitis (una inflamación del intestino) de forma periódica y ser diabético desde los 35 años. En una disputada final en la prueba de cuatro sin timonel, seguidos muy de cerca por sus rivales italianos, Redgrave y sus compañeros de remo lograron el quinto oro en la quinta olimpiada de Redgrave. Hasta entonces nadie había conseguido una hazaña así en un deporte de resistencia.

**Llegan las Superáguilas**
En los Juegos de Atlanta de 1996, el equipo de fútbol de Nigeria, apodado las Superáguilas, participó en uno de los partidos más emocionantes de la historia olímpica. Cuando perdían 3-1 frente a la favorita Brasil en la semifinal, respondieron con dos goles en el tiempo de descuento. Marcaron de nuevo y consiguieron una victoria 4-3 frente a los campeones del mundo. En la final derrotarían a Argentina, convirtiéndose en la primera nación africana que obtenía el oro en fútbol.

# VOCABULARIO

**Abanderado:** Deportista que porta la bandera de su equipo nacional en la ceremonia de inauguración de las olimpiadas.

**Amateur:** Persona que practica un deporte sin cobrar. Las primeras olimpiadas eran solo para deportistas amateur, pero hoy participan tanto amateurs como **profesionales**.

**Anabolizantes:** Drogas que potencian el crecimiento muscular y dan más fuerza al atleta. Están prohibidos en los deportes olímpicos.

**Antorcha olímpica:** Antorcha utilizada para llevar la llama olímpica desde Grecia hasta la ciudad anfitriona antes del comienzo de cada olimpiada.

**Apartheid:** Sistema político que mantenía separadas a las personas blancas y negras de Suráfrica. Fue abolido en la década de 1990.

**Aros olímpicos:** Símbolo de los juegos olímpicos, formado por cinco aros entrelazados que representan los cinco continentes que participan: África, América, Asia, Australasia y Europa.

**Boicot:** Negativa a asistir a un acontecimiento, como las olimpiadas, con frecuencia por motivos políticos.

**COI:** Siglas correspondientes al Comité Olímpico Internacional, la organización que dirige y controla los juegos olímpicos de verano e invierno.

**Combate:** Pelea de un deporte como boxeo, lucha o judo.

**Comisario:** Persona que colabora en la organización de un evento.

**Coreografía:** Representación de una rutina al ritmo de la música.

**Deporte de exhibición:** Deporte realizado en las olimpiadas sin que se otorguen medallas a los ganadores.

**Deporte de resistencia:** Deporte en el que los participantes deben rendir durante mucho tiempo, como el remo o el maratón.

**Deporte no olímpico:** Deporte que no forma parte de los juegos o que ha quedado fuera del programa olímpico.

**Deportista olímpico:** Atleta que participa en los Juegos Olímpicos.

**Descalificación:** Exclusión de un atleta de una carrera o, si ya se ha corrido, retirada del puesto y récord de dicho atleta.

**Deshidratación:** Pérdida de agua. Los atletas pueden sufrirla en condiciones de mucho calor.

**Doping:** Uso ilegal de una sustancia que puede mejorar el rendimiento de un atleta y que puede ser perjudicial para la salud del mismo.

**Ejecución:** Realización de un movimiento en un deporte como la gimnasia o los saltos.

**Eliminatoria:** Carrera clasificatoria en las primeras fases de una competición.

**Era moderna:** En términos olímpicos, el período que va desde los primeros juegos olímpicos, celebrados en 1896, hasta la actualidad.

**Estilo libre:** En natación, estilo libre significa que el nadador puede elegir el estilo que prefiera para la carrera, aunque en la práctica siempre se usa el crol. En deportes como la natación sincronizada y la doma ecuestre, significa que los participantes realizan su propia rutina en lugar de la oficial.

**Fatiga:** Cansancio causado por el esfuerzo de realizar una actividad.

**Foto finish:** Final muy disputado de una carrera. Los jueces estudian una fotografía especial, tomada de forma electrónica, para decidir los puestos en el podio.

**Guerra fría:** Período de hostilidad política entre EE.UU. y la Unión Soviética tras la II Guerra Mundial. Acabó con la disgregación de la Unión Soviética a principios de la década de 1990.

**Lanzamiento de penalti:** Forma de decidir el resultado de un partido de fútbol cuando los marcadores están igualados al final de la **prórroga**.

**Ligamento:** Tendón que conecta un músculo con la parte posterior de la rodilla.

**Llama olímpica:** Fuego que arde en un pebetero en el estadio olímpico durante los juegos.

**Mecenazgo:** Dinero procedente de empresas privadas que se utiliza para promover deportes o deportistas.

**Mercadería:** Artículos a la venta en un acontecimiento, como recuerdos, ropa y juguetes.

**Mérito artístico:** En deportes como la gimnasia, la originalidad, fluidez y elegancia de la rutina de un gimnasta.

**Mérito técnico:** Nivel de dificultad de una rutina en deportes como gimnasia y natación sincronizada.

**Tiempo muerto:** Interrupción del juego en deportes como baloncesto, en la que los jugadores descansan, comentan tácticas o se realizan cambios en la alineación.

**Movimiento olímpico:** Todos los individuos y organizaciones que ayudan a promover y acoger los juegos olímpicos.

**Nación anfitriona:** País que acoge un evento como los juegos olímpicos.

**Paralímpico:** Participante de los juegos paralímpicos para deportistas con discapacidades o necesidades especiales.

**Podio:** Plataforma elevada en la que se sitúan los deportistas para recibir una medalla. En el podio olímpico, el oro ocupa el peldaño más alto.

**Profesional:** Persona que cobra dinero por practicar un deporte. Consulta también **amateur**.

**Prórroga:** Período adicional que se añade al término de un partido si los dos equipos empatan.

**Relevos:** Carrera entre dos o más equipos, en la que cada miembro del equipo corre una parte de la distancia total.

**Resistencia:** Capacidad para rendir casi al máximo durante largos períodos.

**Salida nula:** Comienzo de una carrera en la que un atleta abandona los **tacos de salida** antes de que el juez dé el pistoletazo. Debe repetirse.

**Salto Fosbury:** Técnica de salto de altura en la que el saltador supera el listón de espaldas. Debe su nombre al atleta norteamericano Dick Fosbury, que ideó y perfeccionó el salto.

**Sprint:** Aceleración que realiza un corredor en la llegada de una carrera.

**Tablón de frenado:** Línea de demarcación al final de la pista de jabalina o en la parte frontal del círculo de disco o martillo. Si un atleta rebasa el tablón, el lanzamiento no es válido.

**Tacos de salida:** Artefactos utilizados por los corredores al comienzo de una carrera. Soportan el pie levantado y sirven para adquirir velocidad.

**Testigo:** Bastoncito transportado por un corredor en cada vuelta de la carrera de **relevos**.

**Trampolín:** Plataforma flexible que los atletas emplean para adquirir altura o velocidad en los saltos o la gimnasia artística.

**Velódromo:** Circuito ovalado con una pista peraltada para carreras ciclistas.

---

# SITIOS WEB

**www.olympic.org (en inglés)**
Página oficial del COI, con información detallada de todas las olimpiadas anteriores, grandes deportistas olímpicos y muchas pruebas de los juegos de verano e invierno.

**www.coe.es**
Página oficial del Comité Olímpico español. Explora la historia de las olimpiadas y los participantes españoles a lo largo de los años.

**www.ado.es**
Página de la Asociación de Deportes olímpicos. Aquí encontrarás récords, datos sobre eventos deportivos y direcciones de interés.

**www.csd.mec.es**
Página del Consejo Superior de Deportes. En este sitio web se recogen novedades, informes, datos, normas, reglamentos, clasificaciones y estadísticas.

**http://paralimpicos.sportec.es**
Página del Comité Paralímpico español, con información sobre los distintos deportes y participantes, con fotos, calendarios, medalleros y enlaces de interés

**www.paralympic.org (en inglés)**
Página oficial del Comité Paralímpico Internacional, con información sobre los juegos paralímpicos y resultados de todos los juegos anteriores.

**www.elcastellano.org/glosatle.html**
En este sitio web hallarás un glosaro de atletismo muy completo y útil.

**http://rfef.sportec.es**
Página oficial de la Real Federación Española de Fútbol. En este sitio web hallarás información histórica, reglamentos y normativa sobre el control de dopaje en el deporte.

**www.wada-ama.org (en inglés)**
Página oficial de la Agencia Mundial Antidoping (WADA), con noticias sobre la lucha antidroga en los deportes. listados de sustancias prohibidas y detalles de las últimas iniciativas de pruebas de control.

**www.athens2004.gr (en inglés)**
Página oficial de las olimpiadas de verano de 2004, que se celebrarán en Atenas, Grecia. Contiene noticias e información sobre las pruebas y sobre los lugares y preparativos de los juegos.

**http://en.beijing-2008.org (en inglés)**
Página oficial de los juegos de verano de 2008, que se celebrarán en Pekín, la capital de China.

**www.clivegifford.co.uk/inprint/Olympics.htm (en inglés)**
Colección de páginas de las olimpiadas del autor de este libro, con tests, noticias actualizadas y datos de los juegos de verano.

# ÍNDICE ALFABÉTICO